ULTIMATE

HORSE

ULTIMATE
HORSE

ELWYN
HARTLEY EDWARDS

LONDON, NEW YORK, MUNICH,
MELBOURNE, AND DELHI

Project Editor   Jo Weeks
Art Editor   Amanda Lunn
Editor   Susan Thompson
Editorial Assistant   Helen Townsend
Managing Editor   Jane Laing
Production Manager   Maryann Rogers

This edition fully revised in 2002
Senior Art Editor   Wendy Bartlet
Senior Editor   Heather Jones
Managing Art Editor   Lee Griffiths
Managing Editor   Deirdre Headon
US Editors   Margaret Parrish and
Gary Werner

Produced for Dorling Kindersley by

13 SOUTHGATE STREET WINCHESTER HAMPSHIRE SO23 9DZ

Project Art Editor   Sharon Rudd
Project Editor   Donna Wood

Commissioned photography by
Bob Langrish, Kit Houghton
and Peter Cross

First published in the United States in 1991
This American Edition, 2002
02 03 04 05 10 9 8 7 6 5 4 3 2 1

Published in the United States by
DK Publishing, Inc.
375 Hudson Street
New York, NY 10014

A CIP record for this book is available from the
Library of Congress
ISBN 0-7894-8928-7
Reproduced by Colourscan, Singapore.
Printed and bound in Hong Kong by
Toppan Printing.
See our complete catalog at
www.dk.com

Contents

Introduction

*"Man, encompassed by the elements which conspired to destroy him …
would have been a slave had not the horse made him a king."*

In the mists of prehistory, when horse herds roamed wild over the Earth and humankind was still struggling to survive in a largely hostile environment, there began an enduring partnership between the two that lasts to this day and will surely continue far beyond the present. The early horses provided food for our primeval ancestors as well as the materials for clothing and shelter. Today, in the twenty-first century, when the role of the horse is overwhelmingly recreational, they still fulfill those needs in the remoter parts of the world, reminding us, perhaps, of our long dependence on the horse.

This new edition of *Ultimate Horse* has been much extended to include more breeds and types of horse and pony, most of them the product of the vigorous, innovative societies of the New World, some from as far afield as India and the Far East and others that represent the continued growth of the warmblood competition horse of Europe.

The expansion of the book has not only facilitated the task of presenting the fascinating jigsaw of the world's equine population more comprehensively, but it has also had the effect of bringing the underpinning cornerstones into sharp relief. So wide-ranging a study emphasizes irrefutably the primary, linking influences in the formation of the puzzle.

While the pervasive founding blood of the Oriental breeds, the enveloping presence of the ubiquitous Spanish Horse, and their relatively modern descendant, the Thoroughbred, becomes increasingly self-evident, it is also possible to discern the powerful contribution of the notable secondary influences.

The European breeds owe much to the prepotent Norfolk Roadsters, the trotting wing of the Thoroughbred creation, and to the impressive Cleveland Bay. On the American continent, there is the Morgan horse, the hugely important legacy of the Narragansett Pacer, and those specialized breeds evolved by the early settlers.

Just as evident is the *éminence grise* of the heavy horse breeds, the sustaining Flanders Horse that carried the primitive genes of Europe's Forest Horse.

A further area of the book's expansion is in the sections devoted to conformation and to the comparison of the structures best suited to encompass the wide spectrum of modern horse activities, many of which are described in the feature pages.

The pictures, which involved journeys around the world amounting to thousands of miles, are remarkable in their variety, as well as for the revealing technique of photographing horses against a white background, a method that was used even on the Ukrainian steppes.

In fact, the technique is similar to something practiced in Persia and the East 500 years ago when the conformation of horses was assessed by standing them against a white sheet (see pp.8–9). However, the original *Ultimate Horse* book was the first to introduce the practice in modern horse photography. By placing a horse against a plain background you are afforded the clearest view possible, for it is impossible for the outline to be blurred or broken by distracting elements behind it.

The new *Ultimate Horse* book is offered as a tribute to the horse after 7,000 years as the indispensable partner of man.

If it adds to the reader's appreciation, understanding, and enjoyment of horses it will have served its purpose.

Elwyn Hartley Edwards
Chwilog, 2002

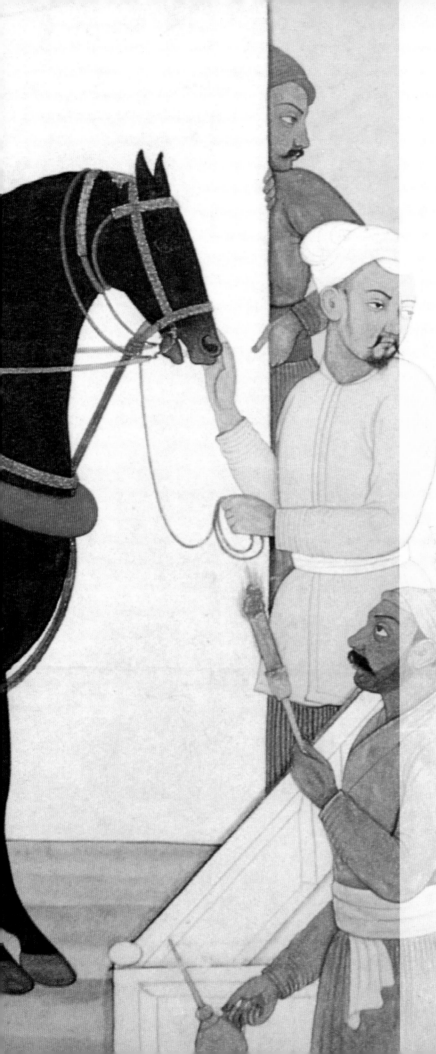

The Essential Horse

The horse's mental character governs its behavior, and its physical structure controls the activities it is capable of and the level of performance it can achieve. The horse's behavior is motivated by instincts acquired over millions of years. These are overlaid and supported by a set of very highly developed senses, giving the horse its particular character.

Selective breeding of high-quality stock; crossbreeding between different types and strains; the employment of "line-breeding" to a common ancestor; or even controlled "inbreeding" of closely related stock belonging to the same family, produced a whole variety of distinctive horses and ponies. Some were bred for strength, others for speed, while some, like the Arabian, developed a unique beauty.

In the course of evolution, horses have acquired senses far more developed than our own, which, although they are of some relevance to communication and sexual behavior, are largely part of a sensitive defense mechanism. Even the position of the eyes, allowing for lateral and almost all-around vision quite unlike human sight, is concerned with the defense system.

ASSESSING CONFORMATION This Mogul miniature shows a horse being assessed for its conformation while standing against a neutral white background, which highlights the outline and clarifies the detail.

Origins

The origin of the equine species can be traced to the Eocene period, some 60 million years ago. In 1867, scientists excavating rock structures of that period in the Southern United States discovered a remarkably complete skeleton of what became established as the first horse. The scientists called it Eohippus, the Dawn Horse, and from it could show a progression on the American continent that culminated in *Equus caballus*, the forebear of the modern horse.

THE EVOLUTION OF THE HOOF

The single hoof in the species Equus *developed over millions of years as a result of the changing environment. In the Eocene period the ancestors of the modern horse lived in forests, and multitoed feet were necessary to prevent them from sinking in soft ground. These toes disappeared as the swamps gave way to open plains and savannah, which were much firmer.*

Four toes
Eohippus had four toes on the front feet.

Three toes
In the Miocene period there were three toes; the central one gradually bore most of the weight.

Hoof The first single-hoofed horse was Pliohippus, with a longer leg and flexing ligaments, whose foot was almost identical to that of the modern horse.

Final form
The final metamorphosis to Equus. The cannon is longer and there is no sign of the vestigial toes.

NUMBER OF TOES The progression from toes and a broad doglike pad to a single hoof involved a gradual reduction in the number of toes. The third toe grew longer and stronger to form a hoof, while the cannon bone lengthened.

EOHIPPUS

Eohippus descends from one of a now-extinct group of animals called Condylartha. The condylarth that was the distant ancestor of Eohippus, and also the ancestor of all hoofed animals, lived on Earth about 75 million years ago. It had five toes, each with a horny nail.

Fifteen million years later, the feet had altered: when Eohippus appeared, the forefeet had four toes while the hind feet had three. The creature is thought to have weighed about 12lb (5.4kg) on average, and to have stood about 14in (36cm) at the shoulder –

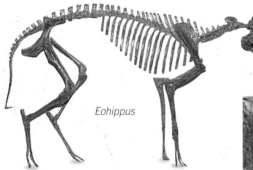

Eohippus

SKELETAL RECONSTRUCTION OF EOHIPPUS
The reconstructed Eohippus skeleton, allowing for the height of about 14in (36cm), the toed feet and the browsing conformation of the skull, is, nonetheless, recognizably equine. Within the species there were, however, numerous variations in height ranging from 10in (25cm) to twice that size. Indeed, during the later Miocene period there was, briefly, a mammoth variety, Megahippus, that may have been as big as an elephant and covered with hair.

about as big as a fox or a medium-sized dog. The color and texture of the Eohippus coat is not known, but it is not improbable that it was like that of a deer, the background dark but with lighter spots or blotches, which would provide camouflage in the dappled, forest surroundings that were the creature's habitat.

Environment is the deciding factor in evolution and, as it changes, so the animals that are to survive adapt to the new circumstances. The toed feet (equipped with pads similar to those of a dog), and the horse's relationship with the tapir indicate that Eohippus lived in an environment that included the sort of soft soil found on jungle

ARTIST'S IMPRESSION OF EOHIPPUS Eohippus was a browsing animal that lived on soft leaves. It was equipped to survive in jungle conditions, being camouflaged by a patterned coat. Its toed feet allowed easy movement over wet ground.

floors and around the edges of pools. The pads enabled the animal to cross wet and marshy ground without difficulty. These pads survive as the ergots of the modern horse, those superfluous horny growths on the back of the fetlocks. Neither the eyes nor the teeth bore much resemblance to those of the modern horse. The teeth were more like those of pigs or monkeys, but they were well suited to a diet of soft leaves growing on low shrubs.

MESOHIPPUS AND MIOHIPPUS

Eohippus was succeeded by two similar and probably overlapping types in the Oligocene period (25–40 million years ago). These were Mesohippus and the somewhat more advanced

ARTIST'S IMPRESSION OF MESOHIPPUS
By the Oligocene period, 25–40 million years ago, Eohippus had been superseded by the three-toed Mesohippus, which had improved dentition, allowing it to consume a wider range of plants.

Miohippus. Both were bigger than Eohippus with longer legs and equipped with teeth that enabled them to eat a variety of soft plant growth. Their toes had reduced to three on each foot, with more weight supported by the central one.

The watershed in the development of the horse occurred between 10 and 25 million years ago in the Miocene period. This was the period when the jungle environment gave way to treeless plains and steppes supporting a low growth of wiry grasses. Adapting to these conditions, the horse developed teeth suitable for grazing and a longer neck to make the grasses easier to reach. The position of its eyes altered to give it all-around vision against the approach of predators; its legs became longer and were equipped with flexing ligaments; and, eventually, the toes fused into a single toe or hoof. All of these changes increased the speed with which it could flee if attack was imminent.

EQUUS CABALLUS
The first single-hoofed horse was Pliohippus, which evolved some six million years ago. Pliohippus was the prototype for the true horse, *Equus caballus*, which was established a million years ago (half a million years before man).

Equus spread from North America over the existing land bridges to Europe and Asia. When the ice packs retreated, perhaps 10,000 years ago, the land bridges disappeared and, for

reasons that can only be a matter for conjecture, the horse became extinct on the American continent. It was not reestablished until the arrival of the Spanish conquistadores.

Following the recession of the ice packs the concensus accepts the existence of four related forms of *Equus*: the horses that inhabited Europe and western Asia; asses from northern Africa; zebras from southern Africa; and onagers, which were found in the Middle East.

Three primitive horses are considered as the foundation for the modern horse: the Asiatic Wild Horse, the lighter, swift-moving Tarpan, and the heavy Forest Horse, *Equus caballus sylvaticus*, of the northern European marshlands, the base for our heavy horse breeds. The last two are extinct but the Tarpan exists in replicated herds bred from animals of pronounced Tarpan character. The Asiatic Wild Horse is preserved in wildlife parks and zoos, and numbers have recently been returned to

ARTIST'S IMPRESSION OF EQUUS CABALLUS *Equus caballus*, the progenitor of the modern horse, evolved about one million years ago and was equipped for life on open, plain-type country, which supported wiry grasses. Unlike his predecessors, *Equus* was a grazing animal with a highly developed system of defence against carnivorous predators.

the wild. By the time of domestication it is suggested that four subspecies had evolved – two pony types and two horse types:

Pony Type 1 was similar to today's Exmoor pony and became established in northwest Europe. It was resistant to wet conditions and thrived in harsh climates.

Pony Type 2 was bigger than Pony Type 1 (14–14.2hh.). It was more heavily built, coarse, and more heavy-headed. It inhabited northern Eurasia and was able to withstand the cold. The Highland pony most nearly resembles it.

Horse Type 3 was about 14.3hh. Long and narrow bodied, goose-rumped, long necked and with long ears, it inhabited central Asia. The nearest modern equivalent is the Akhal-Teke, a breed that is able to tolerate the heat.

Horse Type 4, although smaller than the others, was nevertheless much more refined, with a concave profile and high-set tail. It came from western Asia and its present equivalent is the Caspian pony. It is postulated as the prototype Arabian.

TARPAN (Above) *Equus caballus gmelini Antonius*, the Tarpan (literally "wild horse") of eastern Europe and the Ukranian steppes was a vital element in the development of the modern horse. It exists today in "reconstituted" herds at Popielno and Bialowieza, Poland.

EQUUS PRZEWALSKII PRZEWALSKII POLIAKOV (Right) The Asian Wild Horse was discovered in Mongolia in 1879 by Col. N.M. Przewalskii.

Domestication

The bulk of evidence points to the horse being domesticated in Eurasia 5–6,000 years ago, at the end of the Neolithic period. The dog was domesticated perhaps 6,000 years earlier. Sheep and reindeer were domesticated around 11,000 years ago, and goats, pigs and cattle some 2,000 years later.

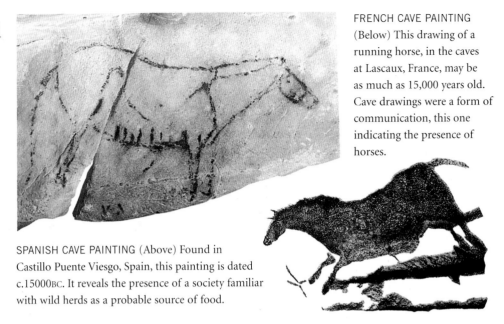

SPANISH CAVE PAINTING (Above) Found in Castillo Puente Viesgo, Spain, this painting is dated c.15000BC. It reveals the presence of a society familiar with wild herds as a probable source of food.

FRENCH CAVE PAINTING (Below) This drawing of a running horse, in the caves at Lascaux, France, may be as much as 15,000 years old. Cave drawings were a form of communication, this one indicating the presence of horses.

HUNTER AND HUNTED

Prior to domestication, the contact between man and horse was that of the hunter and the hunted. During the last stages of the Ice Age, there is much evidence to show that primitive man used the wild horse herds as a source of food. The favorite tactic was to kill the animals by driving a group of them over a cliff, a method with obvious advantages over individual pursuit.

The cave drawings at Lascaux in France and Santander in Spain vividly illustrate the pursuit of horses, as well as providing a remarkable record of primitive life. Huge depositories of horse bones – relics of horse herds driven to their destruction – have been found in many parts of France, particularly at Lascaux and Salutré but also in a number of other places.

FIRST DOMESTICATED HERDS

The people responsible for domesticating the horse herds were probably nomadic Aryan tribes moving about the steppes bordering the Caspian and Black Seas. There is evidence of this happening, but it is probable that domestication was also taking place simultaneously elsewhere in Eurasia, in areas supporting a horse population.

These nomads possibly began as herders of semiwild flocks of sheep, goats, and, more importantly, of the tractable reindeer. The switch to horses would have been made out of practical considerations. In the harsh steppe lands, horses were a better proposition than other animals, being better equipped to find food. Furthermore, horses are not migratory animals like the reindeer, whose movement is governed by the incidence of the "reindeer moss" on which they feed.

Initially, then, horses were herded. Their flesh provided food, their hides were used to make tents and clothes, and the dung could be dried to make fires. Mares supplied milk, which could be fermented into kummis, the fiery brew of the steppes. In time, the mobility of the tribes was increased by employing the quieter animals to transport the household

GREEK POTTERY (DETAIL) (Left) This piece of pottery is decorated with a portrayal of a Greek chariot. The Greek association with horses began around 2000BC but the earliest accounts of horses being used in battle occurs in Homer's *Iliad* (c.800BC), when the "heroes" fought from chariots.

ROCK CARVING (Above) This rock carving of the Native American culture depicts a mounted hunter, armed with a bow, surrounded by the animals which provided food and the materials for clothing and shelter. The use of horses ensured mobility and created a new life concept for the tribes.

effects. The natural consequence thereafter was for men and women to ride the horses, an accomplishment which made the task of herding that much easier. To this day, horse herds are kept in the same fashion throughout the Asian steppe lands, and still provide the very staff of life for the horse-peoples of the twenty-first century.

RIDING AND DRIVING

In rough, mountainous countries, men rode horses, even though these animals would have been of small stature. For the first time in history, in the flat, valley lands of the Middle East, horses provided the key to the establishment and maintenance of a succession of great empires. Their role was almost wholly confined to drawing the chariot. Two horses, however small, could pull a light chariot carrying two or even three men. The addition of two more horses, hitched abreast, reduced effort and increased speed potential. The solid wheel was being used in the Tigris-Euphrates valley around 3500BC, and spoked chariot wheels were commonplace in Egypt by 1600BC.

VALUABLE ANIMAL

As methods of agriculture improved, horses could be handfed. This, combined with selective breeding, produced bigger, stronger, and faster horses suited to the particular requirements of the day. For the most part,

VIKING TAPESTRY The great sea-faring Vikings brought horses with them on their raids to the coasts of Britain and the Scottish islands. This detailed tapestry, which is held at Baldishol, Hedmark, Norway, shows a Viking horseman (c.1180).

those requirements were concerned with warfare and transportation, as well as for the purposes of sport in the great circuses of the classical civilizations of Greece and Rome.

At no point in the early civilizations was the horse employed in cultivation or in menial tasks. The horse was considered altogether too

valuable, and work of that sort was left to oxen. Indeed, in the pre-Christian era the horse had been an object of veneration, occupying an important place in mythology and religious ritual – often being regarded as the supreme sacrifice. In Ancient Greece, Ares, the god of war, traveled the firmament in a chariot drawn by white horses; the image of the goddess Demeter was the head of a black mare and her priests were known as "foals." White horses were occasionally drowned in honor of Poseidon, the god of the sea and the creator of horses, while horses belonging to kings and chieftains were frequently interred with their masters.

Possession of horses ensured mobility; it was the means of creating and extending civilizations, and sometimes it created new societies and a new concept of life. It did this for a short time with the Native Americans. They formed the last of the world's true horse cultures, although they were not in the same class as the archetypal horse societies of the Mongols and Huns. Those nomadic horsemen of the steppes, under their greatest leader, Genghis Khan, built an empire on the backs of shaggy Mongolian ponies. Their contribution to mankind was nonetheless minimal. Genghis Khan's Empire lasted for less than 100 years and was never a factor in the world's progress. In the words of the Chinese general Yeh-lu T'su T'su, "the Empire was won on horseback, but you cannot govern on horseback."

GREEK MOSAIC (Above) This mosaic of a charioteer leading a horse clearly shows the small size of the horse in relation to the man. The mosaic dates from the second or third century AD.

BAYEUX TAPESTRY (Right) The famous eleventh-century tapestry shows mounted men at the sport of hawking. The horses are incomparably bigger than that in the mosaic above.

Conformation

The term "conformation" refers to
the formation of the skeletal frame
(see pp.18–19), and its accompanying
muscle structures, when viewed in
terms of the symmetrical proportion
of the individual parts comprising
the whole. It is the perfection of each
component and their proportionate
relationships that contributes to the
perfection of the overall form. In
the well-made horse, whatever the
breed, no one feature disturbs
the overall symmetry.

PURPOSE – THE GOVERNING FACTOR
Basic conformation, in terms of the correct
and harmonious proportion and placement
of the component parts, is common to all
equidae. But the proportions, while combining
to produce a symmetrical shape, are governed
by the purpose for which the horse is required.

The conformation necessary in the draft
horse, for example, which is required to draw
heavy loads at slow speeds, will be the opposite
of that of the racehorse bred to gallop at speed.
At one extreme there is the strength structure
of the heavy horse, characterized by short,
thick proportions and heavy musculature; at
the other there is the conformation conducive
to speed, based on a light frame and length of
proportions and musculature. In between
there are horses inclined more or less to one
structure or the other. And there will be further
variations in the specialized breeds such as the
American Saddlebred.

VALUE OF SYMMETRY
Correct symmetrical proportions contribute
to a natural balance and free, economical
movement. The mechanically efficient horse is
less prone to unsoundness and strain and will
have a longer working life. The performance
level, all else being equal, will exceed that of
the less well-made animal.

Poor conformation, resulting in discomfort
when the horse is persuaded to attempt to
carry out movement outside the limitations
of the structure, can have a significant effect
on the temperament and behavioral pattern.

THE UNDERPART OF A HEALTHY FOOT
The white line on the foot divides the
insensitive laminae from the sensitive inner
foot; the wall bears the shoe. Both the forefeet
and the hind feet should form an exact pair.
Odd feet on a horse indicate disease or
malformation of the structure.

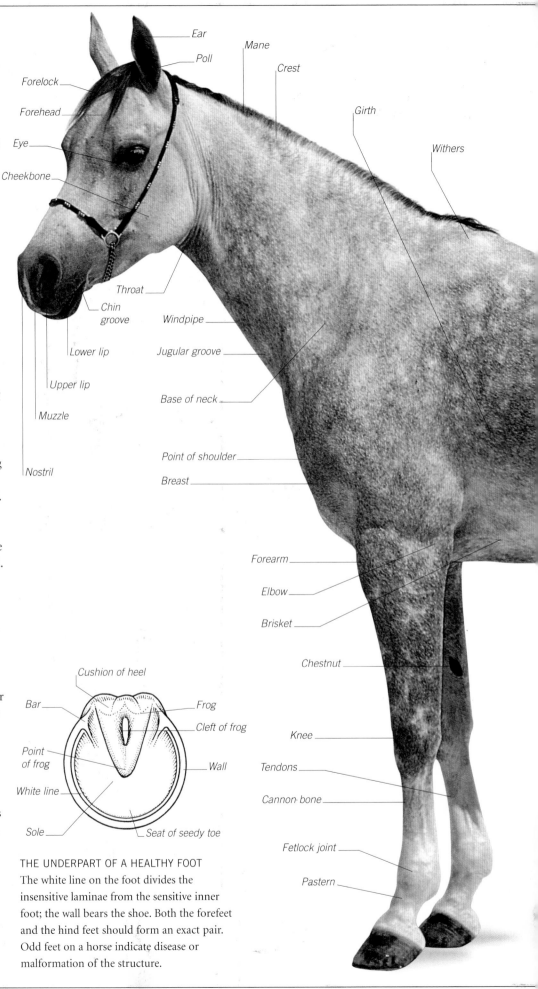

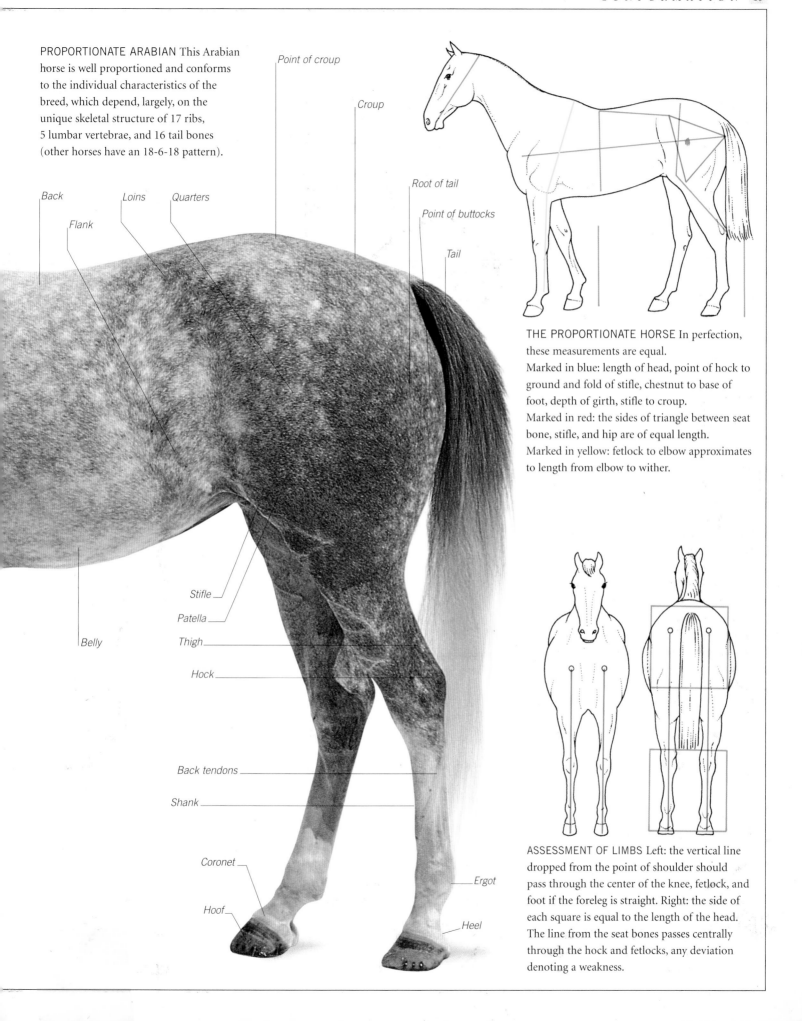

PROPORTIONATE ARABIAN This Arabian horse is well proportioned and conforms to the individual characteristics of the breed, which depend, largely, on the unique skeletal structure of 17 ribs, 5 lumbar vertebrae, and 16 tail bones (other horses have an 18-6-18 pattern).

Point of croup

Croup

Root of tail

Point of buttocks

Tail

Back

Flank

Loins

Quarters

Belly

Stifle

Patella

Thigh

Hock

Back tendons

Shank

Coronet

Hoof

Ergot

Heel

THE PROPORTIONATE HORSE In perfection, these measurements are equal.
Marked in blue: length of head, point of hock to ground and fold of stifle, chestnut to base of foot, depth of girth, stifle to croup.
Marked in red: the sides of triangle between seat bone, stifle, and hip are of equal length.
Marked in yellow: fetlock to elbow approximates to length from elbow to wither.

ASSESSMENT OF LIMBS Left: the vertical line dropped from the point of shoulder should pass through the center of the knee, fetlock, and foot if the foreleg is straight. Right: the side of each square is equal to the length of the head. The line from the seat bones passes centrally through the hock and fetlocks, any deviation denoting a weakness.

ASSESSING PROPORTION

A useful guide in assessing conformation is that provided by the diagram Proportionate Horse (see p.15). These measurements were the result of extensive research by Professor Wortley-Axe and his nineteenth-century French contemporaries, Professors Bourgelat, Duhousset, Goubaux, and Barrier. However, there are some basic rules-of-thumb which are invaluable in any visual assessment.

Of great importance is the depth of girth, which allows room for the expansion of the lungs. The length from wither to elbow should equal or exceed that of the length from the elbow to the ground.

For speed the neck has to be relatively long (short, thick necks are associated with the strength structure). As a guide the length of the neck equals approximately 1½ times the measurement taken from the poll, down the face, to the lower lip. The head needs to be of proportionate size. If it is too big it overweights

MOVEMENT The active, powerful movement of this Welsh Part-Bred is the result of good, basic conformation allied to exemplary muscle development, particularly over the powerfully rounded topline.

CONFORMATION This Standardbred, reared to race in harness, is a good example of conformation to suit the purpose. It would be less ideal in the racehorse.

the forehand; if too small, which is less usual, it will detract from the proper balance. The head acts as the balancing agent for the body and has been likened to a 40lb (18kg) blob on the end of a pendulum. Raised upward it lightens the forehand, transferring weight to the quarters.

It is just as useful to make a visual check of the length of the back from the rear of the withers to the highest part of the croup and to compare it with the length from the point of the shoulder to the last of the "false" ribs

(see Skeletal Frame, pp.18–19). To achieve perfection the last measurement should be twice the length of the former.

The correctness of the limbs can be established by standing directly in front of and behind the horse and following the principles of assessment detailed on p.15.

HEAD STUDY

The proportions of the head are of great importance but it has to be borne in mind that no other part can be so revealing of the individual character. It has been termed "the center of intelligence and the seat of vice."

In the performance horse a lean, refined head with no fleshiness is expected. The ears are mobile and there is an absence of the coarse, wiry hair that denotes a common background. The eyes are large and bright, the nostrils wide and open to permit maximum inhalation of air, and the jawbones are set well apart to allow flexion at the poll. The whole is indicative of intelligence and quick response. The opposite condition, found in heavy or common-bred animals, disposes its owner to slower responses and a far less alert outlook. Occasionally, one will find the small, piggy eye or even that which shows a lot of white.

FAULTS OF CONFORMATION

Conformational faults are the result of weaknesses, or failings, in the basic structure which affect the way of going (the movement) and, in consequence, the level of performance, where that depends on free, straight, and economic action. However, what might be seen as a failing in one discipline might be an asset in another field demanding different criteria. Selective breeding can produce conformation that may depart from the norm but endows the stock with the ability to perform specialized gaits.

DISHING The round circular action when the toe is thrown outward is regarded as a major fault in Europe. However, it is a much-prized characteristic of the Peruvian Paso in which it is encouraged by careful selective breeding.

A SWAY BACK This is a fundamental breakdown in the skeletal formation and is often associated with old age. It adds to the difficulties of saddle fitting and in pronounced cases can adversely affect the movement.

COW HOCKS The points of the hock are carried close together, and the lower limbs incline outward, producing uneven wear in the joint and reducing speed potential.

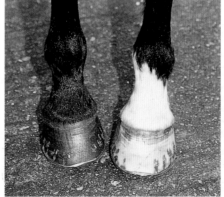

PIGEON TOES These are a feature that also contributes to uneven wear in the joint and may affect the action more or less seriously while encouraging dishing.

SPLAY FEET Such feet will usually induce "brushing," i.e., one foot striking the other as the horse moves. Again, this fault will cause uneven wear in the lower limb.

Skeletal Frame

The framework of the body is the skeleton, made up of variously shaped bones. They support the body mass and their movement; when activated by joints, and in concert with muscle, they result in the locomotion of the body.

A *joint* is formed at the junction of two bones. The ends of the bones, the articular surfaces, are of greater density than elsewhere so as to be better able to withstand the friction occurring between the two surfaces.

As an additional preventative against wear, the surfaces are separated by a layer of gristle, called *cartilage*. The whole is encased within a two-layer capsule, the outer layer giving support and the inner secreting an oily fluid (*synovia* or joint oil) so that the joint works within a vessel of oil and is in a state of constant lubrication.

The whole is held together by connecting *ligaments*, tough, fibrous, and flexible tissues attached to each bone. While permitting free movement they also prevent any risk of over-extension which might result in damage.

The rib cage is notable for its dual attachment. The first eight "true" sternal ribs are attached to both vertebrae and sternum bone; the next 10 "false" ribs are attached only to vertebrae. In a state of perfection the true ribs are long and flat if the ride is to be comfortable. The "false" ribs must be rounded and well sprung if the horse is not to "run up light" in work, with a pronounced hollow immediately after the last rib.

IDEAL SLOPE The shoulder is critical to economical riding movement. The scapula needs to be long in relation to the humerus and sloped forward from the clearly defined wither.

The bones of the riding horse are slender and long, as opposed to thick and short (as they are in the heavy horse), and of greater structural density. The measurement taken around the bone below the knee provides a general guide to weight-carrying capacity: 8in (20cm) is calculated to carry a 150–170 lb (70–76kg) weight, 9–10in (23–25cm) will carry up to 180-195 lb (82–89kg), and 10–11in (25–28cm) 210 lb (100kg) and over. Nonetheless, much depends on the proportions. The denser "bone" of the Arabian and Thoroughbred carries more weight inch for inch than the coarser structure of a common-bred horse.

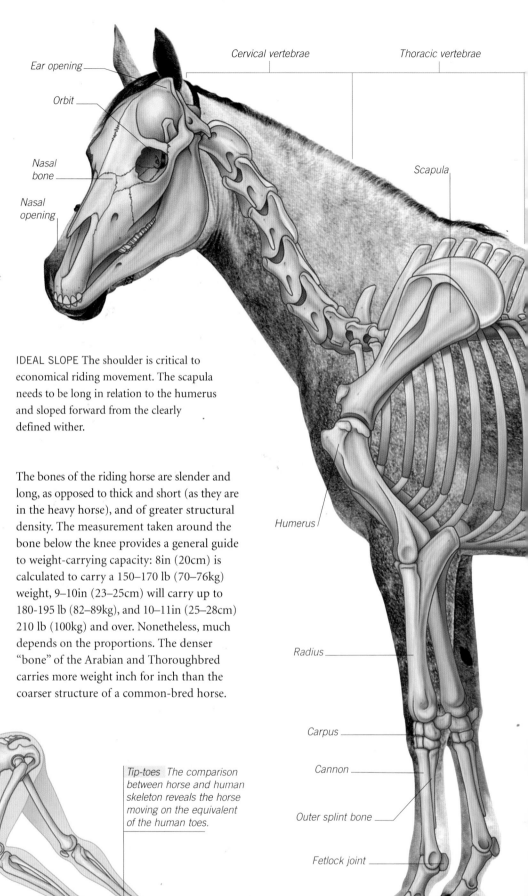

Ear opening

Orbit

Nasal bone

Nasal opening

Cervical vertebrae

Thoracic vertebrae

Scapula

Humerus

Radius

Carpus

Cannon

Outer splint bone

Fetlock joint

Fingertips The horse moves on the equivalent of the human fingertips in front.

Tip-toes The comparison between horse and human skeleton reveals the horse moving on the equivalent of the human toes.

Dorsal vertebrae   Lumbar vertebrae   Sacral vertebrae   Caudal vertebrae

Pelvis

Femur

Tibia and Fibia

Ribs

Point of hock

Outer splint bone

Sesamoid bone

Tarsus
(Hock)

TEETH

The incisor teeth provide a fairly accurate guide to the age of the horse in its first 10 years, but experience is required to estimate the age thereafter.

At birth the foal has no teeth. Then, when it is 10 days old, the central incisors cut through the gums. By the time it is six to nine months old, the foal has acquired a full set of baby teeth. The full set of permanent teeth are in place when the foal is between five and six years old.

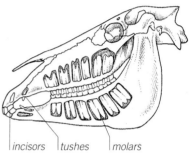

incisors   tushes   molars

MATURE HORSE The two jaws of the mature horse each have 12 molar (grinding) teeth as well as six incisor (biting) teeth.

flat, oval tables
long, small cups

FIVE YEARS Central, lateral, and corner incisors are permanent; cup marks appear on "tables."

round tables
oval cups

TWELVE YEARS At 12 years, the slope of the teeth has increased and cup marks are less distinct.

triangular tables
rounded cups

OLD AGE In old age, the slope of the teeth is very pronounced and the groove on the corner teeth has almost disappeared.

Muscle Structure

Muscle is the substance covering the skeletal frame. Muscles are connected to the bones by *tendons*, tough, inelastic ropes braided into the latter and without which the muscle would be torn. Muscle, by being attached to joints, causes movement whenever it is contracted or extended.

MUSCLE PROPERTY

Muscle itself is elastic and has both the ability to contract and extend, thus producing movement in the body mass.

A peculiar property of muscle contraction, however, is that the degree of contraction possible is in direct ratio to the extent to which the muscle can be stretched. It follows that the greater the muscle's capacity to contract, the greater will be the degree of flexion possible in the joint it activates, and the nearer the movement will approach maximum efficiency. A primary object in the training of the horse has, therefore, to lie in exercise designed to stretch the muscles.

Muscles are either *voluntary* or *involuntary*, the latter occurring in the internal organs, like the bowel and the independent *cardiac* muscle. Muscles are then divided into *flexors* (those that contract to flex the joint), and *extensors* (those that extend, to operate in the opposite fashion).

Muscles act in pairs but can also act in opposition. An example of the former are the dorsal muscles on either side of the spine and those covering the stomach wall. When the horse bends the body, as when making a turn, they become compensatory in their action. The muscles on the inside of the movement contract, while those on the outside stretch correspondingly to allow the turn to be made.

IN OPPOSITION

Muscles act in opposition when the back is rounded (see the diagram on the right). The big, dorsal muscles are then extended, while the rounding is completed by the raising of the abdomen and the engagement of the hind legs under the body, a matter accomplished by three muscles on the side of the abdomen, and three running from the fifth and ninth ribs to

the pubis, acting in opposition as *flexors*. Similarly, the tension of muscles on the underside of the neck in the chest region is counterbalanced by dorsal muscles on top of the neck. Between the two tensions the horse is able to carry head and neck without conscious effort.

The term "tension" is here used in the sense of "muscle tone" or *tonus*, a state that is necessary to prevent any violent extension or flexion that might cause serious damage. Muscle can suffer damage as a result of fatigue caused by severe physical exertion, when an insufficient supply of oxygen will cause the muscle to seize up or "tie up." It can also be damaged by a combination of high-protein feeding and insufficient exercise. *Azoturia*, "Monday morning disease," when the muscle of the loin stiffens painfully, is a case in point.

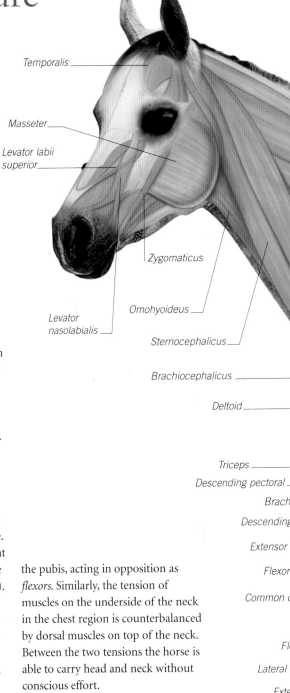

Temporalis

Masseter

Levator labii superior

Zygomaticus

Levator nasolabialis

Omohyoideus

Sternocephalicus

Brachiocephalicus

Deltoid

Triceps

Descending pectoral

Brachialis

Descending pectoral

Extensor carpi radialis

Flexor carpi ulnaris

Common digital extensor

Ulnaris lateralis

Flexor carpi radialis

Lateral digital extensor

Extensor carpi obliquus

Tendon of common digital extensor

Superficial digital flexor tendon

Suspensory ligaments

Palmar anular ligament

Splenius

Subclavius

Trapezius (cervical part)

Serratus ventralis (thoracic part)

Trapezius (thoracic part)

THE OUTLINE The end purpose in training is to produce a correct outline in the young horse. It is achieved by exercises directed at building up muscle on the topline and producing a rounded form with the hind legs well engaged beneath the body.

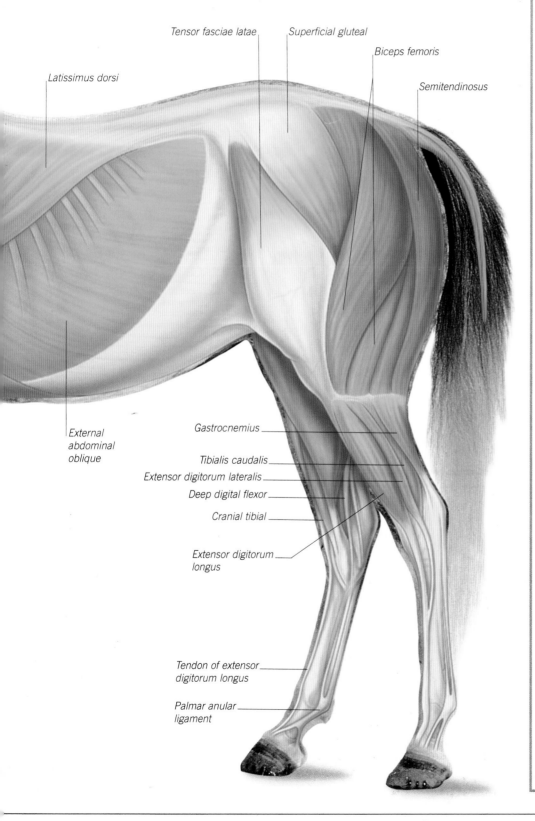

Latissimus dorsi

Tensor fasciae latae

Superficial gluteal

Biceps femoris

Semitendinosus

External abdominal oblique

Gastrocnemius

Tibialis caudalis

Extensor digitorum lateralis

Deep digital flexor

Cranial tibial

Extensor digitorum longus

Tendon of extensor digitorum longus

Palmar anular ligament

MUSCLE DEVELOPMENT

Correctly developed muscles equip the horse to move with minimal effort under the weight of the rider. The converse results in a hollow, stiff-backed horse carrying the nose in the air and trailing the hind legs behind – in short, an inefficient outline, leading to discomfort and undue strain on the structure. The development of muscles in opposition to effective performance is caused by poor training and bad riding allied to a lack of understanding of the principles and practice involved.

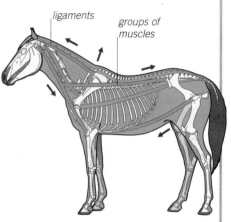

ligaments

groups of muscles

DIRECTION OF TENSION The diagram shows the principal groups of muscles (marked red) and ligaments (marked blue). The arrows indicate the direction of exerted tension, a matter that will be assisted by proper basic training and good riding.

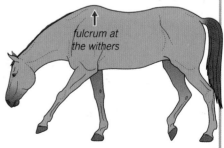

fulcrum at the withers

CERVICAL LIGAMENT Training to encourage the stretching of the neck and rounding of the back causes the cervical ligament, stretching from the poll along the back, to stretch over the fulcrum provided by the wither and encourages the buildup of muscle over the topline.

Hot and Cold

For convenience the horse population can be divided into three types: light horses, heavy horses, and ponies, all three exhibiting conformational differences appropriate to usage and environment. Even then, there will be numerous subdivisions, each with their own individual and often specialized characteristics.

Light horses are looked upon as being of "riding type" or of light "driving type." They will include everything from Arabians and Thoroughbreds, through the American gaited families and the harness racers, to Hackneys and the legion of warmbloods. There are therefore considerable variations in conformation, though not so much in terms of general proportion.

Heavy horses encompass all the members of the draft breeds, the natural successors to the primitive Forest Horse of Europe. There will be variations in size and detail but they share a common, basic conformation and there will be little difference in the proportions.

Ponies are almost a law unto themselves, and their conformation is usually closely related to their environment and usage. That is certainly the case with the native ponies of the British

mountain and moorland areas. Indeed, they are often referred to as the "Mountain and Moorland" breeds. The same is true of some of the European ponies, like the Haflingers,

THE MELTING POT
A The Arabian, the hotblood fountainhead of the world's breeds.
B The Thoroughbred, sole hotblood derivative of the Oriental foundation, was "invented" in England in the seventeenth and eighteenth centuries as the super-horse and has been purebred for over 200 years.
C Warmbloods – horses carrying a percentage of hot blood. The mix of hot and cold.
D The coldblood heavy horse, descendant of the primitive Forest Horse.
E The pony, a warmblood animal of small stature suited to the environmental demands.

B Thoroughbred

C Warmblood

D Coldblood

E Pony

A Arabian

Fjords, Gotlands, and, of course, the remarkable Icelandic Horse.

There used to be a convention that made an arbitrary division between horse and pony at 15hh. Above that height were horses, below were the ponies. In fact, the issue is altogether more complex and is just as much concerned with proportion as with size.

Pony proportions are in general shorter than those of the horse, and the true "native" pony has a conformation derived from its original environment, particularly in respect of its action. The slope of the shoulder and its position relative to the humerus results in a pronounced lift and bend to the knee – an essential requirement in animals that live in rough and uneven terrain, where a long, low action would be entirely impractical.

To complicate matters further, Arabians, often under 15hh., are always known as horses; similarly, the Icelandic Horse is never referred to as a pony. Polo ponies are mostly over 15hh. but are still called ponies.

The Arabian, unique in its proportions, is nonetheless of horse conformation but that is certainly not the case with the Icelandic Horse; polo ponies are in reality small Thoroughbred horses.

HOT, COLD, WARM

There are then divisions between *hotblood* horses, *coldbloods*, and *warmbloods*. (These terms are not a reference to body temperature.) The first term describes the prepotent progenitor of the modern light horse population, the Arabian, which has been purebred for as many as 3,000 years, and its equally purebred and prepotent derivative, the Thoroughbred. The stud books of both do not allow the admission of any outside blood.

"Coldblood" is the term used to describe the heavy horse breed that carries no hot blood, but there are one or two cold-blood ponies, notably the Austrian Haflinger.

Warmblood is the term applied to horses having a percentage of hot blood. These were once known as half-, three-quarter- or even seven-eighths-bred, the terms indicating the percentage of usually Thoroughbred blood in the genetic makeup. "Part-bred" allows the addition of crosses other than hotbloods. While the hotblood influence is paramount in the development of the world's light horses and ponies, there are other powerful underpinning elements, notably the Spanish or Iberian Horse and the Barb. It would not be

PROPORTIONS

Proportions between the light horse, carrying a greater percentage of Thoroughbred blood, the pony, and the heavy horse, reveal distinct differences. The presence of Thoroughbred blood will encourage length in the limbs, which is consistent with the speed structure, while the heavy horse, at the opposite end of the spectrum, has the short, thick proportions associated with strength but not speed. The pony has more in common with the latter.

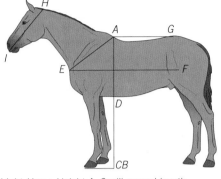

Light Horse Height A–C will exceed length of the body E–F. Legs D–C may be longer than depth of body A–D. Length of back A–G may exceed length of head H–I and head measurement will be shorter than shoulder A–E.

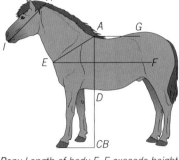

Pony Length of body E–F exceeds height A–C. Depth of body A–D equals and may slightly exceed length of leg D–C. Length of head H–I equals shoulder A–E and back A–G. The proportions relate directly to the environmental factor.

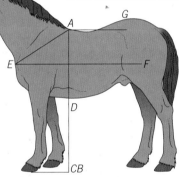

Heavy Horse The proportions are nearer to those of the pony. Length of back A–G may be shorter than length of head H–I. Length of body E–F exceeds height A–C. It would be desirable for depth of body A–D to exceed length of leg D–C.

unreasonable for the student of hippology to question the exclusion of those breeds from the category "hotblood" and, indeed, devotees of both lay claim to hotblood status.

The origins of the Barb are obscured as much by loose nomenclature as anything, and the use of the word in the early evolution of the Thoroughbred, and for some centuries before and after, remains a source of confusion. Of course, there is a Barb contribution, but there is no evidence to support the claim of its being a hotblood, on the grounds of sustained purity or anything else. Nor is the Iberian Horse that runs like a golden thread through so much of the equine history of the Americas, and was for so long "the foremost horse of Europe," accepted by hippologists as being "hotblood" in the modern usage (unless, perhaps, they are Spanish or enthusiasts of all things Iberian). It does have an enviable prepotency in *most* respects. It does not

approach that of the Arabian, but it had a greater influence in Europe from the sixteenth century for some 200 years.

Nonetheless, its homeland of the Iberian Peninsula was continually subjected to occupation by Romans, Vandals, Visigoths, and others for over 400 years before the Muslim invasions of the eighth century.

All these peoples introduced their own horses to the native stock. The Moors brought in thousands of Barbs from North Africa and there was always a significant Arabian presence. Arabian horses were particularly numerous in the region of Córdoba, where an early Emir kept a stud farm of at least 200 at the royal stables by the Guadalquivir River.

It is inconceivable to imagine that the Moorish imports had no effect on the Iberian horse population. The argument will continue, but the essential part played by these horses can never be an issue.

Natural Gaits

The horse has four natural gaits as well as a number of specialized ones, which are based largely on the old ambling, or pacing, gait. This peculiar gait occurs naturally in some breeds, notably the Tennessee Walker, the Saddlebred, the Fox Trotter, and the Standardbred, as well as in the Icelandic Horse.

THE SEQUENCE

The natural gaits are simply walk, trot, canter, and gallop. The sequence of footfalls at walk, when it is begun with the left hind leg, is: 1. left hind; 2. left fore; 3. right hind; 4. right fore – four distinct and regular beats.

The trot is a two-beat gait in which the horse puts one pair of diagonal legs to the ground simultaneously and, after a moment of suspension, springs on the other diagonal. Two beats can be heard, the first when the left hind and right fore touch the ground, and the second when the opposite diagonal pair of legs touches down, following a brief interval.

The canter is a three-beat gait. If it begins on the left hind, the sequence is: 1. left hind; 2. left diagonal (the left fore and right hind touching the ground simultaneously); 3. right fore, which is then termed the "leading leg." On a circle to the right, the horse "leads" with the inside foreleg, i.e. the right fore. On a circle to the left, when the sequence is reversed, he leads with the left foreleg. A horse cantering a right-handed circle on the left lead, or vice versa, is said to be on the "wrong leg" or moving with a "false lead." However, in the advanced school balancing exercise of counter-canter, the horse is required to canter on just such a false lead. The gallop is usually a gait of four beats, but the sequence varies according to the speed. As a four-beat gait, when the right fore leads, the sequence is: 1. left hind; 2. right hind; 3. left fore; 4. right fore, followed by full suspension when all four feet are off the ground.

DEVELOPMENT

The requirements of modern dressage further subdivide the gaits, apart from the gallop. The walk and trot are both divided into four subdivisions.

In the medium walk, there is moderate extension, with the hind feet touching the ground in front of the prints of the forefeet. The collected walk is shorter, more energetic, and more elevated, and the hind feet touch ground behind the prints of the forefeet.

In the extended walk, when the head and neck are stretched, the horse is expected to cover as much ground as possible while maintaining the regularity of the four, distinct footfalls. In this case, the hind feet touch the ground in front of the prints of the forefeet. In free walk, a pace of rest, the horse moves again in extended outline, but with the four beats remaining distinct.

The working trot is between the medium and collected trots and inclines more toward the latter. Medium trot lies between extended and collected, inclining more to the former, and the hind feet touch down in the prints of the forefeet. The canter is similarly divided and the same criteria apply as in the trot.

DEFINITIONS

The perfection or otherwise of the natural gaits and their subdivisions depends, in the dressage context, on the understanding of certain criteria and, in particular, of the accepted definitions. *Rhythm*, for instance, is the regularity and correctly ordered flow of the pace; *tempo* is the rate of the stride or footfall; *cadence* is the extra quality, expression, and animation given to the rhythm and successive footfalls by an increase in upward *impulsion*, which is defined as energy originating in the quarters, directed by the hand of the rider.

GALLOPING GAUCHO The *gaucho's* horse is depicted in the manner of the school of British sporting art of the seventeenth and eighteenth centuries, with legs extended front and rear. The camera sequences of Eadweard Muybridge (1885) proved this to be fallacious.

The four natural paces should have regularity, so that the sound of the hoof beats can be heard separately and distinctly, although at the gallop the sound of the beats may become blurred. The unschooled horse lacks this regularity of movement. Only in a horse that has been properly trained is it possible to alter the outline to meet the requirements of the gait subdivisions. The collected gaits demand a shortening of the horse's base and overall outline, combined with a near-vertical head carriage, increased elevation, and a lowered croup.

TROT A medium trot with a good, swinging, hacking pace. The head carriage is pleasing and there is particularly good engagement of the hind leg under the body.

CANTER A pleasant, smooth, three-beat canter on the left lead is shown here, with the horse going freely in good contact with the bit and extremely well balanced.

GALLOP The gallop is the fastest and most exhilarating gait, in which there is always a period of suspension when all four feet are off the ground.

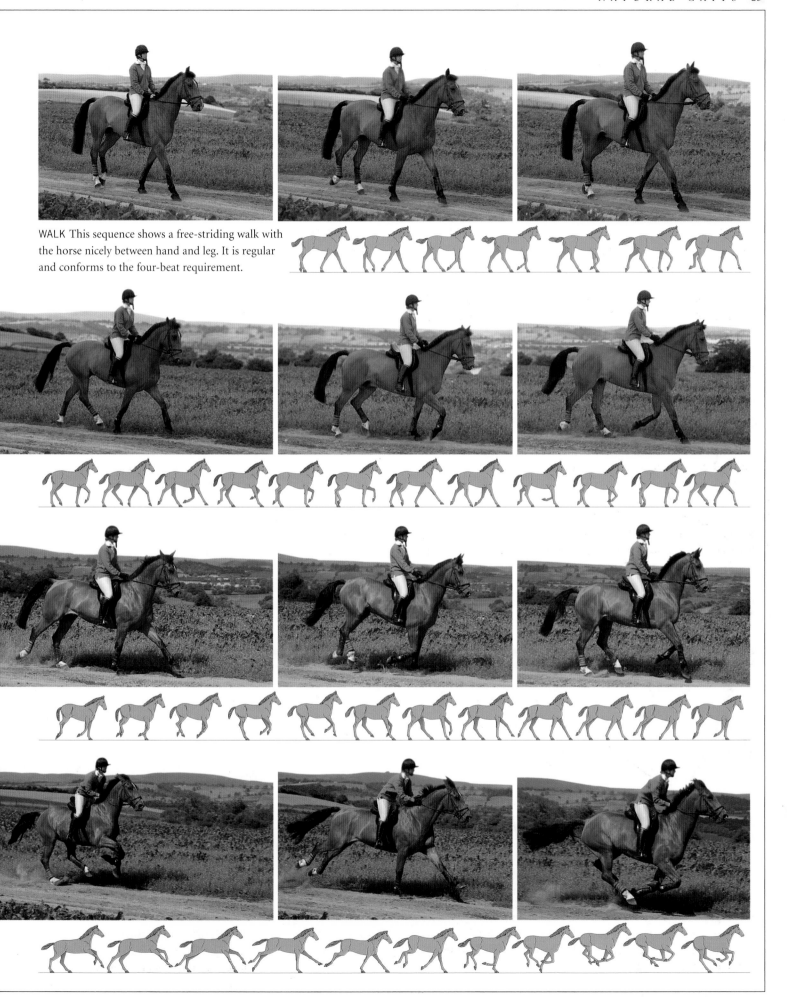

WALK This sequence shows a free-striding walk with the horse nicely between hand and leg. It is regular and conforms to the four-beat requirement.

Specialized Gaits

Largely associated with the American breeds, specialized gaits are also found in Asia. With the exception of the Western horses, the gaits are based on the lateral ambling or pacing movement in which the horse moves its legs in lateral rather than diagonal pairs.

THE GAITED TRADITION

A number of Russian breeds still pace naturally, and Spain was the home of smooth-gaited horses exhibiting a swift, lateral running walk that were much in demand throughout Europe. The most famous were reared in Galicia and their descendants, the Galiceno of Mexico, are still noted for their natural gait.

Both the Kathiawari and Marwari of western India retain a natural lateral pace, the fast and comfortable *revaal*, but it is in the Americas that the gaits have been refined and perfected. In South America the famous Peruvian Paso exemplifies the gaited tradition, but the most unique grouping belongs to the North American continent. Apart from the Standardbred harness racer, the world's fastest pacing horse, there are the three gaited specialists: the Saddlebred, the Missouri Fox Trotter, and the Tennessee Walker. While the action of these horses is undeniably brilliant and their production a matter of the greatest skill, the breeds suffer from artificial, high-gloss, show-ring image.

ARTIFICIAL AIDS

Of those three gaited specialists, only the Missouri Fox Trotter is prohibited by the breed society from employing artificial appliances. Excessive weighting of the feet is not permitted, nor is the use of chains around the fetlock to encourage the lifting action. Conversely, the other two breeds make considerable use of artificial aids to enhance the action, and they also use tail sets.

THE UTILITY HORSE

While the Saddlebred is associated primarily with its performance in the show ring and brilliant, artificial movement, it was initially a totally practical animal. With its feet trimmed normally it can still be used as a utility horse. It can be trained to cut cattle, jump, hunt, or compete in dressage competitions.

Similarly, the Tennessee Walker was primarily developed as a practical plantation horse of endurance and stamina and would have needed the addition of very little in the way of modern artificial aids to do its work.

INHERITED GAITS

The horse heritage of the Americas is the largest, the most varied, and probably the most colorful in the world. The development of the Western working horse, for instance, with gaits entirely suited to the purpose for which it was required and the often inhospitable terrain in which it lived, is as unique as the carefully preserved grouping of gaited horses which had their origin in practical, working usage. For the most part, these gaits are inherited, and the artificialities of the show ring no more than an enhancement of that which nature has provided.

SADDLEBRED The Rack. The five-gaited Saddlebred show horse performs the "slow gait" and the full-speed, four-beat "rack," as well as the basic gaits.

QUARTERHORSE The lope. The definitive Western gaits are the jog and the smooth lope, the Western scaled-down version of the canter, ridden on one hand.

TENNESSEE WALKER The famous running walk is a soft, gliding gait that can be maintained at 6–9 mph (9–14km/h). It is described as "bounce-free."

ENHANCING THE GAITS

Action and lift is encouraged by growing the feet long and fitting heavy shoes in combination with shaped wedges. Chains may also be fastened around the fetlocks with the same end in view and can cause soreness.

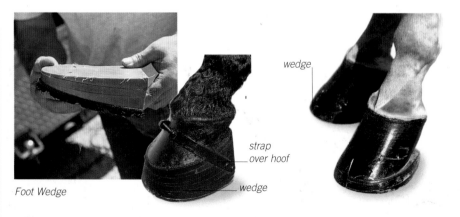

wedge

strap over hoof

wedge

Foot Wedge

TENNESSEE WALKER (Above) Specially designed wedges and a straight foot contribute materially to the running walk.

SADDLEBRED (Above) The long foot is characteristic of the show horse and carries a heavy shoe to exaggerate the lift.

STANDARDBRED The world's fastest harness racer
is a pacing horse, employing the legs in lateral pairs.
The "Standard" is set at 145 sec per mile (1.6km).

Markings and Coat Colors

Coat color originates in the genes of the breeding stock. The genes are carried on chromosomes, of which the horse has 32 pairs (each parent contributing one half of each pair). The combination of genes on each chromosome determines an animal's characteristics, including coat color.

COLOR POSSIBILITIES

Some genes are dominant, which means that they mask the effect of their recessive counterparts. In horses, gray dominates black,

bay, and chestnut; bay dominates black; and chestnut (also called sorrell) is recessive to all colors. Therefore, the combination of a bay gene and a chestnut gene will result in a bay foal because the bay gene is dominant. If two such foals were eventually mated, it is possible that the two recessive chestnut genes (one from each animal) would be united to produce a chestnut foal. Since chestnut horses must carry only chestnut genes, the mating of two chestnuts always produces a chestnut foal.

Horses are described by their coat color and any markings, although color is not always constant – Lipizzaners are born black and mature to gray. Doubtful cases are decided by the color of the hair on the muzzle.

PART-COLORED HORSES Pintos ("paints") in the US have two colors. Odd-colored have patches of more than two colors. Pintos can be Tobiano – white with large patches; or Overo – colored with white patches (see pp.182–3). The Anglo-Saxon terms are piebald – white and black; and skewbald – white on another color. "Bald" is the old term for a white-faced horse.

COAT COLORS

GRAY Black skin with a mixture of white and black hairs.

PALOMINO Gold coat, white mane and tail, with a minimum of black.

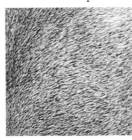

BAY Reddish coat with black mane, tail and points.

STRAWBERRY-ROAN Chestnut body color with white hairs interspersed.

SPOTTED This coat is often referred to as Appaloosa coloring.

FLEABITTEN Chestnut or black specks of hair fleck an otherwise gray coat.

CHESTNUT (or sorrell) Various shades of gold, from pale gold to a rich, red gold.

BROWN Mixed black and brown in coat; black limbs, mane, tail.

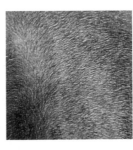

BLUE-ROAN Black or brown body with a percentage of white hair.

SKEWBALD Large patches of white on another base color.

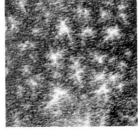

DAPPLE-GRAY Dark gray hairs form distinct rings on a gray base.

LIVER-CHESTNUT This is the darkest of the chestnut shades.

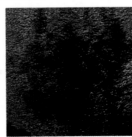

BLACK Black pigment throughout, with occasional white marks.

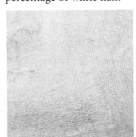

DUN Yellow, blue, or mouse, depending on diffusion of pigment.

PIEBALD Usually irregular, large patches of white and black.

Star

Stripe (or race)

Blaze

Interrupted stripe

WHITE FACE A white face is defined as one in which white hairs cover the forehead and the front of the face and extend laterally toward the mouth, possibly also encompassing the muzzle and lower ear.

White muzzle

White lips

NATURAL MARKINGS The common forms of natural markings occur in areas of white hair on the face and the legs, although "flesh marks" occur on the underside of the belly, flanks, and so on.

Snip

ACQUIRED MARKINGS

Acquired markings are also used as identifications. They include brand marks as well as saddle and girth marks that appear as white hair.

BRAND MARKS Brand marks constitute positive identification of animals. They comprise the herd or stud mark and often the herd number of the animal.

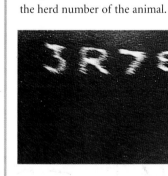

FREEZE MARK A freeze mark is another form of positive identification used as a precaution against theft. The animal can be identified by its number.

DORSAL EEL STRIPE The dorsal eel stripe (also called a list or ray) occurs most usually in conjunction with a dun coat color. It is a primitive characteristic originating in early equidae like the Tarpan and Asiatic Wild Horse.

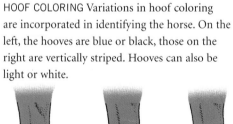

Striped

Blue/black

HOOF COLORING Variations in hoof coloring are incorporated in identifying the horse. On the left, the hooves are blue or black, those on the right are vertically striped. Hooves can also be light or white.

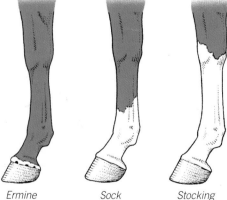

Ermine   *Sock*   *Stocking*

LEG MARKINGS Three main types exist. Ermine markings are black on white, and can be found around the coronet. Socks denote white coloring up to the knee; stockings cover the knee.

ZEBRA BAR MARKINGS Zebra bar markings on the leg are a form of primitive camouflage. They are to be seen on ancient breeds, such as the Fjord (see pp.254–5) and the Highland (see pp.230–1).

The Senses

The horse personality is made up of a number of deeply ingrained instincts that were acquired in the process of evolution. Horses, like humans, are possessed of the five senses: taste, touch, hearing, smell, and sight. In the horse, however, these five senses are far more developed than in ourselves. Furthermore, there is that enigmatic sixth sense, a heightened perception, which is apparent in the horse but rare in our species.

TASTE

Little is known about the horse's sense of taste, although we know it is associated with touch and plays an important role in mutual grooming. We presume that horses like sweet things, and feed manufacturers add sweeteners to their products to make them more palatable, but there is no proof to support this assumption. Many horses, indeed, appear to relish bitter herbs found in hedgerows and on old pasture.

TOUCH

The sense of touch is more relevant to our understanding of the horse. It is used as a means of communication between horses, and between humans and horses. Grooming is one example, and in riding the horse much of the language of the aids is concerned with touch. The leg, for instance, exerts pressures on the receptor cells on the horse's sides and the hand communicates by touching the mouth through the rein and the bit.

The whiskers on the muzzle evaluate by touch objects that the horse cannot see, such as the contents of the manger. Inexplicably, it is the practice to trim off these whiskers for fashion's sake, thus depriving the animal of a natural faculty.

FLEHMEN (Right) Flehmen, the curling back of the lip, can be caused by a stallion licking, or touching, an in-season mare, but it can also occur in response to strong and/or unusual tastes and smells, such as garlic, lemon, or vinegar.

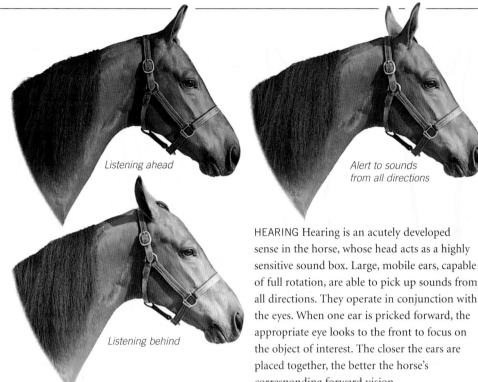
Listening ahead
Alert to sounds from all directions
Listening behind

HEARING Hearing is an acutely developed sense in the horse, whose head acts as a highly sensitive sound box. Large, mobile ears, capable of full rotation, are able to pick up sounds from all directions. They operate in conjunction with the eyes. When one ear is pricked forward, the appropriate eye looks to the front to focus on the object of interest. The closer the ears are placed together, the better the horse's corresponding forward vision.

SMELL AND TOUCH Relationships are established by touching and smelling, as when horses blow into each other's nostrils. Foals instinctively recognize the smell of their dam, just as the dam knows her foal. It is likely that members of a group are further identified by a corporate smell.

HEARING

A horse's hearing is far more sensitive than our own. Indeed, its head may be likened to a sound box served by the large, extremely mobile ears that can be rotated to pick up sounds from any direction. The horse is particularly responsive to the human voice, probably the most valuable training aid. Combined with a firm, soothing hand (touch), the voice is effective in reassuring and calming the horse. Used sharply but not loudly, it can encourage the sluggard or the faint-hearted.

SMELL

Smell is similarly acute and, like hearing, plays an obvious part in the defense system, enabling horses to recognize each other and probably their home surroundings, too. It is suggested that the sense of smell may be related to the horse's pronounced homing instinct (its ability to find its way home). Horses can smell human odor and by this detect any nervousness in the handler. They are particularly sensitive to the smell of blood, often showing disquiet and nervousness when near a slaughterhouse, for instance. Smell also plays a large part in sexual behavior (see Behavior and Communication pp.32–3).

SIGHT

Equine sight is unusual in many respects. The horse's eye is large in comparison with that of other animals, such as pigs and elephants, suggesting a heavy reliance upon sight. Unlike humans and other animals, the horse focuses on objects by raising and lowering the head, rather than altering the shape of the eye lens. Much of its ability to focus on objects in front depends upon the position of the eyes. Placed on the side of the head, as in many heavy breeds, there is wide lateral vision but much poorer frontal vision. In the riding horse such a conformation would be an obvious disadvantage. All horses, as part of the defense mechanism, have a degree of lateral vision, and are able to move the eyes independently. In fact, when grazing, the horse has all-around vision without needing to raise or turn the head, and it is quite possible that it can see something of its rider. Although not nocturnal, the horse can see very well in the dark due to the size of its eyes.

THE SIXTH SENSE

There are numerous examples of horses demonstrating an almost inexplicable perception. The reluctance of horses to pass reputedly haunted places is well documented. They also have an uncanny ability to sense impending danger, and they can be hyper-sensitive in detecting the moods of their riders.

TOUCH Horses gain confidence by touching strange objects with their nose and also with the foot, involving both the senses of touch and smell. They will often touch or paw at a ground pole in training before crossing over it.

Behavior and Communication

Horses have a sophisticated language of communication, which involves physical and tactile signals, or body-language, such as the laying back of ears and mutual grooming. Smell is also an important form of communication: the animals produce and receive pheromones, smell messages, which are produced by the skin glands.

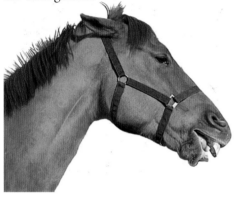

EARS AND EYES (Above) The ears reveal clearly the horse's state of mind and possible intentions. Should they be laid back in intense irritation or aggression, the action is usually accompanied by the animal showing the whites of the eyes.

THE IMPORTANCE OF SMELL

Foals instinctively recognize the smell of their dam. Furthermore, members of a group are identified by what may be a corporate odor. Smell also plays a significant part in sexual behavior. The pheromone sent by a mare in estrus is a clear message to the stallion that she is ready to mate. She also sends physical messages, the flashing of the vulva, for example, and the adoption of the mating posture when she holds the tail to one side. She communicates just as clearly if she is not ready to accept the stallion's attentions, by baring her teeth and attempting to bite or kick him. Indeed, she may further indicate her displeasure vocally by squealing.

Though horses are not as territorial as other animals, stallions do scent-mark their territory with urine and feces piles. The stallion will also urinate over the urine or feces of mares within his group, sending a clear message to outsiders that the mares are part of his harem.

FLEHMEN

Stallions check the reproduction cycle of mares by sniffing their vulva and urine. As the mare approaches estrus, the stallion becomes excited and indulges in a form of foreplay. He licks the mare and engages in tactile stimulation, which may be accompanied by flehmen, the peculiar curling back of the lip. Flehmen is not always associated with sexual excitement, and it is not the sole prerogative of the male horse. It can be provoked in both sexes by strong and unusual smells and tastes, such as garlic, lemon, or vinegar.

VOCAL COMMUNICATION

Horses communicate vocally, although in a limited way. Squeals and grunts are usually signs of aggression or excitement. Snorts are made when horses see or smell something that interests them particularly or something that is potentially dangerous. Horses whinny for separated companions, and may whinny out of excitement. A mare will neigh softly to reassure her foal, and both sexes make the same noise in anticipation of being fed or receiving a titbit. Some horses even learn to attract human attention by whinnying loudly if their feed is delayed.

COMMUNICATION WITH HUMANS

It seems certain that humans do communicate unconsciously with horses by the smells they exude. Frightened people and, perhaps, aggressive ones, too, give off odors that reveal their state of mind to the hypersensitive equine, causing it to become either apprehensive or aggressive, depending on

GROOMING (Above) Mutual grooming cements a relationship between the two participants. Mares groom their foals in this way, and stallions use it to stimulate mares sexually.

INSTINCT (Left) In the wild, the horse lives in herds composed of a number of groups. In part, it is possible that members of a group recognize each other by a corporate smell.

PLAY FIGHTING Young horses fight in play in the process of growing up, but they are also engaged in establishing a pecking order within the group. These encounters rarely result in either of the protagonists coming to any harm.

whether the animal is recessive or dominant in nature. Old-time horsemen smeared their hands in aromatic fluid when dealing with young or difficult horses. The saying "a bold man makes a bold horse" is revealing of the horse's hypersensitivity and another example of communication between the species.

TASTE AND TOUCH

Horses also communicate through the closely related senses of taste and touch. They do so when they groom each other, thus creating a friendly relationship. Humans seek to communicate or introduce themselves by touching and patting horses. In fact, it might be more effective to do as horses do and blow into the nostrils. Grooming is another way to communicate with horses and it builds up a relationship between the two.

UNDERSTANDING SIGNALS

It is not difficult to understand that a horse standing with a hind foot rested, head down, ears held slightly back, lower lip hanging and eyes partially closed, is in a relaxed state. The posture of tension is equally easy to interpret. Horses that turn their quarters to a human who enters their box are sending an unmistakable message. Stamping a hind leg, shaking the head and/or swishing the tail are signals of irritation.

THE EARS

Horses' ears give crystal-clear messages. Enormously mobile, they can be rotated at will, controlled as they are by 13 pairs of muscles. Their positions reveal the horse's state of mind. Pricked firmly forward, they indicate a strong interest in some object and a corresponding lack of attention to the rider. When relaxed or dozing, the horse lowers the ears and allows them to become flaccid. When laid hard back, they indicate displeasure, temper, or aggression. When one is stuck sideways, the horse has probably heard a wasp or fly. Twitching, mobile ears are comforting to a rider for they assure him that the horse is attentive.

REARING Horses may rear if startled. They also rear in play and as a way of displaying their dominant qualities. They may also rear out of excitement or sheer *joie de vivre*, particularly if they are being restrained. Stallions are prone to rearing for many of those reasons, but only a very few horses indulge in rearing as a "vice."

Pregnancy and Birth

Mares usually reach puberty between the ages of 15 and 24 months, but it may be later. It is possible to breed from a two-year-old, but three is more acceptable.

COMING INTO SEASON

From early spring through the fall, mares come into season (a condition referred to as being in "heat" or estrus) at regular intervals between 18 and 21 days. Each heat lasts five to seven days. During heat, a mare will accept a stallion. There are a number of unmistakable signs that indicate a mare is in season, although they do not all occur simultaneously. Mares may appear irritable and unsettled, and will seek the company of other horses more than usual. The tail is swished fairly constantly and the clitoris (the small, sensitive organ lying within the lips of the vulva) is protruded. Urine is passed frequently in small quantities and mucus is present around the lips of the vagina.

It is possible to establish the phase of the mare's cycle by internal examination, but the most certain way of finding out whether she is ready to be mated is by trying her with a stallion – a practice known as "teasing." At stud farms, it is usual to have the mare brought to one side of a padded partition and the stallion to the other. The partition prevents either animal from being injured. If the mare is ready, she will adopt the mating posture and hold her tail to one side. If she is not, she will bare her teeth at the stallion and attempt to bite or kick him.

PREGNANCY AND BIRTH

The average gestation period of the horse is 11 months and a few days. Obviously there are variations between broodmares but, as a rule, a colt foal is carried longer than a filly. The term for colts is approximately 334 days and for fillies 332 ½, but there is a possible variant of 9 ½ days either way.

When full term is reached, highly bred horses, like the Thoroughbred, require more

MATING Mating, when the semen enters the vagina and uterus, eventually reaching the Fallopian tubes, occurs two to five days before the end of estrus.

attention than the self-reliant pony breeds. It is usual for highly bred mares to foal in a foaling box with attendants keeping watch on closed-circuit television. Pony stock is nearly always allowed to foal outside and problems rarely occur. The pony mares give birth quickly, as they would under feral conditions where a protracted birth might attract the unwelcome attention of predators.

FOAL DEVELOPMENT IN THE WOMB

Two months (right) At two months, the length of the embryo is approximately 3–3¾in (7–10cm) from poll to dock. The limbs are distinctly formed and the sex is recognizable.

Four months (left) The foal now weighs about 2lb (1kg) and measures between 8–9in (20–23cm). The first traces of hair occur around the lips. The hooves have formed.

Six months (right) Hair over the body is much more apparent. External sex organs are formed. The length has increased to about 22in (56cm) and the weight may be upward of 12½lb (5.5kg).

SIGNS OF FOALING The foal's presence is apparent from the fifth month of pregnancy, and the foal's movements can be seen from the sixth month. As the pregnancy approaches its completion, the mare's belly drops. Signs of foaling are the udder enlarging and wax appearing on the teat extremities.

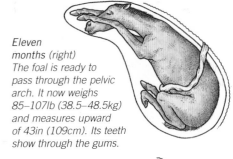

Eleven months (right) The foal is ready to pass through the pelvic arch. It now weighs 85–107lb (38.5–48.5kg) and measures upward of 43in (109cm). Its teeth show through the gums.

Ten months (right) Weight increases to 64–74lb (29–33.5kg); length to 34–37in (85–92cm). Coat and long hairs are fully grown and the foal is ready to turn for birth.

Eight months (left) The foal assumes an upright position. Both mane and hair along the spine grow. Weight increases to 36–42lb (16–19kg); length 27–29in (68–73cm).

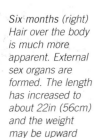

LABOR AND BIRTH Labor has three phases: involuntary uterine contractions as the fetus is positioned for expulsion, and the cervical and associated structures relax; voluntary expulsive effort when the foal enters the pelvis, passes through the cervix and is born; and the expulsion the afterbirth. Before and during contractions, the mare is restless, lying down and getting up again. During labor, contractions become more frequent until they occur every few minutes. This stage lasts up to six hours until the water bag ruptures and allantoic fluid is emitted from the vagina.

1 *After the water breaks, the mare lies down and strains as the labor pangs increase in strength. She will often grunt loudly and will sweat noticeably as the birth sequence approaches its climax.*

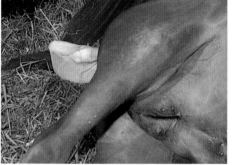

2 *In a normal presentation the forefeet of the foal are the first to appear between the distended lips of the vulva. They are covered in transparent membranes, the caul, which burst as the birth progresses.*

3 *The head lies on the extended forelegs and appears after the forefeet. Once the shoulders appear, the heaviest part has been delivered and the rest follows. As this happens, the membranes over the nose break and breathing starts.*

4 *The foal kicks free from the mare, at which point the umbilical cord may be broken off. Nature's "blood valve" will close, precluding the exit of blood from the foal while allowing an inward flow from the placenta.*

5 *Within a short time of birth, the mare will have gotten to her feet, breaking the umbilical cord if it has not already been severed. Within half an hour or so, the mare will lick the foal. This warms her newborn.*

THE AFTERBIRTH

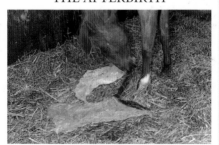

The afterbirth is expelled up to four hours after foaling. If it has not appeared after that time, veterinary attention is necessary. If any afterbirth is retained within the mare, septicemia can occur.

6 *After half an hour, the foal will be nuzzling the mare. The colostrum, the first milk the foal receives, is essential to its well-being. It acts as an antibiotic and ensures the passing of the meconium in the first bowel action.*

Foal Development

A new foal will be on its feet and suckling its dam within half an hour of its birth, and its development is correspondingly rapid when it is viewed in human terms. Foals born inside can be turned out with the mare on the second day, so long as the weather conditions are not impossible. If it is cold and wet, the mare and foal must be brought in at night.

EARLY DAYS

The foal's relationship with human beings begins almost as soon as it is born. In some instances, it is necessary to clear the mucus and membranes from around the nostrils at the time of birth, and during the first 24 hours of life it will need to be injected against joint-ill and tetanus. Initially, the mare may act

defensively toward her foal, placing herself between the attendant human and her helpless youngster. A good-tempered, kindly mare will soon get over this understandable apprehension, and if she demonstrates her confidence in humans the foal will quickly follow suit.

HANDLING

It is best to begin handling the foal in the stable rather than outside, and to this end the mare should be brought in for a short period each day. At this stage, the foal will naturally follow its dam without outside encouragement.

When the foal is no more than three days old, it should be possible to handle it with the help of someone holding the mare. The mare is placed alongside the stable wall and the foal needs no persuasion to come up along the nearside of its mother. The trainer or owner can then place the right arm around the foal's rump and the left around the chest. In a few days, the young animal will consent to stand quietly within the embracing arms so long as it is allowed to be close to its mother, its flank touching her side to give it confidence.

The next step should be to teach the foal to lead in hand and that, too, begins within the confines of the box. The mare is led quietly around and the foal will instinctively seek to follow her. It can be encouraged to do so by being pushed gently forward with the right arm, while the left is held ready to restrain any violent forward plunge. In a day or so, the left arm can be replaced with a soft stable rubber

placed around its neck and, in a short while, it will be possible to lead the foal in this fashion both to and from the paddock and stable. The foal can be reassured by the attendant scratching its chest, withers, and quarters in simulation of the dam's affectionate "love-nibbles" which she gives at those places.

Within a week, the foal can be fitted with a soft leather foal-slip and by then should submit happily to being led, so long as it is not too far from the mother. The slip is first put on in the stable, the foal being gently pushed into it from behind, rather than risking a battle and possible injury by trying to pull the slip over the foal's nose.

From the second week onward, the foal should be made used to being touched and stroked all over by humans. Its feet can be picked up for a second or two as well. This

TWO WEEKS OLD At two weeks, the foal will have become accustomed to the presence of humans.

AT REST Young foals need a great deal of rest and therefore spend a lot of time lying down.

SIX WEEKS OLD (Above) At six weeks, foals have become increasingly self-reliant as they have become stronger. When they reach this age they may share their dam's feed but they still need a regular supply of her milk (right).

READY, SET, GO Foals are on their feet within half-an-hour of birth and in an incredibly short space of time are able to keep up with their dams – a necessary accomplishment in the wild.

exercise will prepare the young animal for the time when the farrier is asked to trim its feet – when the foal is about three months old.

At three or four months, the foal learns to load into a box or trailer in company with its mother. The technique for trouble-free loading is for the foal to be loaded first, two people encircling the animal in their arms and propelling it firmly up the ramp. The mare, anxious not to be separated from her foal, will follow quickly into the box or trailer. In this way the object will be achieved quietly and securely without any stress to mare or foal.

FEEDING AND CARE

If the grazing is good and the mare has been fed well, her milk and the grass will be ample food for the foal up to the age of two months. Toward the end of that time, the foal should be sharing the dam's concentrate feeds. As a guide, a foal requires 1lb (0.5kg) of concentrate food per day for up to five to six months. In addition to oats, boiled linseed, and barley, the feed should include powdered milk, 2oz (60g) rising to 8oz (227g) per day, and cod-liver oil to promote bone growth. In winter, the foal needs an ample supply of soft, meadow hay, which will not overtax its immature teeth or its digestion. Apart from nutrition, a foal's other needs are plenty of sleep (rather like a young baby), as well as the company of other horses and enough space to romp in.

It is usual for colt foals, other than those intended for use as stallions, to be gelded before weaning takes place. Gelding can be carried out later but yearling colts can become unacceptably boisterous if left entire. Worming is an essential measure to be taken before weaning. (Courses of anti-tetanus injections are administered after.)

WEANING

Weaning takes place between four and a half and six months, when the milk hairs have darkened and the foal is able to feed on its own. Practically, it is an unavoidable step, but it can cause stress to both mare and foal and must, therefore, be handled sympathetically.

Foals can be prepared for the final separation by being kept away from the

TWO TO SIX MONTHS OLD (Left) Foals lose their furry, milk hairs any time after two months. (Above) By the time it is five to six months old, the foal is strong enough to be weaned from its dam.

dam for short periods. The mare can be exercised, for instance, while the foal remains in the box with a companion and with food available. The eventual, full separation must be total for at least four weeks, the mare being kept off the premises if possible while the foal is kept in a deeply bedded and very secure box. After a week, the foal can be turned out for short periods in the paddock so long as the mare can be neither seen nor heard.

Good feeding for youngstock is essential, as well as the freedom that allows them to develop naturally. By the time the foal is a yearling, it should be having not less than 7lb (3kg) concentrate feed a day, plus salt, an appropriate mineral supplement, cod-liver oil, and so on. Hay should be fed ad lib and ample supplies of clean, fresh water must be at hand.

Proper management of youngstock will pay dividends in terms of strong, healthy physical development that equips the horse for work and training later in life. It also contributes to an equable mental state. Well fed, and allowed to develop naturally under supervision, the youngster will learn to accept humans calmly.

AT SIX MONTHS After weaning, foals will be healthier if turned out during the day.

A YEAR Yearlings, when shown, are expected to be turned out immaculately, like this one.

The Breeds

Initially, horse breeds and types developed gradually by adapting to their environment, and through the natural kinship that existed between groups of horses occupying particular regions. Once the horse was domesticated, however, human intervention accelerated and altered the development of specific breeds and types. The practice of gelding male horses, allowing breeding to be carried on by a selective process from only the best stock, increased the quality and accentuated the characteristics most suited to the purposes to which the animals were put. Better methods of agriculture and husbandry produced more nutritious feedstuffs, and from the earliest times the chariot people of the Middle East were feeding grain to their horses. As a result, horses became bigger, faster, and/or stronger, according to the purposes for which they were required.

The world's light horse population is founded on prepotent breeds of largely Eastern origin. Foremost among them is the hotblooded Arabian, acknowledged as the fountainhead. Then there is the Barb of North Africa, also an Eastern horse; the Thoroughbred, an Arabian derivative; and finally the pervasive Spanish Horse, itself much influenced by the Barb.

BRED TO THE SADDLE This young Mongolian boy is representative of the horse people of the steppes, whose lives were bound inextricably to the horse on which their primitive economy depended.

Arabian

The Arabian horse, arguably the most beautiful of all, is unmistakable in character and appearance. It is also the purest and oldest of all breeds, having been carefully bred for thousands of years.

ORIGINS

While the exact origin of the Arabian is unclear, the evidence from art shows that a race of horses of fixed "Arab" type was in existence on the Arabian Peninsula at least 2,500 years before the Christian era. The Bedouin, the people who were most intimately concerned with this "desert horse," trace their association, albeit tenuously, from around 3000BC to the mare, Baz, and the stallion, Hoshaba. Baz is claimed to have been captured in the Yemen by Bax, the great-great-grandson of Noah, tamer of the wild horses. The spread of the all-pervasive Arabian blood throughout the world was made possible by the Muslim conquests, which were initiated by the Prophet Mohammed in the seventh century when the green banners of Islam, and the desert horses, swept through Iberia into Christian Europe.

INFLUENCE

The influence of the Arabian is apparent in the greater part of the world's equine population. It is acknowledged as the foundation of the Thoroughbred, which exceeds its progenitor in size and speed but cannot compare in terms of soundness and stamina.

The ideal height for an Arabian is between 14.2 and 15hh.

Withers The neck curves gracefully into rounded withers, and into shoulders that are distinctly set.

Neck A distinctive feature of the Arabian is the mitbah, a word applied to the angle at which the head meets the neck. This results in an arched curve that allows the head to turn freely in all directions.

Mane Both the mane and the tail are uniquely fine and silky.

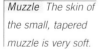

Muzzle The skin of the small, tapered muzzle is very soft.

HEAD The head is unmistakable and unforgettable. It is short and of great refinement, the face being pronouncedly concave or dished. The nostrils are exceptionally large and so are the eyes, which are widely spaced and lower than in other breeds. The ears are small, fine, and sometimes curve inward. A feature of the head is the *jibbah*, the shield-shaped bulge between the eyes, which extends from the ears to the nasal bone. It is unique among equines.

ENDURANCE The modern Arabian excels naturally at endurance riding, although it is outclassed in the other competitive disciplines. Nonetheless, it is bred in great numbers throughout the world with rare dedication, and is still a major upgrading influence on other breeds.

SKELETON The Arabian outline is governed by the unique skeletal formation. The Arabian has 17 ribs, 5 lumbar bones, and 16 tail vertebrae in comparison with the 18–6–18 arrangement of other breeds. This difference in formation contributes to the high carriage of the tail.

Body The Arabian back is short and slightly concave, the loin is strong, and the croup is long and level.

Color Chestnut, gray, bay, as here, and black are the Arabian coat colors.

MARENGO This etching is of the Emperor Napoleon mounted on his favorite charger, Marengo, which he rode in his last battle at Waterloo in 1815. Napoleon made a point of riding gray horses and had his personal stud farm of gray Arabian chargers. He greatly encouraged the use of Arabians at the French national stud farms.

Tail The root of the tail is set noticeably high in the croup. In movement, it is carried arched and well up.

STAMINA Arabian stamina is legendary, and there are numerous records of the breed's remarkable powers of endurance. In the nineteenth century, races were often held over long distances in the desert and could last for three days.

Limbs Arabian limbs are hard and clean, but without excessive bone measurement under the knee of the forelimbs. The tendons are clearly defined and the feet are near perfect in shape and size. Hind legs in the Arabian were, for many years, a failing, but for all that the breed is inherently sound and the movement is remarkably free.

ACTION The action is described as "floating," the horse moving as though on springs. The Arabian is fiery and courageous but also possesses an exceptionally gentle nature.

Endurance Riding

The expanding sport of endurance riding, now an International Equestrian Federation (FEI) discipline with European and world championships run under Federation rules, derives from the military rides held in the early twentieth century to test cavalry horses, but owes more to the US cavalry tests conducted in 1919.

CIVILIAN RIDES

The military rides conducted in Germany and the old Austro-Hungarian Empire were sometimes marred by their severity. In contrast, the American rides, conducted to assess the quality of Arabian and Thoroughbred horses as remounts, were carefully supervised and models of good horse management.

One of the first civilian rides was the 1936 Vermont 100-mile, and it served to encourage the formation of numerous trail ride associations all over the US. Today, over 500 rides are held annually.

The most notable of the American events is the Tevis Cup Ride initiated by Wendell T. Robie in 1955. It runs from Tahoe City, Nevada, over the Sierras, to Auburn, California, and the terrain is hazardous. Robie won the Tevis three times on Arabian horses, and the Arabian is acknowledged as the supreme endurance horse.

In Australia, where the sport continues to gain popularity, the Tevis equivalent is the Tom Quilty, just as demanding and run over similarly punishing country.

European distance riding in its modern form also evolved around the Arabian horse and was organized in the 1920s by the British Arab Horse Society, which is still much involved and runs a unique annual marathon.

The first rides were used to show the suitability of Arabian horses for the breeding of cavalry remounts. The horses carried 182 lb (82.5kg) and covered the 300-mile (480km) course in just five days.

The first 100-mile rides in Britain were held in 1937 and 1938. Today, in the UK and other European countries, there is a full program of pleasure rides up to 25 miles (40km), competitive trail rides run at faster speeds, and endurance rides of between 50–100 miles (80–160km).

All events are subject to rigorous veterinary checks, with penalties incurred for respiration, pulse, and recovery rates outside the set limits.

THE DESERT RIDES

As with the racing industry, the involvement of the Maktoum family, the rulers of Dubai, has given a huge boost to the sport. Sheik Mohammed and his sons are enthusiastic and successful competitors and the first endurance ride center has been built in the United Arab Emirates.

ON YOUR FEET (Above) To ease stiffening and aching muscles, and to relieve the horse of weight on his back, endurance riders will often dismount to run part of the course on foot. Riders wear safety helmets, but dress is otherwise informal and designed for comfort and safety rather than a stylish appearance.

FITNESS FOR BOTH (Above top) Horse and rider need to be physically fit to cover the distances without strain. Comfortable saddlery, meticulously fitted, is an essential, and the horse is encouraged to go in a relaxed manner while maintaining an easy rhythm.

DESERT RIDES (Left) The well-mounted Maktoum family, rulers of Dubai, compete regularly and successfully in endurance events both in their own desert country and in rides held throughout Europe.

Barb

The Barb is second only to the Arabian as one of the foundation breeds of the world's equines. Like the Arabian it is a desert horse, but it is unrelated in appearance and character. Its habitat is Morocco, in North Africa. There is a theory that the Barb may have constituted a pocket of wild horses that escaped the Ice Age.

PRESENT TO QUEEN VICTORIA (Left) This etching from the *Illustrated London News* of April 1850 shows some Barbs that the Sultan of Morocco presented to Queen Victoria.

ORIGINS

Crossings with Arabian horses have occurred throughout history, and the modern Barb must have a percentage of Arabian blood. Some authorities hold that it belongs to a desert (Arabian) racing strain that resembled a horse very like the Akhal-Teke (see pp.128–9) prior to domestication. Whatever the origin, the breed possesses a massively dominant gene, for there is no sign of the Arabian pre-potency in the Barb's long, convex profile, nor in its sloping quarter and low-set tail.

INFLUENCE

The Barb played a major part in the development of the Andalucian (see pp.50–1), and was just as influential in the evolution of the Thoroughbred and a dozen or more European breeds. Perhaps because it is less numerous and less attractive than the Arabian, the Barb has never received due recognition.

Tail Unlike the Arabian, the Barb tail is usually low set in sloping quarters that are also quite different to that of the Arabian in their proportions.

Quarters The hind legs and quarters are by no means exemplary, but the Barb can go very fast over short distances and has unplumbed depths of stamina and endurance.

Limbs The limbs are slender and certainly not perfect, and the feet are often narrow – but no horse is tougher and more frugal than the Barb.

MOROCCAN FESTIVAL Moroccan horsemen, descendants of the Berbers who led the Muslim conquest, display their riding skill in the wild, rifle-firing charge that is a feature of the North African festival.

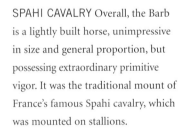

SPAHI CAVALRY Overall, the Barb is a lightly built horse, unimpressive in size and general proportion, but possessing extraordinary primitive vigor. It was the traditional mount of France's famous Spahi cavalry, which was mounted on stallions.

Head Arabian blood has improved the head, but the Roman nose is often evident and is indicative of primitive genes.

Withers The withers are reasonably well defined, but the shoulder is flat and often surprisingly upright for a horse of such agility.

Skull The Barb's skull verges on the primitive, its shape being pronouncedly narrow.

Body The back is short and very strong and runs up to an often pronounced croup. Usually, there is depth through the girth.

Color Originally, the Barb colors seem to have been bay, dark bay, and black, but the addition of Arabian blood has produced a large proportion of gray horses. This Barb is black.

NORTH AFRICAN FIGHTERS For centuries the Barb was the mount of the fierce, North African horsemen who penetrated Spain and were eventually repulsed by Charles Martel and his Frankish knights at Poitiers in AD732.

ACTION The Barb is renowned for its speed over short distances. It does not have the ethereal, floating action of the Arabian, but it is just as enduring, just as sound, and just as tough.

The Barb is between 14.2 and 15.2hh.

Thoroughbred

The Thoroughbred is the fastest and most commercially valuable of the world's breeds, and around it has grown a huge racing and breeding industry. It evolved in England in the seventeenth and eighteenth centuries as a result of the crossing of imported Arabian sires with a native stock of "running horses."

ORIGINS

Successive British monarchs from Henry VIII onward founded royal stud farms where the "running horses" were created by mixing Spanish and Italian imports with the Irish Hobby and the Scottish Galloway, subsequently reinforcing these with Oriental blood. Further impetus was given by Charles II following his coronation in 1660, after which the town of Newmarket became the headquarters of racing.

The breed has three foundation stallions – the Byerley Turk, the Darley Arabian, and the Godolphin Arabian. The Byerley Turk was captured by Robert Byerley at the Battle of Buda and ridden by him at the Battle of the Boyne in 1690. He is responsible for the first of the four great Thoroughbred lines: Herod, Eclipse, Matchem, and Highflyer (who was Herod's son). The Darley Arabian came from Aleppo in 1704 and stood in Yorkshire. He was the sire of the first great racehorse, Flying Childers, and the founder of the Eclipse line. The Matchem line is the responsibility of the Godolphin Arabian, brought to England in 1728.

Girth Depth through the girth allows for maximum expansion of the lungs, essential in a racehorse.

Forehand A long, graceful neck running into well-defined withers and a long, sloping shoulder is typical of the Thoroughbred.

Eyes The eyes are large and alert.

Nostrils The nostrils are large.

HEAD The head of the Thoroughbred is clean cut, lean, and very fine, with a covering of skin thin enough for the veins to be seen beneath. The profile, unlike that of the breed's Arabian ancestors, is straight. The eyes are big and alert, and the nostrils are large. There is no thickness through the jowl, and the ears are alert and mobile.

The average Thoroughbred racehorse is 16–16.2hh., but horses above and below that height are frequently found.

IROQUOIS (Left) This engraving is of Iroquois, American-bred winner of England's Epsom Derby in 1881 when he was ridden by the legendary figure of the turf, Fred Archer. Archer, who started racing at 13 years old, was champion jockey for 13 seasons, winning a total of 2,748 races. In 1886, when he was 29 years old, he committed suicide at Newmarket, where he is buried.

Body Length of proportion characterizes the Thoroughbred and is indicative of speed. However, there must be strength in the back, loins, and quarters.

Coat The Thoroughbred refinement extends to the body and the coat. They are both fine, and the coat is thin and silky.

Color Principal Thoroughbred colors are brown, bay, as here, chestnut, black, and gray, the last a color attributed to the seventeenth-century Alcock Arabian.

TEMPERAMENT The Thoroughbred possesses both physical and mental stamina and is very courageous, battling on when less well-bred horses will have given up. Not surprisingly, it is highly strung, nervous, and sensitive, and can be difficult temperamentally.

MATURING YOUNG The modern Thoroughbred is bred to mature at an early age, and horses are raced at two years old. This practice is wasteful and many youngsters break down under the strains imposed. It continues largely on account of the economics involved.

ACTION The action of the Thoroughbred is long, low, and economical. The length of the hind leg from the hip to the hock is long so that the hind legs attain the maximum possible thrust when galloping.

SECOND Second was bred by the Duke of Devonshire in 1732. He was, by the great Flying Childers out of an unnamed mare (who was sired by Basto, a son of the Byerley Turk). He was not a remarkable racehorse but he won two King's Plates, ran in heats of 2 and 4 miles (3.2 and 6.4km) and he carried 168lb (76kg)! The portrait is by James Seymour (1702–52).

Racing

Modern racing, called "the sport of kings" because of its association with the British monarchy from its formative years in seventeenth- and eighteenth-century England, has its origins in the evolution of the Thoroughbred during that period (see pp.46–7). Since then it has been the British pattern of racing that has been followed worldwide.

A MULTINATIONAL INDUSTRY

Although Britain may still claim to be the center of the international racing industry, the greatest world influence in the twenty-first century is that of the royal house of Dubai, the enormously wealthy Maktoum family. The Maktoums' Godolphin enterprise is based at Newmarket, the headquarters of British racing, while in Dubai they have created one of the greatest racing complexes in the world and stage some of the most valuable races in the international calendar.

Betting is a central element in the sport, as it has been from the outset, and is largely responsible for the unimaginably high sums changing hands for star performers.

THE CLASSICS

All racing countries stage a group of classic races based more or less on the British races and designed to set and raise standards of performance.

The British classics for three-year-olds are the St. Leger, the 2,000 Guineas and the 1,000 Guineas, the Derby, and the Oaks. The Triple Crown, racing's greatest accolade, is the composite term given to the 2,000 Guineas, the Derby, and the St. Leger.

The American equivalent of the British classics are the Kentucky Derby, the Preakness Stakes, the Belmont Stakes, and the Coaching Club American Oaks. The first three of these races constitute the American Triple Crown.

THE WINTER GAME

Winter is traditionally the time for racing over fences – steeplechasing and point-to-point racing – and the spiritual home of the sport is in Britain and Ireland. Steeplechasing is the professional side of the sport, while point-to-point meetings are organized for amateurs by the recognized hunts.

The greatest steeplechase in the world is the British Grand National, held at Aintree, and first run in 1839. It is run over a course of 4 miles 856 yds (7.22km) and has 30 fences, some with big drops on the landing side. Its best-known fence, which must be jumped twice during the race, is the awesome Becher's Brook. It was named after Captain Martin Becher, who fell into it, and it continues to take its toll. Although the Grand National is the best-known race internationally, the focal point for steeplechasing is the Cheltenham National Hunt Festival, which stages the prestigious Gold Cup. The most testing race in mainland Europe is the Czech Republic's Gran Pardubice, run over 4 miles (6.4km) and numerous natural and formidable obstacles.

A GLORIOUS VICTORY (Above) The joy of winning a great race on a brave horse is expressed in the ecstatic mud-stained figure of the jockey, while the horse, ears pricked and full of running, looks quietly pleased with himself.

THE GREATEST (Above top) The Grand National is the most famous jumping race in the world and a national institution. The first National, in 1839, was won by Lottery, and the greatest performer over the Aintree fences was Red Rum, who won the race three times, in 1973, 1974, and 1977.

RACING IN THE BLUE GRASS (Left) First race on the opening day at the Keeneland track in the heart of Kentucky's Blue Grass country. Keeneland is surrounded by some of the world's greatest stud farms.

Andalucian

In the development of modern horse breeds, the most significant influences are the Arabian and then the Barb. Discounting the Thoroughbred, whose history goes back only about 200 years, there is a third presence, the *éminence grise* of the equine race. This is the Andalucian, for centuries known as the Spanish horse.

ORIGINS

The center of Andalucian breeding is in old Spain, in Jerez de la Frontera, Cordoba, and Seville. In these areas, Carthusian monks preserved the purity of the breed with dedication. However, the precise origins of so old a breed are difficult to establish. Before the Ice Age, a land bridge, now the Straits of Gibraltar, existed between Spain and North Africa. Barb horses could have crossed over it into Spain. At the time of the Muslim occupation of the Iberian Peninsula, between AD711 and 1492, the indigenous stock was exemplified by the Sorraia Pony, a primitive type with a Barb connection. It seems likely that the Spanish horse evolved from crossbreeding between this native stock and that of the largely Berber invaders – the North African Barbs.

Head The handsome head is often hawklike in profile, and it owes much to the Barb (see pp.44–5). The appearance is always arresting.

Color The usual colors are bay and shades of gray, as here, and a characteristic mulberry shade that is very striking. There were strains in the old Spanish horses that were spotted and parti-colored. The coat patterns of the American Appaloosa and Pinto are inherited from Spanish stock imported by the conquistadores in the sixteenth century.

CARTHUSIAN INFLUENCE
In the seventeenth and eighteenth centuries, outcrossing, to heavy stallions to breed bigger horses nearly ruined the Andalucian, but the Carthusian monks of Jerez selectively bred the Andalucian, and the best lines today trace to those original Carthusian horses.

BULLFIGHTERS AND HERDERS The Andalucian, the mount of the *rejoneadore* (Spanish bullfighter, see p.54), is also the riders' favorite at the colorful *ferias*.

INFLUENCE The Lipizzaner is an almost direct descendant of the Andalucian. Other breeds that owe much to this noble horse include the Friesian, Frederiksborg, Kladruber, Connemara, Cleveland Bay, and Welsh Cob. The Alter Real and Lusitano are its blood brothers. Also, most American breeds descend from Spanish Horses.

BABIECA Babieca, for over 20 years the mount of Spain's national hero Ruy Diaz – El Cid (c.1040–1099) – died at the age of 40 and was buried at the monastery of San Pedro de Cardena. A memorial stands there in his honor.

Quarters The strength of the quarters and the degree of articulation that is possible in the hind joints make the Andalucian particularly suitable for the advanced movements of the manège.

SORRAIA PONIES The Iberian Peninsula was the first European area in which the horse was domesticated. The ancient base stock, primitive in character, is represented by the Sorraia Pony and the more refined Garrano of Portugal. The Sorraia is probably a descendant of both the Asian Wild Horse and the Tarpan, bearing an extraordinary resemblance to the latter. In height, the ponies vary between 12 and 13hh. and in appearance they are less than attractive. Their heads are large, with a typical, primitive, convex profile; the shoulders are straight and the tails low set. There are grays, and yellow duns with black points, and, in particular, duns with a dorsal eel-stripe and barred, zebra legs – the hallmarks of the primitive equine. Like their primitive forebears, Sorraias are incredibly tough and hardy, resistant to both cold and heat, and able to thrive on poor soils and forage.

ACTION The action is proud and lofty. The walk is showy and rhythmical, the trot high-stepping and full of impulsion, the rocking canter smooth and spectacular. The natural balance, agility, and fire of the Andalucian, together with its spectacular paces and docile temperament, make the breed well suited to the *Haute Ecole*.

STRONG AND ENDURING The short-coupled Andalucian, sometimes having a sloped croup and low-set tail, is not fast, but it is enormously strong and enduring.

Tail A feature of the Andalucian is the long, luxuriant, and frequently wavy tail and mane, which enhances the natural presence of the breed.

Generally, the Andalucian stands at 15.2hh.

Lusitano

The Lusitano is the Portuguese wing of the Iberian Horse. There are differences in the detail of the conformation, possibly resulting from the breeding policies employed, but the horse is, nonetheless, indisputably Iberian in appearance and character. It has an awesome reputation as the mount of the *campinos*, who herd the wild black cattle, and the *cavalheiros* who challenge and ultimately subdue the fighting bulls of the *corrida* (see pp. 54–5).

HISTORY AND CHARACTERISTICS

While the precise origin and development of the breed is uncertain in some respects, the Lusitano is the definitive horse of Portugal and, allowing for the occasional experiment, has been bred selectively in that country for centuries. Even so the name Lusitano (from *Lusitania*, the old Latin for Portugal) has been officially recognized only since 1966.

The Lusitano was the all-around horse of the country, used in light agricultural work as well as for general riding and as a showy carriage horse. It was also the mount of the Portuguese cavalry formations. Above all it is notable for its dominance of the Portuguese *corrida* as the highly schooled, supremely courageous horse of the *cavalheiro*.

In Portugal it would be unthinkable for the bull to be killed, as it is in Spain, and it would be a disgrace for the horse to be injured. The principles of this highly dangerous sport were laid down in the eighteenth century by Portugal's greatest Master, the accomplished Marquis de Marialva (1713–99).

Neck The neck is short, thick, and muscular, melding perfectly into the shoulder.

Shoulders The shoulders are enormously powerful and encourage the elevated, vigorous action of this supremely intelligent horse.

Limbs The forearm is muscular, and there is considerable length in the overall proportions of the leg which does not detract from the brilliance of the action.

The Lusitano is 15–16hh. on average.

REAR VIEW The full wavy tail, a little low in the quarter, is an Iberian characteristic. The strength of the quarters and second thigh is notable.

Girth The depth of girth may seem less than perfect but is appropriate to a horse of this athletic agility.

PERSONALITY There is an innate fire about this otherwise gentle and highly responsive horse. It is intelligent, courageous beyond belief, and possessed of an extraordinary agility.

Color Gray and bay are the most common colors; never chestnut, which would suggest an Arabian outcross. Dun is less usual, and there is the occasional and very striking mulberry shade.

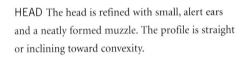

HEAD The head is refined with small, alert ears and a neatly formed muzzle. The profile is straight or inclining toward convexity.

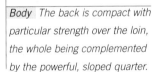

Body The back is compact with particular strength over the loin, the whole being complemented by the powerful, sloped quarter.

COMPETITION While the Lusitano performs a full range of dressage movements in the *corrida*, and does so at speed, he is less appreciated in competitive dressage events. The Lusitano is beginning to find acceptance, but his exceptional elevated movement does not attract marks in a field dominated by powering, specially bred European warmbloods, and he may suffer from a lack of conventional extension.

HISPANO-ARABIAN The breed is the result of judicious crossbreeding between the Spanish (Iberian) Horse and Arabian or Anglo-Arabian blood to produce a very refined, spirited riding horse. It retains much Arabian type, particularly about the head, but combines that special refinement with the substance and powerful back and quarters of the Spanish Horse.

Bullfighting

The subject is emotive and frequently misunderstood. Nonetheless, the elemental contest between the fierce black bull and the man, whether mounted or on foot, belongs to an age-old tradition, deeply rooted in both Spain and Portugal, although there are significant differences between the two that should be recognized.

BULLFIGHTING IN SPAIN

Bulls were fought by horsemen in the circuses of Ancient Greece and Rome and it is claimed that Julius Caesar was the first to fight a bull in Spain.

The proud Spanish *rejoneador* rides Andalucian horses schooled to the highest levels of the *Haute Ecole*. Using a string of valuable horses, the *rejoneador* goes through the sequence of placing the *rejones*, short steel blades, in the bull's neck. The *rejones* are followed by shorter darts, the *banderillas*. Finally the electrifying climax, "the moment of truth," is reached when he kills the bull with the long blade of the *rejon de muerte*.

In the Spanish ring, the entry of the *rejoneador* is preceded by the picadors, mounted men on horses protected by a quilted covering, who are armed with lances. They prepare the bull for the entry of the *rejoneador* by weakening the animal.

While the mounted horseman is an acclaimed feature of the Spanish ring it is really the *matador* (the killer), who, dressed in his tight-fitting "suit of lights" fights and kills the bull on foot. The *matador* is at once the hero and the star of the *corrida* (bullfight).

BULLFIGHTING IN PORTUGAL

There are no *picadors* or *matadors* in the Portuguese rings, and there is no moment of truth, for the bull is never killed and it would be a disgrace for the horse to be scratched let alone wounded. Unlike the stark, severely dressed *rejoneador*, the Portuguese *cavalheiro*, mounted probably on a Lusitano, dresses magnificently in eighteenth-century costume, all velvet, lace, and gold braid, surmounted by an extravagant tricorne hat.

He and his noble horse give a performance that is arresting in its beauty, artistry, and courage, and that displays the very peaks of the equestrian art. It is given in perfect balance at breakneck speed as the horse brushes the bull in a ballet in which the excitement is heightened by the element of danger and possible death.

The whole is performed as a controlled ritual governed by the rules laid down by Portugal's first classical Master, the 4th Marquis de Marialva (1713–99). In his honor it is known as the Art of Marialva.

THE COMMON GROUND

What is common to both Spain and Portugal are the fighting bulls, which have been the inspiration for a school of practical, classical horsemanship as old and sometimes even older than that of the other European schools (see pp.96–7).

THE CLIMAX (Above) The Portuguese *cavalheiro* delivers the *banderilla*, his horse, ridden on one hand, turning around the bull so closely that it would be difficult to separate them even by a whisker. This is the nearest approach to the famous and dramatic Moment of Truth that dominates the Spanish ring.

REJONEADOR OF SPAIN (Above top) Dressed traditionally in the somber clothes of the Spanish horseman, the *rejoneador* challenges the bull to charge. The horse, though coiled like a spring, maintains his composure as he awaits the terrifying onslaught.

THE FINAL DART (Left) With the bull charging toward him at full speed the Portuguese *cavalheiro* prepares to place the final dart with accuracy and precision. The turnout of both man and horse is especially noteworthy.

Alter Real

The Portuguese Alter takes its name from the town of Alter do Chao where it was first bred at the royal stud farm (hence *real*) in 1748. The stud provided the royal stables with horses for Haute Ecole riding and the bullring (see pp.54–5) as well as for carriage work.

DISASTROUS OUTCROSSES

In the turbulent history of Portugal, the Alter has on more than one occasion suffered from ill-advised crossbreeding experiments. Hanoverian, Norman, and English blood were all introduced as well as a massive and disastrous Arabian infusion.

The breed was saved by the introduction of the purest Andalucian strains (see pp.50–1) toward the end of the nineteenth century. The acquisition of mares from the famous Zapatero strain was particularly successful and, together with line-breeding to two exceptional stallions at the beginning of the twentieth century, was responsible for the wonderfully impressive modern Alter Real, which, it is claimed, closely resembles the original eighteenth-century stock.

DISTINCTIVE APPEARANCE

This breed differs distinctively in character from the other Iberian breeds, particularly in the back formation and the comparative length of pastern, cannon, and forearm, while the chest is exceptionally broad and deep. These conformational characteristics result in the extravagant action of the Alter and the notable knee flexion, both of which are useful attributes in a horse dedicated to the baroque principles of classicism.

The Alter is physically well suited to Haute Ecole riding and is the preferred mount of the Portuguese School of Equestrian Art.

Head and neck The head is noticeably Iberian in every respect. The neck is short, very muscular, and is naturally carried high, but there is no suggestion of fleshiness in the jowl that might inhibit flexion. The mane is fine and luxuriant.

Shoulder and chest The shoulder, running to flattish withers, is comparatively short and very powerful. The chest is exceptionally deep and broad and in this respect differs noticeably from that of other Iberian breeds.

Limbs The cannons are short and so, too, is the muscular forearm. The pastern is of proportionate length, with the slope being characteristic of the breed.

Back The back and topline, with the croup sloping characteristically to a low-set tail, are especially distinctive in the Alter but there is particular power through the loins.

Quarters Hips are broad and the whole quarter well muscled and strong throughout, while the development of the second thigh is notable.

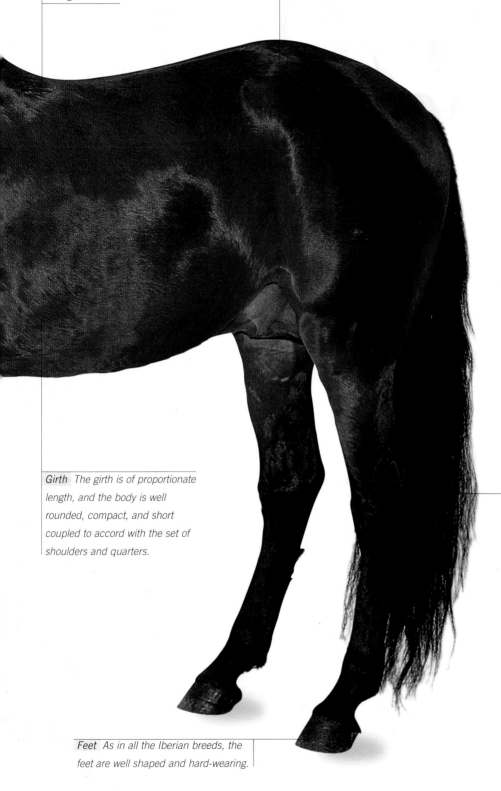

CARRIAGE ELEGANCE The Alter Real, bred in the eighteenth century at the royal Vila de Portel stud in Alter do Chao, was required as an impressive, quality carriage horse for court purposes, as well as for riding and demonstrating the Art of Marialva (see pp.54–5) when facing the fighting bulls. The strength, balance, and noble presence of the Alter make the breed especially suitable for both pursuits.

Girth The girth is of proportionate length, and the body is well rounded, compact, and short coupled to accord with the set of shoulders and quarters.

Hocks If the horse is to withstand the rigors of advanced Haute Ecole work, the joints must be very strong, clearly defined, free from any fleshiness, and formed so as to allow maximum flexion.

Feet As in all the Iberian breeds, the feet are well shaped and hard-wearing.

The Alter Real stands between 15 and 16hh.

Anglo-Arabian

The Anglo-Arabian originated in Britain but is also bred elsewhere. In France great attention has been paid to producing a specialized all-around horse. In Britain and France this is a composite breed, but no standard has yet been laid down.

Withers In the Anglo, withers are more prominent than those of the Arabian. The well-set neck is longer.

ORIGINS AND CHARACTERISTICS

In Britain, an Anglo-Arabian is a cross between a Thoroughbred stallion and Arabian mare, or vice-versa, with their subsequent recrossing. These are the only two strains in the pedigree. In France several permutations are possible, though to be entered in the stud book there must be a minimum of 25 percent Arabian blood, and ancestors must be Anglo-Arabian, Thoroughbred, or Arabian.

In theory, the Anglo should combine the best of Arabian and Thoroughbred. It should retain the Arabian's qualities of soundness, endurance, and stamina while incorporating the scope and some of the speed of the Thoroughbred, but without its excitable temperament.

BREEDING FOR SIZE In Britain, the popular practice is to use an Arabian stallion with a Thoroughbred mare, when the progeny are likely to exceed either of the parents in size. Crossing the Thoroughbred stallion with an Arabian mare is considered to produce smaller offspring of less monetary value than the purebred.

Mane The mane is fine and silky, as are the tail and coat.

BREEDING THE ANGLO-ARABIAN IN FRANCE In France, the principal breeding centers are the stud farms of Pau (shown here), Pompadour, Tarbes, and Gelos. The breeding of Anglo-Arabians in France began in 1836, when E. Gayot was director at Pompadour. It was based on two Arabian stallions, Massoud and Aslan (a Turk), and three Thoroughbred mares, Dair, Common Mare, and Selim Mare.

HEAD The head is more Thoroughbred than Arabian. The profile is straight, ears mobile, and eyes expressive. Although there is no breed standard, the Anglo also tends toward the Thoroughbred, rather than the Arabian, in overall appearance. French Anglo-Arabians from the southwest are lighter in type and have specific races reserved for them.

TOUGH HORSES The Anglo-Arabian from Pompadour is a large, muscular specimen, noted particularly for being an excellent jumper. The overall object is to produce tough horses of the best riding type that will race, jump, go cross-country, and compete at dressage.

Body The back of the Anglo is usually short, the chest is deep, and the shoulder is very oblique and powerful.

Quarters The quarters have a tendency toward being long and horizontal. The frame is well up to weight and is more solid than the Thoroughbred.

GEORGE IV DRIVING ON THE BRIGHTON ROAD This etching of Britain's George IV driving "Mrs Q" in his elegant, private carriage on the road to Brighton (c.1800) shows a pair of horses that were probably Thoroughbred. At that time, however, they would have displayed a pronounced, Oriental influence.

Color Colors vary in this excellent saddle horse. Chestnut, as here, and bay are usual, but brown also occurs.

ACTION The speed of the Anglo is not as great as that of the Thoroughbred (see pp.34–5), but the best are enormously agile and athletic and are distinguished by the correctness of their action.

Limbs The limbs are sound and uniformly good. Any lightness of bone is compensated for by its density and good quality.

The height of the Anglo-Arabian is between 16 and 16.3hh.

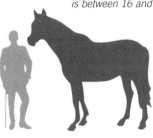

Shagya Arabian

Until its collapse in the early part of the twentieth century, the Austro-Hungarian Empire dominated horse breeding in Europe. At the end of the nineteenth century it had a horse population in excess of two million and some of the greatest stud farms in the world. Hungary's oldest stud farm, Mezöhegyes, was founded in 1785, and in 1789 the stud farm at Babolna was established. Hungary is famous for its superb Arabian horses, and Babolna became the center for their breeding.

ORIGINS AND CHARACTERISTICS

After 1816, the Babolna stud farm concentrated on the production of purebred "desert" Arabians and on part-breds, which were called Arab Race. Arab Race were the progeny of purebred stallions crossed with mares of very Oriental appearance that carried strains of Spanish, Hungarian, and Thoroughbred blood. This last policy produced the Shagya Arabian, which is now bred throughout central and Eastern Europe as well as in Hungary.

The race was founded on the Arabian stallion, Shagya, a horse of the Kehil/Siglavi strain, born in Syria in 1830 and imported to Babolna in 1836. He was a cream-colored horse and big for an Arabian, at 15.2½hh. He was the sire of many successful stallions, and his direct descendants are at Babolna and at stud farms throughout Europe.

The Shagya typifies the Arabian horse in every respect, but possibly displays more bone and substance than the modern "straight" Egyptian type, for example. It is, above all, a practical horse used for every purpose under saddle and in harness.

Color The predominant color is gray, as here, but all Arabian colors occur. The superb O'Bajan XIII, the "Black Pearl of Hungary," and his son, both stallions at Babolna following World War II, were black, the rarest of Arabian colors.

Limbs The Arabian horse has a largely undeserved reputation for having poor hind legs. Little criticism can be made of the Shagya Arabian in this respect since the breed's hind limbs are notably correct.

Height is usually around 15hh.

BRAND MARK
Throughout Europe it is customary to brand stock on the quarter or shoulder. This is done to denote the family and the stud farm of the horse's origin.

Outline The outline of the Shagya Arabian is identical to that of the purebred Arabian. In general, however, the Shagya is larger and more substantially framed.

Head The foundation stallion, Shagya, was noted for the beauty of his head, and his descendants inherit his great quality. The profile is pronouncedly dished, the muzzle tapered and small, and the skin especially fine, while the very large eyes dominate the head.

Body Like purebred Arabians, the Shagya has 17 ribs, 5 lumbar bones, and 16 tail vertebrae (other horses have 18–6–18). This largely accounts for the high-set carriage of the tail and the distinctive line of the back.

Shoulders Bred as a saddle horse, the Shagya has the necessary oblique shoulder that contributes to the freedom of movement and the length of the stride. If anything, the withers are more prominent than in many Arabian strains.

Bone In the Shagya Arabian, a practical riding horse, the measurement of bone (taken around the cannon below the knee) will rarely be less than 7½in (19cm).

ACTION The action of the Shagya, like that of all Arabians, is unique. Free and elastic, it is as though the horse moves on springs.

Feet Shagya feet, as with the great majority of Arabian horses, should be, and usually are, near perfect in both shape and size.

AT LIBERTY At the home of the Shagya at the Babolna state stud farm, it is customary for small herds of mares, often accompanied by a stallion, to run out at liberty for much of the year, although under supervision.

Belgian Warmblood

Traditionally, Belgium has specialized in massive heavy horses such as the Brabant (or Belgian Heavy Draft, see pp.208–9). However, to meet the modern demand for competition riding horses, the emphasis has shifted to the production of a warmblood in the mold of the other European competition horses. The average annual foal crop is now over 4,500, and in a short space of time the Belgian horse has achieved considerable success.

PURPOSE-BRED

The breed was founded in the 1950s by crossing the lighter Belgian farm horses with the Gelderlander (see pp.112–13) to produce a heavyweight riding horse. This was a solid, reliable animal but not one endowed with great talent or gymnastic ability. The Gelderlander was later replaced by Holstein stallions (see pp.82–3) and the more athletic Selle Francais (see pp.72–3), both having a strong Thoroughbred background and both moving notably well. Finally, to produce the best type of competition horse, pure Thoroughbred blood was introduced (see pp.46–7). Later, Anglo-Arabian and Dutch Warmblood crosses were added to establish the desired temperament. The result is a powerful, straight-moving horse of about 16.2hh., combining agility with good limbs, sound feet, and the calm temperament necessary for top-class competition. In fact, this newcomer to the warmblood scene is virtually specially-bred for both dressage and jumping. The stride, shorter than that of the Thoroughbred and more elevated, is an advantage in both disciplines, together with real strength through the loin.

Neck and head The neck is relatively short. It does not contribute to speed but it is strong and ideally suited to either dressage or jumping. The head is plain, but workmanlike, and the impression is that of intelligence.

Shoulders The shoulders and neck correspond to the shorter neck formation – a conformation inclined more to strength than to speed. The chest is big, wide, and deep with room between the forelegs.

Limbs Good, solid, short limbs, with well-formed joints and sufficient bone, are a feature of the breed, as are the good feet. They are open, well sloped, and equal in size.

GENETIC MIX *The Belgian Warmblood is bred all over its native country but particularly in the traditional horse-breeding area of Brabant. Wisely, much use has been made of neighboring breeds for outcrossing but, as with all the warmbloods, the Thoroughbred is the essential element in the genetic mix.*

Quarters The hips are broad and the quarters are powerful. Strong muscles carry through to the second thigh and there is notable strength in the loin.

Tail The quarters slope attractively, and the tail is set high and carried well.

THE RECORD The Belgian Warmblood has an enviable record of success in international jumping competitions, and this has been achieved in a comparatively short space of time. The gymnastic ability of today's breed is exceptional, and the level temperament is a great advantage in the potentially exciting atmosphere of the big jumping arenas, as it is in the training program.

Body The body is well rounded, with adequate depth through the girth. The withers could be more clearly accentuated, but the structure is compact.

Thigh A very strong, short second thigh is a plus point for the overall assessment of the hindleg and adds to the impression of strength.

Hind limbs These are acceptable and set well under the compact body, although the hock joint, in this instance, tends to be puffy.

The Belgian Warmblood stands at about 16.2hh.

Welsh Part-Bred

The Welsh Part-Bred has been in existence for much longer than most of the European warmbloods, but it is only in recent years that it has begun to be seen as a serious competition horse and to be promoted in a positive fashion, albeit to a limited extent.

INHERENTLY SOUND

That the Welsh Part-Bred has not had the impact of the warmbloods of mainland Europe is owed to the fragmentation of the British horse-breeding industry, a lack of purpose, and the absence of government support. It is, nonetheless, a very fine competition horse, versatile, very active, inherently sound, and courageous.

The Welsh breeds have for centuries provided a reliable base for up-breeding, passing on the sagacity of the pony breeds as well as their strength of constitution. The Riding Pony (see pp.236–7), acknowledged, after the Thoroughbred, as "the most notable achievement of selective breeding in equestrian history" is just one example.

PREFERRED CROSS

In the context of the competition horse, the preferred cross is that of the Thoroughbred/ Welsh Cob (see pp.224–5) with perhaps a second cross to the Thoroughbred to give greater speed and scope.

It is usual to put the Thoroughbred stallion to the Cob mare, when the character of the Thoroughbred will normally tend to predominate, but the opposite arrangement can also produce excellent horses, particularly when the progeny is then put back to the Thoroughbred.

Neck The good neck is sufficiently long to give a more than adequate length of rein.

Head The head is well formed, with large, expressive eyes, an intelligent outlook, and some quality.

Shoulder A strong shoulder, with reasonable slope runs from defined withers to an exemplary forearm.

BOLD PERFORMER This Welsh Part-Bred, result of a second cross to the Thoroughbred, competed successfully at Badminton (see pp.66–7) as well as in other international events. Constitutionally sound, fast, and strong, he is a bold, courageous jumper. Nevertheless, he still retains the native pony's "sense of self-preservation."

Back *This is a good back of appropriate length. It runs smoothly through to the croup and is powerful over the loin. It contributes materially to the attractive topline.*

Quarters *There is a lovely line over the quarter, good length from hipbone to hock, and breadth between the hips. The conformation allows for maximum engagement of the hind legs.*

CONDITION MAINTAINED This horse is by a Thoroughbred sire out of a Welsh Cob. The mare has passed on the palomino color. He is not built to gallop but his proportions are well suited to jumping or dressage. Indeed, he was a notable performer at advanced medium dressage level. Although an old horse, he has retained magnificent condition and his legs remain clean and hard.

Tail *The tail, which is set well up in the quarter, is of good length and without any tendency to fall away behind.*

Thigh and hock *The second thigh is muscled and of good length, while the hock is clean, very well defined, and without any suggestion of puffiness.*

Body *The body is compact and entirely proportionate, with very good depth through the girth. The ribs are particularly well sprung.*

VERSATILE HORSE The Thoroughbred/ Welsh Cob cross is a notably hard horse, free from unsoundness, hardy, and long-lived. It inherits the jumping ability and surefootedness of the Cob and is sensible while being courageous across country.

Limbs *The limbs are well made, muscular, and with the best of joints all around.*

Feet *The Welsh breeds invariably pass on their inherent soundness in the well-formed feet.*

The Welsh Part-Bred stands between 15.2 and 16.1hh.

Eventing

The French use the term *concours complet* – the complete test – to describe eventing, the most demanding of the equestrian disciplines. It is an accurate description of the most comprehensive test of horse and rider that could be devised. Like so many equestrian sports, it developed from nineteenth-century cavalry tests.

THREE PHASES

Civilian participation in eventing began after World War II. The sport grew with remarkable speed and attracted a majority of female riders. British riders are the most numerous in the sport, and their teams have an enviable success record. In recent years, Australia and New Zealand have produced outstanding teams and individuals, although it is English-and Irish-bred horses that today remain the principal influence in the sport.

The three phases of an event, held over three days (hence the term three-day event) are: the dressage phase, to demonstrate submission and obedience; the cross-country (or speed and endurance) phase, which includes a course of fixed obstacles designed to test ability, courage, and stamina; and the final arena jumping phase, to confirm that the horse remains "fit for further service" after the exertions of the cross-country.

The relative values of the three phases are calculated as follows: dressage 3; speed and endurance 12; arena jumping 1. These ratios are, however, under constant review.

Event horses are graded according to performance records, and there is a carefully devised progression from one-day pre-novice events to the full three-day championships.

World and international championships are held in the years between the Olympic Games.

BADMINTON

Eventing gained the greatest impetus and encouragement from the Badminton Horse Trials, first held on the Duke of Beaufort's estate in 1949. Badminton remains preeminent in the eventing calendar, setting the standard for other worldwide events.

At Badminton, the endurance phase covers about 16 miles (5.2km) and takes 1½ hours. The first roads and tracks section is 3½ miles (6km) long and the second is 6 miles (9km). In between there is the steeplechase over 2 miles (3km), with a time limit of 4½ minutes calling for an average speed of 25mph (42km/h). After a compulsory 10-minute break, riders tackle the 4½-miles (7km) cross-country course over 32 fences and a varied terrain. Since many fences are combinations, the horse jumps considerably more than 32 fences.

SAFETY

Although the organization of horse trials has always taken safety into account, a series of fatal accidents in 1999 compelled the sport to place even greater emphasis on "horse-friendly" courses.

ROADS AND TRACKS (Above) This section covers some 9 miles (15km) and has a time limit, although it is undemanding in any other respect. There are two roads and tracks sections divided by the steeplechase over a 2-mile (3km) course. The roads and tracks and the steeplechase precede the 4½-mile (7km) cross-country course, which is central to the event.

COMPULSORY BREAK (Above top) After the second roads and tracks section there is a compulsory 10-minute break in which the horse is prepared by the back-up team for the gruelling cross-country section.

THE WATER OBSTACLES (Left) All courses include a water complex. It is usually spectacular and always demanding of a high degree of courage and skill on the part of both members of the partnership.

Dutch Warmblood

No other European warmblood has been so skillfully promoted as the Dutch Warmblood, but in fairness, it has been produced with equal skill. There have been some notable performers: for example, the showjumper Calypso, and the immortal Marius, sire of the charismatic Milton. There are also dressage horses, such as Dutch Courage, which are of the classic warmblood breeding pattern.

ACTIVE HORSE (Above) The Dutch breeders were skillful in producing horses suited to the market needs. This elegant carriage, typical of the nineteenth century, is drawn by a surprisingly active little horse.

ORIGINS

The Dutch Warmblood is essentially the product of two of Holland's indigenous breeds – the Gelderlander (see pp.112–13) and the Groningen. It was then refined by Thoroughbred blood and adjusted by using French and German warmbloods. The Gelderlander was created in the last century by the breeders of the Gelder province.

The heavier Groningen was derived from the Friesian and Oldenburg. It had powerful quarters, but its front was not as good as the Gelderlander's. The two were put together, and the mix was adjusted by outcrosses to create a base for a competition horse. The carriage-horse action and the long, harness back were eliminated by the Thoroughbred. Temperamental deviations were corrected by a return to the related warmbloods.

Quarters The powerful draft quarters of the old Groningen farm horse have been refined by the extensive use of the Thoroughbred.

Color Any color is acceptable, but bay, as here, and brown are probably the most common. (There was once a skewbald strain in the Gelderlander, but it does not appear in the Dutch Warmblood.)

Limbs Dutch breeders have succeeded in producing a horse with good, sound limbs and feet, and one with bone and substance. The short cannon is a noticeable feature.

DUTCH COURAGE One of the greatest promoters of the Dutch Warmblood is Jennie Loriston-Clarke, the British dressage rider, who competed so successfully on Dutch Courage. Her displays in long reins, as here, and under saddle established the breed's reputation in Britain.

PERFORMANCE The Dutch Warmblood is already a proven performer in the show-jumping ring and the dressage arena, although like so many warmbloods, it is far less successful as a cross-country horse. The Gelderlander, from which in part it derives, is an excellent carriage horse that makes its mark in international events.

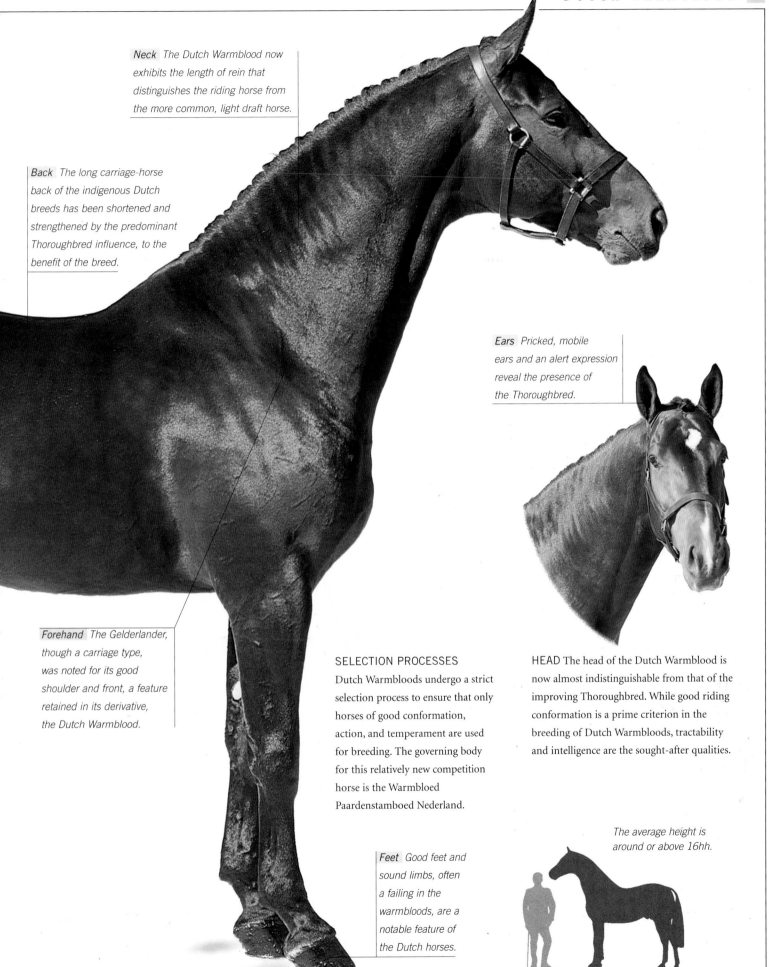

Neck The Dutch Warmblood now exhibits the length of rein that distinguishes the riding horse from the more common, light draft horse.

Back The long carriage-horse back of the indigenous Dutch breeds has been shortened and strengthened by the predominant Thoroughbred influence, to the benefit of the breed.

Ears Pricked, mobile ears and an alert expression reveal the presence of the Thoroughbred.

Forehand The Gelderlander, though a carriage type, was noted for its good shoulder and front, a feature retained in its derivative, the Dutch Warmblood.

SELECTION PROCESSES
Dutch Warmbloods undergo a strict selection process to ensure that only horses of good conformation, action, and temperament are used for breeding. The governing body for this relatively new competition horse is the Warmbloed Paardenstamboed Nederland.

HEAD The head of the Dutch Warmblood is now almost indistinguishable from that of the improving Thoroughbred. While good riding conformation is a prime criterion in the breeding of Dutch Warmbloods, tractability and intelligence are the sought-after qualities.

Feet Good feet and sound limbs, often a failing in the warmbloods, are a notable feature of the Dutch horses.

The average height is around or above 16hh.

Dressage

The word dressage comes from the French term *dresser*, which in the equestrian context refers to the training of the riding or harness horse. The modern sport has its immediate origins in the military "best-trained charger" tests, but its roots stretch back in time to the development of the classical art of the Renaissance period.

DEVELOPMENT

Sweden was the major force in the sport until 1956, despite a remarkable performance by the German teams at the 1936 Berlin Olympics. After 1956, Germany came to the forefront of world competition, dominating the sport and influencing the type of horse used, as well as the criteria of judgment, with their strong and now extremely expensive specially-bred warmblood horses.

The classical Haute Ecole movements of *passage* and *piaffe* were not introduced to the advanced tests until the Los Angeles Olympics in 1932, and the classical airs, or leaps, above the ground have no part in modern competition.

Dressage is probably the fastest-growing of all equestrian disciplines, certainly in Europe and particularly in Britain, where there is no tradition of school riding. The sport has generated a small industry devoted to its needs: specialized equipment and riding clothes, for instance, as well as an increasing demand for schooling arenas.

THE TESTS

Dressage tests range from those at the introductory levels to the ultimate Grand Prix test, which involves all the advanced movements. There is also the visually attractive *kur*, the freestyle competition to music, which brings the sport nearer to the otherwise disregarded art form of the past. The *kur* apart, the four international competitions are: the Prix St. Georges, Intermediate One, Intermediate Two, and the Grand Prix. These advanced-level tests are all ridden, as are the tests at medium level, in a large arena. Lower grade tests from preliminary upward take place in a smaller arena.

Each movement in a test is marked on a scale signifying the standard achieved: 10 excellent; 9 very good; 8 good; 7 fairly good; 6 satisfactory; 5 sufficient; 4 insufficient; 3 fairly bad; 2 bad; 1 very bad; 0 movement not performed. Today, overall marks are increasingly presented as a percentage.

DEFINITIONS

The FEI (the international authority for equestrian affairs), defines the objective of dressage as follows: "By virtue of a lively impulsion and the suppleness of his joints, free from the paralyzing effect of resistance, the horse obeys willingly and without hesitation." It speaks also of the "harmonious development of the physique and ability of the horse," which results in his being "calm, supple, loose, flexible … confident, attentive and keen…"

DRESSAGE DISPLAY (Above) A team of riders presenting a popular display of dressage riding and movements at the British national championships held at Goodwood, UK, the seat of the Duke of Richmond and Gordon.

ABOUT FACE (Above top) The advanced pirouette at canter in which the horse pivots on the inside hind leg. The movement, hallowed in the classical art, was not performed in competitive dressage until the 1920 Olympics.

EXTENSION (Left) An excellent extended trot performed with admirable composure, in balance, and with maximum flexion of the driving hock joint. The rider's contact through the rein and the head position are exemplary.

Selle Français

Since 1958, the French Warmblood has been called *le cheval de Selle Français* (French Saddle Horse). As versatile as the Trakehner (see pp.76–7), the Selle Français is both tough and agile. It is a mix of breeds, but owes much to fast trotting blood.

ORIGINS

In the nineteenth century, the skillful Normandy breeders imported English Thoroughbred stallions and half-bred stallions to cross with their tough but common, all-purpose Norman stock. Most of those half-bred stallions had a background of robust Norfolk Roadster (see p.98). They produced two crossbreds, the fast harness horse, which was to become the French Trotter (see pp.102–3) and the Anglo-Norman, which was subdivided into a riding horse and a draft cob. The former was the prototype for the Selle Français.

After World War II, the production of a riding horse possessing speed, stamina, and ability was accelerated. Trotters, Thoroughbreds, and Arabians have all contributed to the development of the type. Primarily, it is a show jumper, but it is also bred to race as AQPSA (*autres que pur sang association*, meaning "other than Thoroughbred"); many also participate in cross-country racing and eventing.

Of the existing breed, 33 percent are by Thoroughbred sires, 20 percent are by Anglo-Arabians, and 2 percent are by French Trotters; 45 percent are by Selle Français stallions, some of whom have trotting connections.

Neck A long, elegant neck, more graceful than that of the French Trotter, is typical of the Selle Français.

Shoulders Early Anglo-Normans, particularly those close to the Trotters, were inclined to straightness in the shoulder, a failing that has been rectified in the Selle Français.

Jowl There is no fleshiness in the jowl.

Medium weight *Small: to 15.3hh; Medium: 15.3–16.1hh; Large: over 16.1hh.* Heavyweight *Small: below 16hh; Large: over 16hh.*

HEAD The head has now lost the coarseness of the breed's Norman predecessors. This increased refinement has come from the Thoroughbred and Arabian influence. Despite increased quality, the head of the Selle Français remains reminiscent of the French Trotter.

Bone The Selle Français should have a very good bone measurement, no less than 8in (20cm). The old fault of small knees in the breed has been eliminated.

Outline The outline is generally that of the Thoroughbred, but there are unmistakable overtones of the more raw-boned Trotter in the body and limbs generally.

Quarters The quarters, very like those of the French Trotter, are broad and very suited to the purpose of show jumping.

LE PIN AND SAINTE LÔ The homes of the Selle Français are the great state stud farms at Le Pin, shown here, and Sainte Lô. The first stallions were installed at Le Pin in 1730, while Sainte Lô was founded in 1806. The old stud farm at Sainte Lô was destroyed by bombing in 1944.

Color All colors are permissible in the Selle Français, but chestnut, as here, is the most common.

FURIOSO One of the most successful stallions of the post World War II period was the Thoroughbred Furioso, bought in England. He had a great career, topping the sire ratings for 10 consecutive years and siring many international jumpers.

Limbs The trotting connection has passed on limbs of exceptional strength; the especially powerful forearms are a feature of both the riding and trotting horses. The joints must be clean, well developed, and correct.

ACTION The movement is active, long-striding, and characterized by a supple agility. The jumping ability is pronounced, and the breed has more spirit than many other warmbloods.

CROSSES Other than those mentioned, crosses that qualify for the name Selle Français are: Thoroughbred/French Trotter; Arabian or Anglo-Arabian/French Trotter; and Thoroughbred/Anglo-Arabian (with under 25 percent purebred Arabian blood).

Danish Warmblood

Denmark has an ancient equestrian tradition. Early in the fourteenth century, the Cistercian monasteries of Holstein (a Danish Duchy until 1864) established breeding farms, where they crossed large, North German mares with the best Spanish stallions obtainable. The modern Holstein and subsequent Danish breeds, such as the Frederiksborg, evolved from this early breeding policy.

ORIGINS

Nonetheless, the Danes were latecomers to competitive sports. A National Equestrian Federation was formed in 1918, but only in the 1960s was a stud book opened for a national riding horse, first known as the Danish Sports Horse and now termed the Danish Warmblood.

   The breed was developed by crossing local-bred mares with pedigree stallions from a variety of breeds and countries. The mares were half-breds, usually of Frederiksborg/Thoroughbred origin. They provided a sound base for breeding an all-around competition horse that was in increasing demand at the time. The stallions used were Anglo-Norman, Thoroughbred, and Trakehner, as well as Polish horses, like those once generally known as Malapolski and Wielkopolski. The Hanoverian influence is, however, notably absent in what can now be looked upon as Denmark's national breed.

Outline The outline can hardly be faulted and displays all the desirable attributes of the competition horse. The Danish Warmblood excels as a dressage horse, being naturally balanced, and is also an excellent cross-country performer. This specimen would not fail in the show ring either.

Color All colors occur in the Danish Warmblood although bay, as here, is the most common.

MODERN COMPETITION HORSE

The Danish Warmblood is one of the best examples of a modern competition horse currently being bred in Europe. It retains an excellent temperament while still possessing spirit and courage.

Feet The slope of the foot and pastern, and the length of the pastern, is exactly right in this superlative example of a modern riding horse.

SWEDISH WARMBLOOD The Swedish Warmblood originated some 300 years ago at the royal stud farm at Flyinge, and a stud book opened in 1874. It was based on a wide variety of imported horses. In this century, increased use of the Trakehner, Thoroughbred, and Hanoverian has been made to breed event and dressage horses of the highest quality.

Withers Well-placed, prominent withers, blending into the slope of the riding shoulder, ensure the best possible placement for the saddle.

Length of rein There is an impressive and reassuring length of rein in this good example of the breed.

Limbs The limbs are powerful, the joints big and well defined, and there is ample bone to carry the horse's body weight and that of his rider. The forelegs are particularly well made. The forearm is long and muscular, and the knees are big, broad, and flat.

Jowl The throat is clean and there is no suggestion of fleshiness in the jowl.

HEAD The head shows clearly the Thoroughbred influence. The expression is at once kind, intelligent, bold, and shows common sense. The overall effect is one of great beauty.

The height varies between 16.1 and 16.2hh.

Trakehner

The Trakehner is a breed of great antiquity. Of all the warmbloods, it is arguably the nearest to the ideal of the modern competition horse. Trakehner blood is often used to upgrade other breeds.

ORIGINS

The Trakehner originated in what used to be East Prussia and is now a part of Poland. In the early thirteenth century, the province was colonized by the Order of Teutonic Knights. They established the Trakehnen stud farms using the indigenous Schweiken as a base. These ponies were plain and often common, but they were also tough and hardy. Schweiken Ponies descend from the Konik Pony – a derivative of the primitive Tarpan. They inherit the Tarpan's natural vigor and powers of endurance.

In 1732, Friedrich Wilhelm I of Prussia founded the Royal Trakehner Stud Administration. This was the main source of stallions for all of Prussia, and the area soon established a reputation for elegant coach horses. Within 50 years, the emphasis shifted to army chargers and remounts of a quality unsurpassed in Europe. Thereafter, increasing use was made of English Thoroughbred and Arabian blood, which balanced deficiencies in temperament and constitution.

By 1913, most Trakehner stallions were Thoroughbred. The greatest influence was Perfectionist, son of Persimmon, who won the English Derby and the St. Leger in 1896. The best of his sons, Tempelhuter, provided a powerful line that is recognized as the foundation for the modern Trakehner.

Neck There is ample length to the elegant neck.

Shoulders The ideal Trakehner has good, well-shaped shoulders.

TEMPERAMENT Because of the influence of Thoroughbred blood, the Trakehner is a highly courageous horse, but careful selective breeding has ensured the retention of great stamina and endurance, as well as an exemplary conformation.

Ears The alert, mobile ears are always held well.

Eyes There is width between the expressive eyes.

HEAD The refined head of the Trakehner exemplifies the background of English Thoroughbred and Arabian blood. It is full of the quality that has earned the breed the title of "noble" – a word much used in describing what may be regarded as Europe's finest warmblood. It also has an unmistakable character and expression, not always so evident in other warmbloods.

Limbs Good, strong limbs and joints are a feature of the Trakehner. It stands close to the ground on short legs and cannons.

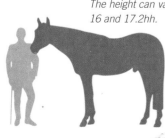

The height can vary between 16 and 17.2hh.

PERFORMANCE The Trakehner has an impressive record in international sports. Trakehners dominated the 1936 German Olympic team, which won every medal at Berlin. Since then there have been many notable Trakehners in the fields of dressage, jumping, and cross-country.

TEMPELHUTER When the famous stallion Tempelhuter died in 1932, his progeny at Trakehnen included 54 stallions and 60 brood mares. The other important line of Dingo owes much to Tempelhuter's daughters.

ELK-HORN BRAND This elk-horn brand is the traditional marking of the Trakehner Horse, which was also called the East Prussian. The horse is branded on its quarter, and the headstall is frequently engraved with elk horns.

Quarters The quarters are particularly powerful – it is interesting that the field for the Gran Pardubice steeplechase in Czechoslovakia is largely Trakehner.

Color The Trakehner coat can be of any solid color. This Trakehner is bay.

CONFORMATION The Trakehner has an excellent conformation, which, overall, is like that of a Thoroughbred of substance. It is a wonderfully balanced specimen – athletic, agile, and with great freedom of movement at all paces.

OUT IN THE FIELDS These mares enjoy the freedom of their pasture. Over half a century ago mares like these, with their foals at foot, trekked 900 miles (1,450km), across war-stricken Europe to escape the Russian troops. Only 1,200 survived, from a registration of 25,000, to continue the breed in West Germany, where the governing body, the *Trakehner Verband*, was formed in 1947.

Hooves Notably good, hard hooves in comparison to some other warmblood breeds.

Hanoverian

Probably the most successful European warmblood is the Hanoverian, which has a worldwide reputation as a show jumper and dressage horse. It is the result of a meticulous mix of compatible bloods supported by a strict process of selection.

ORIGINS

The Hanoverian breed was founded in 1735 on the stud farm at Celle, established by George II, Elector of Hanover and King of England. The object was to create strong stallions that, when mated with the heavy local mares, would produce all-purpose agricultural horses.

Initially, Celle relied upon 14 black Holsteins. These were powerful coach horses, based on native mares crossed with oriental, Spanish, and Neapolitan blood. Then the Thoroughbred was introduced, which at that time was more oriental in character than otherwise. The result was a lighter, better-quality horse that could be used in harness and as a cavalry remount, as well as for general farm work. The Thoroughbred influence was continued, but it was carefully monitored so the Hanoverian would not become too light.

By 1924, the stallion population at Celle was 500. After World War II, the policy was directed to the production of the riding competition horse. Trakehners – refugees from East Prussia – were used to reinforce the stallion band. Some Trakehners, as well as Thoroughbreds, remain at Celle and still exert a beneficial influence on the continuing development of the Hanoverian breed.

CAREFUL SELECTION

The selection of Hanoverian breeding stock includes controlled performance testing and takes into account the temperament of the individual horses. Hanoverians are bred very carefully for their equable and willing temperament, and for their reliability.

Neck The neck of the Hanoverian is noticeably long and fine. It runs into large, sloping shoulders, and the withers are particularly pronounced.

Color This Hanoverian is a bright bay. Every sort of solid color is found in the breed, no single color being predominant. The original Holstein foundation stallions were black.

HEAD The introduction of Thoroughbred blood has given quality to the formerly heavy and somewhat coarse head of the old-type, all-purpose agricultural Hanoverian. Modern Hanoverians have a lighter head of medium size, which is clean cut and expressive, with a large and lively eye.

BRAND MARK (Left) The stylized back to back "H" motif has been the distinctive brand of the stallion depot at Celle since the latter's formation by George II in 1735. It is estimated that over 8,000 mares are served each year by selected Celle stallions.

HANOVERIAN FOAL This powerful black foal was bred in England from imported and English warmblood stock. The color is reminiscent of that of the old, black, Holstein coach stallions on which the breed was founded at Celle. Hanoverian warmbloods are well represented in England.

Back The back is of medium length and is a strong structure; the loins are particularly powerful, as suits a jumper.

Tail The tail is always well set on the quarters and sometimes appears to be set noticeably high.

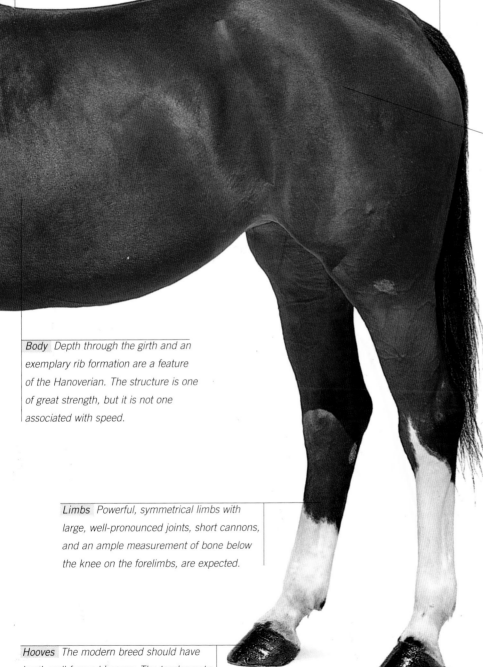

Quarters The quarters are exceptionally muscular, and sometimes there is a characteristic flattening at the croup.

Body Depth through the girth and an exemplary rib formation are a feature of the Hanoverian. The structure is one of great strength, but it is not one associated with speed.

WESTPHALIAN Though the Hanoverian is associated with Celle, it is used in the production of another warmblood strain, the Westphalian, notably at Warendorf. The Westphalian is, for all intents, a Hanoverian bred in Westphalia.

ACTION The action of the breed is impressive. It is straight, true, very energetic and has a particular elastic quality. There is little or no knee action and the stride is long.

Limbs Powerful, symmetrical limbs with large, well-pronounced joints, short cannons, and an ample measurement of bone below the knee on the forelimbs, are expected.

Height is approximately between 15.3 and 16.2hh.

Hooves The modern breed should have hard, well-formed hooves. The tendency to poor hooves has been largely eliminated.

Jumping

The first jumping competitions were designed as tests for hunters, and the first recorded organized competition was in 1865 when the Royal Dublin Society staged a high and wide "leaping" competition on Leinster Lawn in Dublin. Jumping competitions were afterward included in the Olympic Games held in Paris in 1900.

CAPRILLI

A watershed in the sport was the first Concorso Ippico Internazionale, held at Turin, in 1903, when the Italian team rode in accordance with the forward system *il sistema*, evolved by Captain Federico Caprilli (1868–1907), chief instructor at the cavalry school at Pinerolo. This forward seat, in contrast to previous practice, centered on the *advancing* hand, supported by the forward inclination of the body, from the basis of a much shortened stirrup. The weight was thus perfectly positioned over the horse's center of gravity. The seat enabled standards to rise and, with slight national variations, it was adopted worldwide.

Between the world wars, international jumping continued to flourish in both Europe and the United States. The backbone of the sport was the International Horse Show at London's Olympia, which staged the first Nations Cup competitions, and the National Horse Show at Madison Square Gardens, New York.

However, the sport was strangled by its own rules, which varied alarmingly from one country to another and were, at best, complex and imprecise.

THE RULES

After the World War II the rules were formulated internationally and time was introduced as a factor. Only then did the sport really begin to develop into its present form.

While international (FEI) rules vary a little according to the competition, basic national rules are straightforward enough. Under British rules, for instance, the first refusal is penalized at four faults, the second results in elimination; the fall of horse or rider earns elimination. Every commenced second over the time allowed incurs one fault. Domestic events are decided by those jumping clear in the first round, jumping against the clock in the second.

PUISSANCE AND DERBY

The long jump is no longer featured, but the high jump lives on in the puissance competition. In this, the final fence is the big wall, which is raised after each round.

The Derby competitions, held over long outdoor courses that include banks, ditches, and water fences, added a new, exciting dimension to the sport. The first of these was the Hamburg Derby held in 1920. In Britain, Douglas Bunn introduced the British Jumping Derby at Hickstead in 1961. It became a feature of the Hickstead meeting and inspired similar courses to be built by the leading equestrian nations between 1969 and 1979.

THE HICKSTEAD BANK (Above) A competitor descends the awesome bank at the Hickstead Derby meeting in excellent style. The Derby-type courses, adding a cross-country element to the sport, gave a new dimension to show jumping around the world. It never fails to provide a great spectacle for onlookers.

THE PUISSANCE (Above top) The malevolent, final wall that decides the outcome in the puissance competitions is raised after each round. From the start, it presents both horse and rider with an enormous test of agility, jumping strength, and courage.

ACTION (Left) An international combination in action during a major event over a big, well built, and imaginatively designed obstacle. Neither horse nor rider can afford to leave any room for error in the execution of the leap.

Holstein

A mix of German, Neapolitan, Spanish, and Oriental blood, the Holstein was in great demand by its European neighbors. They valued it because of its ability as a tough and powerful, but not inelegant, carriage or coach horse, and as a strong riding horse.

HISTORY

The main influences on the Holstein were the English Thoroughbred and Yorkshire Coach Horse. The Thoroughbred improved the gallop while the Yorkshire Coach Horse gave a high, wide action and an excellent temperament.

Thoroughbreds have been used to produce a lighter competition horse. The modern Holstein resembles a quality hunter and is successful as a show jumper, dressage horse, and eventer.

Forehand The chest is wide and deep, but the sloping shoulder of the modern Holstein, and the long, slightly arched neck, conform entirely to the riding horse requirement and do not reflect the coaching background.

Eyes Large, bright eyes are characteristic of Holsteins.

HEAD The old Holstein was plain and heavy around the head, and often had a convex profile. The infusions of Thoroughbred have given refinement to the head of the present-day Holstein, which is now that of a quality hunter; it is expressive, with large, bright eyes and well-placed ears. The tendency toward heaviness in the lower jaw, a failing in the past, has now been almost entirely eliminated.

Bone The pastern corresponds to the slope of the shoulder, while the bone measurement under the knee is expected to be 8–9½in (20–24cm).

DRESSAGE HORSE Its temperament and regularity of paces make the Holstein a natural choice for dressage. Probably the best eventing prospect of the German breeds, Holsteins have also produced some of the postwar period's finest show jumpers, such as Fritz Thiedemann's Meteor.

THE PACES Much emphasis is given to the quality of the paces. The walk is long, free, and elastic, and the action straight. The trot is active, very balanced and rhythmic, and covers a lot of ground; a little knee action (inherited from the carriage type) is permissible. The canter is smooth, straight and, again, in easy balance.

Body Body structure is one of strength combined with quality. The withers are of pronounced riding type, the chest is deep, and the back and loins are strong and muscular.

Color All colors are permissible. The most typical are bay, with black points, and brown, as here. Grays are quite common, but chestnuts less so.

TANDEM TEAM In the nineteenth century, the Holstein was used extensively as a harness horse. This illustration shows Holsteins harnessed in tandem. As a carriage horse, the Holstein had strength and presence, as well as a tractable disposition. The pronounced knee action has been reduced to a slight bend in modern horses, and the coaching shoulder has disappeared.

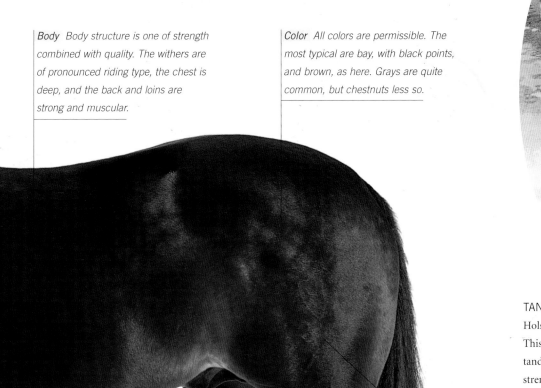

Quarters The tail is always carried well, but it is not set over-high in the powerful quarters, which run into strongly muscular stifles, thighs, and gaskins.

Limbs The limbs are exemplary with big, flat knees, well-formed hocks, and short cannons. The forelegs are set well apart and the elbows are clear of the body.

Feet The Thoroughbred influence has improved the feet, which were a failing of the old coaching breeds of mainland Europe. Breeders of the Holstein pay careful attention to the correctness of size, shape, and density of horn.

Holsteins are 16–17hh. (For registration, three-year-old fillies should be 16hh., and premium stallions of two-and-a-half years should be 16.1–16.2hh.)

Oldenburg

The Oldenburg, the heaviest of the German warmbloods, was established in the 1600s, largely through the efforts of Count Anton Gunther von Oldenburg (1603–67). He used the half-bred stallion, Kranich, and a base of Friesians.

Neck *The neck is long and very strong but still reflects the coaching background.*

HISTORY

To this Friesian base were added Spanish Horses, Barbs, Neapolitans, and English half-breds, and during the nineteenth century the breeders introduced Thoroughbreds, Cleveland Bays, Hanoverians, and French Norman strains. The resultant coach horse, or *karossierpferd*, was 17hh. and heavily built. Despite its size and build, it was noted for its early maturity. With the decline in demand for heavy coach horses, the breed developed as a general-purpose farm horse. When demand changed again, after 1945, more Thoroughbred and Norman blood was introduced to make the Oldenburg closer to a riding type. Today it is an all-purpose riding horse, still big and powerful; and although it retains some of the harness horses' knee, this is much freer than its ancestors.

HEAD The head can be described as plain but honest. The profile is straight, but a tendency toward a Roman nose is not unknown. There is occasionally some thickness of the jowl. Nonetheless, the expression is essentially kind and genuine, and the eye has a hint of boldness.

IMPRESSIVE AND VERSATILE The modern Oldenburg is lighter than its forebears and moves with greater freedom. A big, impressive horse, it is well suited to the dressage discipline on account of its kind temperament and regular paces, but it still retains its ability as a powerful harness horse.

Limbs *To carry so big a frame, the limbs are strong and short, with large, well-developed joints, short cannons, and a bone measurement below the knee that is upward of 9in (23cm). The placement and length of the humerus in respect of the scapula accounts for the fairly high knee action.*

Feet *When stallions are tested before licensing, particular attention is paid to the feet. In so big an animal, they must be well open at the heels, large enough in proportion to the horse, and of sound quality.*

Build Of all the warmblood riding horses, the Oldenburg is the most powerfully built. The chest is exceptionally deep, which contributes to the action. The shoulder does not approach that of the Thoroughbred in length and shape and, combined with the width of the chest, is not conducive to speed. However, the paces are rhythmical and even elastic, the horse moving very correctly.

Quarters The quarters and the hind limbs are very strong. Although the Oldenburg is not built for speed, it is known as a powerful jumper, as well as being a good performer in dressage competitions.

Tail The tail is set and carried noticeably high in the strong quarters.

THE DUTCH GRONINGEN An offshoot of the Oldenburg, the Dutch Groningen played its part in the evolution of the Dutch Warmblood. It derives from crosses between the Oldenburg and the Oldenburg's close relation, the East Friesian (from which the former was once indistinguishable), and the heavier Friesian mares. It was a strong, steady carriage horse, noted for its good quarters, that could be used for farm work and as a useful, if undistinguished, heavyweight riding horse. The old pure type, which was very similar to the Oldenburg of the period, probably does not exist today.

SOCIETY OF BREEDERS Under Acts of 1819, amended in 1897 and again in 1923, the responsibility for the breed and licensing of stallions lies with the Society of Breeders of the Oldenburg Horse, in the area of Oldenburg. The society pursues a policy of careful selection, resulting in uniformity of type. Its stallions are performance-tested in their third year.

Color Colors in the breed are mostly brown, black, and bay, as here. Chestnuts and grays are unusual if, indeed, they are seen at all.

CHARACTERISTICS The coach-horse characteristics, particularly in respect of shoulders and the length of the back, have been largely eliminated in the modern Oldenburg riding horse by the use of Thoroughbred blood. The German breeders, however, have ensured that the Oldenburg retains its reputation for being temperamentally reliable.

The height of the Oldenburg is 16–17.2hh.

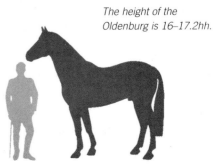

Hunter

By definition, a hunter is any horse used for the purpose of riding to hounds. It is a type of horse and may vary according to the requirements of the country in which it is used. It does not share common characteristics, such as color, and so it is not a breed.

ORIGINS

The best hunters are those bred in Ireland, Britain, and, to a degree, the US, where the Thoroughbred element is equally paramount. The Irish hunter is often based on the Irish Draft/ Thoroughbred cross, as is sometimes the case with those bred in Britain. Any cross is permissible, and many good hunters have a background of pony blood such as Connemara, New Forest, Fell, Highland, or Welsh Cob. However, the best hunters will always carry a good proportion of Thoroughbred blood.

CHARACTERISTICS

A good hunter is sound, well proportioned and with all the conformational attributes of the top-class riding horse. It is well balanced, with easy, comfortable paces, and fast enough to keep with hounds. The animal requires courage, agility, stamina, and jumping ability, to cope with every kind of obstacle during a long day in the field. Temperate and well mannered, the hunter must have a robust constitution that allows him to hunt up to two days a week throughout the season.

Height in the hunter is variable. The average, except for small hunters, is around 16–16.2hh.

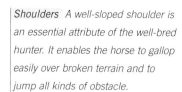

Shoulders A well-sloped shoulder is an essential attribute of the well-bred hunter. It enables the horse to gallop easily over broken terrain and to jump all kinds of obstacle.

CONFORMATION A quality hunter has all the attributes of a riding horse combined with substance, strength, and good bone. A well-made horse stays sound for longer than one of poor conformation.

Color All colors are acceptable in the hunter. This one is dark bay.

THE HUNTER AND HIS HUNTER For 300 years, hunting has been the sport of the countryside. "Go anywhere in England where there are natural, wholesome, contented, and really nice English people; and what do you always find? That the stables are the real center of the household." G.B. Shaw.

THE SECOND HORSE (Left) This nineteenth-century etching illustrates the practice of employing "second horses." This is continued today in the fast, galloping grass countries of the English shires. The owner rides his first horse in the morning and changes to his fresh "second horse" for the afternoon's hunting. The groom, or second horseman, follows the hunt quietly on lanes and tracks until the replacement horse is required.

HEAD Hunters are not always as beautiful as this one, but they should show some quality and give the impression of being workman like and honest. The good ones have a look about them that denotes intelligence and an equable disposition.

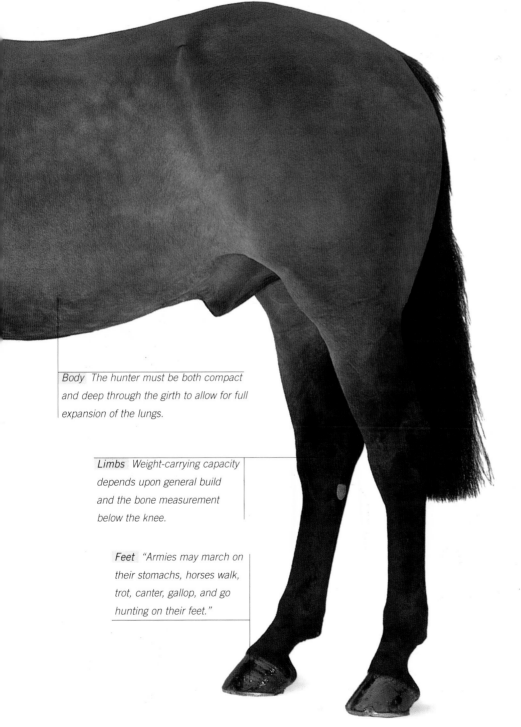

Body The hunter must be both compact and deep through the girth to allow for full expansion of the lungs.

Limbs Weight-carrying capacity depends upon general build and the bone measurement below the knee.

Feet "Armies may march on their stomachs, horses walk, trot, canter, gallop, and go hunting on their feet."

REAR VIEW An exemplary rear view of a quality horse. Quarters and gaskins are powerful, joints clean and hard, and the cannons of the hind legs are straight, not being offset below the hock joints. The overall impression is that of strength and of galloping potential.

Hunting

The oldest tradition of organized hunting in Europe belongs to France, where some 75 packs, termed *equipage* when the quarry is the stag, and *vautrait* when it is the wild boar, continue to hunt in visually spectacular style, to the musical accompaniment of the curled French horns sounding the *fanfares de circonstance.*

BRITISH FOX HUNTING

It was the French who introduced the sport of hunting to England following the Norman Conquest of 1066. At that time the recognized "beasts of chase" were the stag, the boar, and sometimes, the wolf.

Not until the seventeenth century did the English begin to hunt the fox, which, by the nineteenth century, was the accepted quarry.

In the UK and Ireland hunting attracts such large fields (mounted followers) that numbers have to be limited in the interests of conservation.

Hunting is controlled by the Masters of Foxhounds Association, each hunt having its own clearly defined country. The pack is usually the property of a committee which appoints the masters, to whom it grants an annual sum from which the kennel and stable staff are paid.

If a master hunts the pack he is said to "carry the horn." He is the only one who actually carries a horn, blowing specific calls to communicate with his hounds, his helpers, and the field.

Although hunting is conducted under strictly enforced regulations and supports a multimillion dollar industry, there is opposition to its continuance, especially in the urban-dominated UK. Irish hunting is less threatened, and the American packs much less so, if at all. As this book went to press, the whole subject of the future of hunting in the UK was once more a highly sensitive social and political issue.

THE CLEAN BOOT

Drag hunting, sometimes put forward as a viable alternative to fox hunting, is a popular cross-country sport in areas where fox hunting is impractical. Hounds hunt a "drag," a strong-smelling lure, largely made up of animal excreta. When bloodhounds are used, the hounds hunt the "clean boot" – the scent left by man.

THE AMERICAN SPORT

In the United States, the enthusiasm for hunting is increasing with each season. The early colonists established the sport, strictly on the British pattern, in Virginia, Maryland, and Pennsylvania, about the same time that the sport was developing in Britain.

The red English fox was once imported into the United States, but for most packs the indigenous gray fox is hunted. In the western United States the quarry is the coyote.

In the British Isles it is the Irish hunter that still reigns supreme as the preferred mount, but in the United States its counterpart is likely to be the big, elegant American Thoroughbred.

LEADING THE WAY (Above) The master or field master (whose job it is to control the field) needs to be able to show the way over the countryside, taking his fences as they come. He has to be a good, bold horseman, to be well mounted, and to know every field and furrow in the hunt country like the back of his hand.

MOVING OFF (Above top) The huntsman, followed at a respectful distance by the field, moves off from the meet, taking his hounds on to draw through the first selected covert – a copse or a piece of gorse, perhaps – likely to harbor a fox.

IN WASHINGTON'S COUNTRY (Left) A Virginian fox hunter, traditionally attired, follows the Fairfax Hounds, which were founded by Lord Fairfax in 1747. The country is as "well-foxed" as it was in Washington's day.

Hack

In times gone by, grooms rode their masters' hunters quietly to the meet, and the owners, after breakfasting, followed in their dogcarts or carriages, or they rode on a "covert hack." This was a Thoroughbred riding horse, elegant, well mannered, and comfortable to ride at a smooth "hack canter." The covert hack was an attractive, showy horse, lighter than a hunter. It did not have to carry weight for a full day's hunt nor, therefore, did it have to have the substance and bone essential for the hunting field.

PARK HACK

Even more refined than the covert hack was the beautiful and highly schooled "park hack." In the fashionable days of riding in Rotten Row in London's Hyde Park, the park hack paraded its well-tailored owner, who often might be escorting a lady, before the appraising and sometimes critical public eye. To show off its rider to full advantage, the park hack was brimful of presence, moving in all the paces with lightness and with great gaiety and freedom. Its manners, like its appearance, could not be less than absolutely impeccable.

MODERN HACK

The same qualities are required of the modern show-ring hack, which must be a model of good conformation. While light and graceful, a modern hack is not a "blood weed" (a horse lacking bone and substance) and it is expected to have not less than 8in (20cm) of bone under the knee.

The majority of entrants in hack classes are Thoroughbred, or nearly so, and are far closer to the park hack than to the stronger covert type. Some, however, may be part-bred Arabians and one or two very good ones are Anglo-Arabians. Show classes are for small hacks (14.2–15hh.), large hacks (15–15.3hh.), and ladies' hacks (14.2–15.3hh.). Ladies' hacks are shown under sidesaddle. Hacks are shown at walk, trot, and canter. They are not required to gallop but must give an individual display. In British shows, entries are also ridden by the judge.

ACTION Hack action must be straight, true, and low to the ground with no tendency toward dishing or lifting the knee. The trot is smooth and floating, the canter is slow, light, and in perfect balance, and the movement is distinguished by a particular brilliance. While the hack is schooled to perfection, the performance is not expected to resemble the disciplined accuracy of the dressage horse.

REAR VIEW Viewed from behind, the immediate impression is one of graceful symmetry combined with strength. No deviation is tolerated in the straightness of the hind limbs or in the construction of the joints. A good second thigh and enough width over the quarters is just as much a requirement of the hack as of any equine. The feet must be of the highest quality.

Outline The overall outline of the hack is that of the Thoroughbred, the structure being designed for speed. The proportions are as near to perfect as possible, and the musculature is long, never short and thick.

Mane When shown, hacks have their manes braided to show off the neck. The tail is either thinned by pulling or it, too, is braided.

Ears Ears should be mobile and attentive.

Color The hack can be any solid color. This one is dark bay.

HEAD A quality head denotes well-bred antecedents, and such a head is essential in the hack. No show class was ever won by a horse that was common in this respect. Big, bold, and generous eyes are a feature.

DEFINITION One telling definition of a hack describes it as a horse to be ridden with one hand while its owner flirts with a lady companion.

Feet Hacks are shown in lightweight shoes to enhance the action.

The height of the hack is 14.2–15.3hh, depending on the class requirement.

Cob

Stocky little horses, big-bodied, and standing squarely on short, powerful legs, cobs are unmistakable in their appearance. Their overall conformation, with short, thick musculature, is that of a structure far more disposed to strength and weight-carrying capacity than to speed. For all that, the true cob is able to gallop, and the action is more low than high.

ORIGINS

The cob is a type, not a recognized breed, and there is no set pattern to its production. Some of the very best cobs are produced as the result of crossing an Irish Draft or a heavyweight hunter with a Thoroughbred, and some recent champions have been pure Irish Draft Horses. Occasionally, there have been examples of cobs bred from or by Shires and Welsh Cobs. However, their breeding is rarely deliberate and often accidental.

CHARACTERISTICS

Until the passing of the UK Docking and Nicking Act 1948, which made the practices illegal in Britain, it was traditional to dock the tails of cobs. This gave a jaunty, sporty appearance, but it was a cruel and unnecessary custom.

   The word most frequently applied to cobs is "confidential," and it suits them admirably. Their job is to provide a steady, unflappable ride for a heavyweight rider who may have passed the first flush of youth. Their manners, therefore, have to be very good and they should certainly never "hot up." Most cobs, indeed, have a particular intelligence and are usually full of character.

   In the past, the cob was a dual-purpose animal, going as well in harness as under saddle. Today, a cob is more likely to be kept as a general family horse, and many of them make great hunters that are easy and economical to keep.

Color Cobs are of any color, but many are gray as a result of the Irish Draft influence. No objection would be made to a skewbald or even a spotted one, although these are extremely rare. This cob is bay.

Quarters Big, strongly muscled, and well-formed quarters are a characteristic of the cob, whose job is to carry weight. They are too thick-set for any great speed, but can usually jump well.

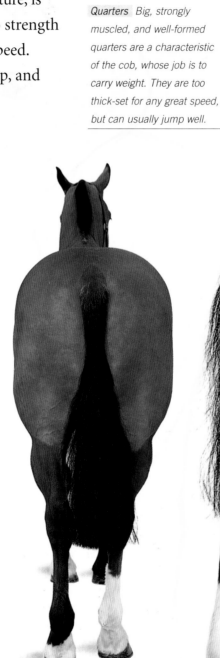

REAR VIEW The cob does not always have a head "like a lady's maid" but he certainly has "the bottom of a cook." The back end may not be conducive to speed, but there is no doubting its strength.

Back The back is short and fairly broad, as suits a weight-carrying structure, and the loins are thick and powerful. A long back, particularly if accompanied by slackness in the loin, is an unacceptable conformational fault in the cob.

Shoulders The shoulders are strong but are sufficiently sloped for low, economical movement and to prohibit any exaggerated action from the knee.

IMPRESSION The cob is a gentleman's gentleman.

Neck The neck, in accordance with the cob's build, is relatively short. It is, however, crested and strong.

Mane The mane is always hogged.

Girth Cobs stand on short, powerful limbs, but the great depth of girth gives them the appearance of being even shorter than they are in reality.

Limbs The cannon below the knee is short, and the bone measurement, which is taken below the knee and governs the weight-carrying capacity, can be as much as 9in (23cm).

Knees The knees are large and flat, and the forearms are strongly muscled and quite free where they join the body at the elbow.

Feet The cob has broad, open feet of a size in proportion to its build.

HEAD The cob head is sensible, workman like, and honest, rather than an example of refinement and quality. However, it is not coarse and has an intelligent look, accentuated by the mobile, alert ears and the generous, widely spaced eyes.

Cobs may be as much as 15.3hh., but in the show ring the limit is 15.1hh., a height that allows a less than athletic rider to mount without too much difficulty.

Lipizzaner

Although the white Lipizzaner is usually associated with the famous Spanish Riding School in Vienna, it is bred all over what was once the Austro-Hungarian Empire. The school horses are raised at Austria's Piber Stud near Graz, but the state stud farms of Hungary, Romania, and the Czech Republic also specialize in the breed. Naturally, variations in type occur, and the smaller Piber Lipizzaner is by no means predominant. Hungary, for example, breeds a bigger, very free-moving horse, which excels as a carriage horse.

ORIGINS

The breed takes its name from Lipizza (Lipica), in the old Yugoslavia, where it originated. The stud farm and breed were founded in 1580 when nine Spanish stallions and 24 mares were imported from the Iberian Peninsula at the command of Archduke Charles II.

The archduke's object was to ensure the supply of a suitably grand horse to the ducal stables at Graz and the court stable in Vienna. The Spanish School (so called because, from the outset, it used Spanish Horses) was established in 1572 to instruct noblemen in classical equitation in a wooden arena next to the Imperial Palace. The present school, the Winter Riding Hall, was built on the orders of Charles VI and completed in 1735.

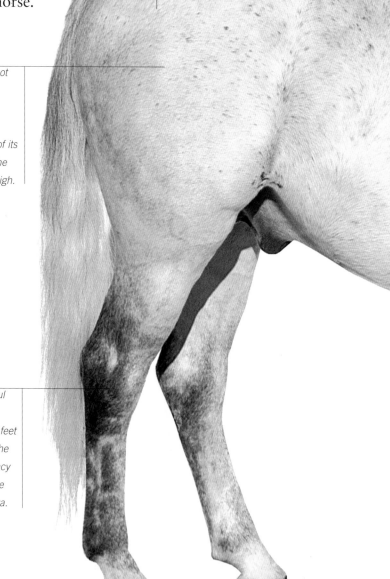

Color The color is uniformly white, although foals are born black or brown. Occasionally, bay occurs. By tradition, a bay horse is always kept at the Spanish School.

Quarters Although not built for speed, the Lipizzaner is ideally suited to the school disciplines because of its powerful quarters. The fine, silky tail is set high.

Limbs Short, powerful limbs, with flat joints, good bone, and hard feet are characteristic of the Lipizzaner, and a legacy of the rocky, limestone country around Lipizza.

KLADRUBER The Kladruber, a carriage horse, was based on Spanish stock and has had considerable influence on the development of the Lipizzaner. The stud farm at Kladrub in the Czech Republic, founded in 1572, is the oldest in Europe.

Shoulders *The withers are often less than pronounced, and the shoulder matches this formation, which is as suited to harness as to riding. As a consequence, the action tends to be high rather than long and low.*

Head *The head is well shaped. The Arabian influence is often in evidence, but the ramlike profile of the old Spanish Horses can also be found.*

Body *The body is compact, deep, and muscular, with considerable depth through the girth.*

LONG LIFE Lipizzaners are slow to mature but are notably long-lived. Many of the Spanish School stallions are working at well over 20 years of age.

CONFORMATION Overall, the conformation, particularly in the Piber Lipizzaners, inclines toward that of a useful, all-around cob. A greater Thoroughbred influence is discernible in the Hungarian type, which has more scope and greater range of movement.

SIX STALLIONS The Lipizzaner breed is based on six principal stallion lines: Pluto (1765), a white Spanish Horse from Fredericksborg; the black Conversano (1767), a Neapolitan; the dun Kladruber, Favory (1779); Neapolitano (1790), a bay Neapolitan from Polesina; Siglavy (1810), a white Arabian; and Maestoso (1819), a Neapolitan Spanish cross. Descendants of these stallion lines are still maintained at the Spanish Riding School, and 14 of the original 23 mare lines are preserved at Piber.

AGILE AND ATHLETIC The Lipizzaner is agile and athletic, and its quiet temperament makes it especially suitable for the school disciplines. The Spanish School and Piber herds owe their survival to American troops, who rescued them from the advancing Russians at the end of World War II.

The height is variable: between 15.1 and 16.2hh.

Classical Equitation

The basis for classical riding was laid in the baroque riding halls of Renaissance Europe. It extended under a succession of masters, beginning with Federico Grisone, whose school at Naples opened in 1532. Its consummation came in the work of Francois Robichon, Sieur de la Guérinière (1688–1751), "the father" of the classical art.

THE LEGACY OF GUÉRINIÈRE

Guérinière – whose book *Ecole de Cavalerie*, published in 1733, was to become the bible of equitation – was the inspiration for the twin streams of classical equitation exemplified by the Spanish Riding School in Vienna and France's famous Cadre Noir at Saumur. Both seek to preserve the principles of Guérinière, while, perhaps, employing a different accent. The same is true of the third classical tradition, that of the Iberian schools, whose own master, the 4th Marquis of Marialva (1713–99), was inevitably influenced by the same teaching.

THE RATIONAL SCIENCE

Guérinière, equerry to Louis XIV from 1730–51, was royal riding master and director of the royal manège of the Tuileries, and it is through his work that the principles of equitation became expanded into a rational science. "Without theory," he maintained, "all practice is aimless."

He introduced progressive systematic training, with exercises – such as the two-track shoulder-in, the flying changes at canter, and so on – to increase suppleness and balance. Moreover, the classical seat position that he defined and taught remains in its essentials entirely valid today.

AIRS ABOVE THE GROUND

The division between dressage, the sport, and the art form of the *Haute Ecole*, practiced by the classical schools, is between the movements carried out on the flat and the "airs above the ground." Dressage (see pp.70–1) includes the parade paces of *piaffe* and *passage* but not, for instance, the classical Spanish Walk performed by the Iberian schools.

The classical leaps are now confined to three movements: *levade, courbette,* and *capriole,* although the Cadre Noir also includes *croupade,* the powerful, high kick of the hind legs. In *levade* the horse raises the forehand while balancing on deeply bent hocks. It provides the base for *courbette,* when the horse bounds forward while maintaining the *levade* position, and the soaring *capriole,* "the leap of the goat." In this ultimate air the horse leaps from all four legs, striking out behind with the body kept horizontal.

The precise form of the leaps varies between the three schools of classicism, although all are similar enough to be recognizable.

SPANISH WALK (Above) The spectacular Spanish Walk is confined to the Iberian Schools and is a feature of the displays of the bullring *cavalheiro* and *rejoneador.* The movement, probably originating in the Byzantine circus, is not practiced elsewhere in Europe, nor included in competitive dressage.

COURBETTE IN HAND (Above top) A stallion of the Andalucian School, Jerez, prepares to bound forward on the hind legs from the basic *levade* position. This and the other "airs above the ground" demand a high state of collection and great strength in the hocks.

SCHOOL QUADRILLE (Left) The Spanish School of Vienna, the world's oldest riding academy, where "the art of riding" is "cultivated in its purest form and brought to perfection."

Hackney

There is no disputing that the brilliant, high-stepping Hackney is the world's most spectacular harness horse. Today, it is largely confined to the show ring but it also has all the courage and ability to compete with equal distinction in driving events. The early trotters, on which the breed was founded, were noted for their speed and endurance under saddle and in harness. One trotter, Bellfounder, trotted 2 miles (3.2km) in 6 minutes, and 9 miles (14.5km) in 30 minutes.

ORIGINS

The origin of the word Hackney is doubtful but it is thought that it probably derives from the French *haquenée*. In Old French *haque*, a word related to the Spanish *haca*, means a "nag" or gelding.

The Hackney, both horse and pony, has its base in the tradition of English trotting horses of the eighteenth and nineteenth centuries. (The pony also has a Fell influence through the Wilson ponies, bred by Christopher Wilson of Kirkby Lonsdale in Cumbria.) There were two recognized English trotters or roadsters, those of Norfolk and those of Yorkshire. Both shared a common ancestor in the Original Shales, a horse born in 1755 out of a "hackney" trotting mare by Blaze. (Blaze, in turn, was related to Messenger, founder of the American Standardbred harness racer.)

Blaze was also a great-great grandson of the Darley Arabian, one of the three founding sires of the Thoroughbred. His equivalent in the evolution of the Hackney Pony was Wilson's pony stallion, Sir George, who traced his descent from Flying Childers, the sire of Blaze and the first great racehorse.

Neck The neck is fairly long and well formed. It rises almost vertically out of the shoulders.

Head The head is small, with convex profile, small, neat ears, and a fine, quality muzzle. The eye is large and very bold.

Shoulders The shoulders are powerful and the withers are low – not like those of a riding horse.

IN HARNESS A hackney turnout is frequently one of the most exciting sights in the show ring. The vehicle used is very light, single-seated, and equipped with four pneumatic-tired wheels.

Feet The feet are allowed to grow longer than is usual to give additional "snap" to the action.

OMNIBUS (Above) Hackney Horses are commonly associated with the hackney cab. Here, a horse is drawing one of the early omnibuses, a vehicle that originated in Paris.

Coat *The coat of both horse and pony is particularly fine and silky.*

Color *Colors in both Hackney Horses and Ponies are usually dark brown, black, bay, as here, and chestnut.*

Hind leg *The quarters and hind legs are enormously powerful and the hocks are of exceptional strength. The conformation contributes to the remarkable driving action of the quarters.*

Body *Without undue length in the back, the body of the Hackney is compact but has great depth through the chest.*

Tail *The tail is set and carried high.*

ACTION Brilliance of action is always paramount in the judging of the Hackney. It has to be straight and true, with no dishing or throwing of the feet from side to side.

Limbs *Limbs must be short, and the hocks strong and "well let down," i.e. not standing high from the ground. At rest, the Hackney stands firm and four-square with forelegs straight and the hind legs back to cover the maximum ground.*

The Hackney Horse is 15–15.3hh. on average; the Hackney Pony does not exceed 14hh.

Driving

Competitive driving was well established in mainland Europe by the late nineteenth century. Benno von Achenbach, winner of the first competition to award a gold medal in 1882, had a special influence on the sport. He perfected the Achenbach, or "English," method of driving he had learned from the English professional Edwin Howlet.

COMPETITION

Achenbach's system – in which all the reins are held in the left hand and manipulated by the fingers of the right – is now generally adopted, other than by the Hungarians who have their own style and use a light breast harness.

While driving competitions had long been a feature of continental shows, it was not until 1969, at the instigation of HRH Prince Philip, then President of the FEI (see p.70), that driving was recognized internationally as a competitive sport. Today, there are European or world championships held every year as well as numerous international trials.

In addition to four-in-hand teams, classes include pairs, tandems, and some single horse turnouts.

The driving trial follows the format of the three-day event, with an arena dressage test followed by the marathon, the equivalent of eventing's speed and endurance phase, which has three times more influence on the result than the dressage test. It is divided into sections, covers about 40 miles (64km), and includes a twisting, often hilly course on which obstacles have to be negotiated.

The last phase is the obstacle competition, called "cone driving." It is carried out over a course of obstacles made up of cones and has a very tight time limit. Penalties are incurred for striking a cone and displacing the ball on top as well as for exceeding the time limit. The competition tests the driver's skill and the fitness of the horse after the punishing marathon.

VEHICLES AND HORSES

Marathon competition vehicles or "battle wagons" are specially-built and are practical rather than elegant, many being equipped with disk brakes.

Most of the driving teams are made up of warmbloods from the European coaching breeds, such as Holsteiners, Oldenburgs, and Gelderlanders. Cleveland Bays and Cleveland crosses are popular, as are the more easily maneuvered Welsh Cobs and Fell ponies. The dashing Hungarian teams use Lipizzaners bred in Hungary, which are faster than the classical Piber type (see pp.94–5).

SCURRY DRIVING

This is the equestrian version of stock-car racing and very popular with spectators. Essentially it is an obstacle race against the clock for pony pairs put to light, pneumatic-tired, four-wheeled vehicles carrying the driver and a groom. The groom maintains stability by the swift, judicious positioning of his weight.

A SINGLE TURNOUT (Above) Single horse turnouts are also part of competitive driving trials, and they compete over the same phase format as the pairs or four-in-hands. This horse, like those above top, is wearing a breast harness rather than the conventional driving collar. It is lighter in weight and therefore more suited to the single horse turnout.

GALLOP ON! (Above top) A pair of well-matched scurry ponies seen as they negotiate a sharp turn through the cones at high speed. Time is the critical factor in these competitions, as well, of course, as successfully completing a clear round, and that requires skill, judgment, and nerves of steel, too.

IN ACTION (Left) A powerful team of Dutch Warmbloods, wearing a breast harness, negotiating an obstacle with confidence and at speed. The horses are all wearing protective boots, which also give some support to the lower limb.

French Trotter

The sport of trotting, both in harness and under saddle, was established in France in the early nineteenth century, and the first custom-built racetrack was constructed at Cherbourg in 1836. The development of the French Trotter from existing horses in Normandy was a result of this.

ORIGINS

Supported by the Administration of the National Studs, the astute and forward-looking Normandy breeders imported English Thoroughbred and half-bred stallions, as well as the incomparable Norfolk Roadsters, to produce lighter, more active progeny from their native mares. Chief among the imports were The Norfolk Phenomenon, a Roadster, and the half-bred son of Rattler, Young Rattler, both of whom exerted a profound influence. The Thoroughbred, the Heir of Linne, was also used. These and other imported stallions resulted in five bloodlines to which most modern French Trotters trace back.

STANDARDBRED BLOOD

In due course, infusions of American Standardbred blood were made. This was in order to give the Trotter more speed, but it has had no effect upon the unique character of the tough French Trotter, which is now capable of taking on, and beating, the best harness racers in the world. In trotting races under saddle – and 10 percent of all French races are for ridden Trotters – the French product has no equal. Ridden races encourage the bigger, more powerful horse, which is invaluable at stud for various purposes.

Apart from its contribution to harness races, the Trotter has been instrumental in the development of the Selle Français (see pp.72–3) and is noted as a sire of jumpers. The French Trotter was recognized as a breed in 1922, and the stud book closed to non-French entries in 1937. Recently, however, it has been opened just a little to permit the entry of selected Standardbred crosses.

Shoulders Formerly the French Trotter tended to have straight shoulders. The modern Trotter has more quality with good shoulders.

Jowl There is no thickness through the jowl.

HEAD As a fixed breed, the French Trotter has a unique, characteristic appearance. The head of the modern Trotter inclines more to the English Thoroughbred than to the old Anglo-Norman type of horse from which it descends. Though it is less refined than that of the Thoroughbred, it gives the impression of intelligence and spirit.

RACES France's leading harness race is the Prix d'Amérique. The all-age championship of Europe, it is run at Vincennes over 1 mile 5 furlongs (2,650m). The premier ridden race is the Prix de Cornulier over the same distance. Ourasi, the leading French Trotter, completed a hat trick of successes in the top Prix d'Amérique in 1988, and broke a new kilometer record of 1 minute 15.6 seconds.

Quarters Immensely powerful quarters are characteristic of the modern French Trotter, which has replaced the somewhat coarse and raw-boned animal of former times. The modern Trotter also has much more quality about him.

RACING RIGS In the 1890s, the original large wheels were replaced by smaller, bicycle-type, ball-bearing wheels equipped with pneumatic tyres. They contributed to a notable increase in speed. The modern, modified rig, racing sulky, perfected by Joe King – an American aeronautical engineer – came into use in the 1970s and immediately produced record-breaking performances.

Color This French Trotter is chestnut. Predominant coat colors for the breed are chestnut, bay, and brown. There are some roans, but it is rare to find grays.

VINCENNES The Hippodrome de Vincennes is the leading French racetrack. This 1¼-mile (2km) track is recognized as the supreme test for both the harness and saddle trotter. It begins downhill, then levels out until the last 1,000 yards (900m), which have a severe uphill gradient. Unique in the trotting world, it has helped to produce a similarly unique breed of trotting horse.

SPEED In 1989, the qualification time permitting entry in races for horses of four years and over was 1 minute 22 seconds over ⅝mile (1km).

FUCHSIA The most prepotent trotting line is that of Fuchsia, an English half-bred foaled in 1883. He sired some 400 Trotters, and over 100 of his sons were the sires of winners.

Average height is 16.2hh. The bigger horses make the best ridden Trotters.

Friesian

The coldblooded Friesian, a descendant of the primitive Forest Horse of Europe, is bred on sea-girt Friesland in the north of the Netherlands. In Holland, it is an object of fervent admiration as much today as it was in the past.

HISTORY

The Romans acknowledged the Friesian as a powerful working horse despite its being ugly in their eyes. A thousand years later, it had become better looking, and it proved itself as an animal of strength, docility, and endurance when it carried the Friesian and German knights to the Crusades. Contact with eastern horses improved the breed still more, as did the infusion of Andalucian blood (see pp.50–1) when Spain occupied the Netherlands during the Eighty Years' War.

Because the Friesian excelled in harness, under saddle, and as a farm horse, it was much used to improve neighboring breeds. The famous Oldenburg (see pp.84–5) was founded largely on Friesian blood. England's Dales and Fell Ponies (see pp.226–9) were also influenced by it when the Frieslanders and their black horses formed the flank-guard for the Roman legions. Through its derivative, the Old English Black, the Friesian also influenced England's Great Horse, now the Shire (see pp.188–9), and the Norwegian Døle Gudbrandsdal.

The Friesian stands 15hh. and up.

Topline The relatively small Friesian has an impressive topline, accentuated by the arched and proudly carried neck.

Head The head is long, with short ears, but alert, finely drawn and very expressive of the breed's cheerful willingness and lovable character.

A SUPERB HARNESS HORSE Because of its agility and temperament, the Friesian makes a good riding horse. However, it is as a harness horse that the breed excels, for it is beautifully balanced and moves impressively at an energetic, active trot. In its own land it is driven, to popular acclaim, to the traditional Friesian gig.

FUNERALS (Left) An engraving of the Duke of Wellington's funeral car drawn by black horses through London's streets. Because of their black coats, their presence, and their notable action, Friesians were much in demand for the "funeral business." These same attributes meant that many also found their way to the circus ring.

DØLE GUDBRANDSDAL (Above) The Døle Gudbrandsdal originates in Norway's Gudbrandsdal valley, yet it is very like the English Fell and Dales Pony, probably sharing similar ancestors, such as the Friesian. The contact between Norway and England resulted in the Friesian being exported to both.

Color The Friesian is always black.

Tail The tail and the mane of the Friesian are very full and luxuriant, and are rarely pulled or braided.

Body The body is compact, strong and deep, denoting a robust constitution. The shoulders, ideally suited to harness, are powerful. Limbs are short, strong, and with good bone.

Feet There is considerable feather on the lower limbs. The hard feet are of blue horn and not prone to disease.

REAR VIEW The quarters of the Friesian are sloping and somewhat low-set, like those of the Dales Pony, which shows Friesian influence. They are strong, but unlike the heavy draft breeds they are not massive.

Irish Draft

There is not much doubt that the Irish hunter is the best cross-country horse in the world. It is produced as the result of a Thoroughbred cross with what has been called "the horse of the countryside"– the Irish Draft, a versatile horse that can help with every kind of work.

ORIGINS

Very early in the breed's development, the indigenous stock of Ireland was upgraded by the Spanish Horse. The size and character came from the heavy European horses, mostly French and Flemish, which were imported into Ireland from the time of the Anglo-Norman invasion of 1172.

Subsequently, these strong mares were improved by more eastern and Spanish, or Andalucian, blood. The progeny were used for every kind of farming purpose on small Irish farms.

Rich limestone pastures and the mild climate produced bone and substance, while the Irish love of hunting resulted in the ability to get over most obstacles.

The cross with the English Thoroughbred gives quality, scope, and speed without detracting from the breed's hunting sagacity.

Color This Irish Draft is dapple-gray. All solid coat colors occur in the breed.

Shoulders The shoulders of the older type of Irish Draft tended to be upright, and the neck was short. These failings have been eradicated in the modern horse.

Forehand The breed is naturally deep chested and, because of the improvement in the shoulder, the forelegs of the modern Irish Draft are well placed to give a longer stride.

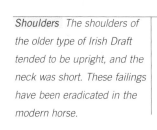

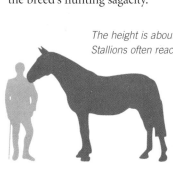

The height is about 16hh. Stallions often reach 17hh.

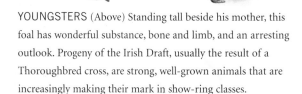

YOUNGSTERS (Above) Standing tall beside his mother, this foal has wonderful substance, bone and limb, and an arresting outlook. Progeny of the Irish Draft, usually the result of a Thoroughbred cross, are strong, well-grown animals that are increasingly making their mark in show-ring classes.

Back Above all, the Irish Draft combines great substance with quality. Sometimes, the back may be a little long and the quarters too sloping, but in most cases the overall structure is one of splendid strength.

TEMPERAMENT AND CHARACTER The modern Irish Draft is a natural jumper, agile, very athletic, and bold. The majority of the Irish Draft stallions that are registered with the Irish Draught Horse Society of Great Britain are regularly hunted and take part in jumping competitions. The breed is temperamentally equable and cooperative, and it is economical to keep.

HEAD The head of the Irish Draft, in relation to the size of the horse, is small and intelligent with a decidedly knowing look about it. The eye is generous and the expression honest – altogether a thoroughly working type.

Body The body is deep, and the coat is fine, not coarse. The withers are nicely formed and the rib cage is distinctly oval. There should be no suspicion of the horse being slab-sided.

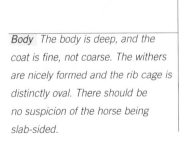

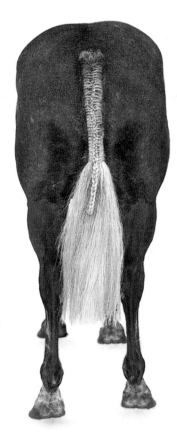

Limbs Irish Draft limbs are massive, with good flat bone and no feather at the extremities. The old fault of being tied-in below the knee on the forelimbs has disappeared.

REAR VIEW Great strength in the jumping quarters is one of the hallmarks of the Irish Draft. The action is straight, level, and balanced. It is not exaggerated, but it is athletic and covers the ground.

Norman Cob

Normandy is one of the world's greatest horse-breeding areas. For centuries, the stud farms of Le Pin and Sainte Lô in Normandy have produced a variety of horses, each one bred to fulfill a specific need. French Trotters, Percherons, Thoroughbreds, Anglo-Normans, and Boulonnais are all kept; but also resident at both stud farms is a lesser-known but very popular horse – the Norman Cob.

ORIGINS

Le Pin was founded as a royal stud farm by Louis XIV in 1665. The first stallions were installed in 1730. Sainte Lô was founded by imperial decree in 1806, and by 1912 it housed 422 stallions.

At the beginning of the twentieth century, half-bred breeders were making the distinction between horses suitable as cavalry remounts and the heavier type that could be used in light draft. The tails of those heavier horses were docked, and soon the animals were termed cob after the English cobs they resembled. No stud book is kept, even though many cob stallions are kept at the national stud farms, but there is performance testing for young stock and the breeding is, of course, documented.

The La Manche region is the cob country of Normandy, and cobs are still regularly worked there. They perform various light draft jobs on the land and work in general farm transportation. Over the years, the Norman Cob has become progressively heavier to meet the demands of the work it is expected to do, but it has never lost its energetic paces or its appealing character.

Neck A crested neck and a sensible head are typical of the Norman Cob.

Build The Norman Cob is stockily built throughout and is obviously strong and powerful, but it is not a true heavy breed and lacks the massive frame and proportions of the heavy horses. On the other hand, it is more active and energetic.

PACK HORSES Normandy has always been a land of horses, and its people have used them for every kind of purpose. They supported this rich agricultural area, working the land, carrying produce to market, and providing a means of transportation. These pack animals are carrying wood in carefully designed panniers, and one carries the woodcutter's wife.

Body *Just like the lighter English riding cobs, the Norman is compact through the body, with a short, strong back running into powerful quarters. The barrel of the horse is characteristically deep and round, and the strong shoulder is nicely sloped.*

Color *The traditional coat colors of the Norman Cob are chestnut, bay, or bay-brown, as here. Occasionally red-roan or gray occurs but rarely any other color.*

MAIL COACH Ancestors of the Norman Cob were the obvious choice to draw the mail coaches of the mid-nineteenth century. They were strong enough to cope with the poor roads and could trot steadily at a fair speed for long distances.

Tail *The tails of the Norman Cob began to be docked early in the twentieth century, a practice still carried out in France although it is illegal in Britain.*

ACTION The modern Norman Cob is heavier than the kind bred earlier in the breed's history, which was closer to the riding type of horse and was bred in vast quantities for military purposes. It still retains, however, much of the activity and freedom of action, particularly at the trot – the working gait of the light draft horse.

Limbs *The limbs of the Norman Cob are short and very muscular, but they are lighter than those of the heavy breeds and do not carry the same profuse feather. Nonetheless, in the forelimbs the bone measurement is more than ample.*

The Norman Cob is bigger than its British counterpart, standing between 15.3 and 16.3hh.

Cleveland Bay

As long ago as the Middle Ages, a bay-colored pack-horse was bred in the north-east of Yorkshire, England's North Riding, an area that includes Cleveland. It was known as the Chapman Horse because it carried the wares of the chapmen, who were the merchants, traveling salesmen, and carriers of the day.

ORIGINS

The Chapman Horse was the foundation for the modern Cleveland Bay, later influenced by infusions of Spanish blood. There were numerous Andalucians in northeast England in the latter part of the seventeenth century, and there was also the Barb, for there was much trafficking between the Barbary Coast of North Africa and the northeast sea ports.

From this amalgam was bred, without recourse to either cart or, in later times, Thoroughbred blood, a powerful, clean-legged horse able, as none other, to work heavy clay lands and to haul considerable loads; a horse that could carry heavy men out hunting and was a notable jumper. Above all, of course, it was a coach horse unsurpassed by any other up to the reign of George II.

With the arrival of the macadamized roads, the Cleveland Bay was judged too slow for coaches able to travel at an average speed of 8–10mph (12–16km/h). As a result, the Yorkshire Coach Horse, a Thoroughbred/Cleveland cross, came into being. The Yorkshire Coach Horse's stud book was closed in 1936 when it was, for all intents, extinct.

Most Clevelands stand between 16 and 16.2hh.

Neck *The modern Cleveland, though lighter than its predecessors, is especially powerful in its neck and through the shoulder.*

Color *The Cleveland is always bay with black points.*

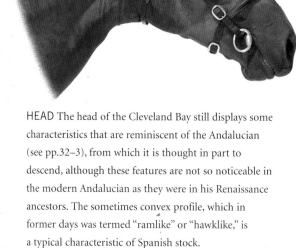

HEAD The head of the Cleveland Bay still displays some characteristics that are reminiscent of the Andalucian (see pp.32–3), from which it is thought in part to descend, although these features are not so noticeable in the modern Andalucian as they were in his Renaissance ancestors. The sometimes convex profile, which in former days was termed "ramlike" or "hawklike," is a typical characteristic of Spanish stock.

MULGRAVE SUPREME By 1962 there were only four Cleveland stallions in Britain. The breed survived largely because Queen Elizabeth II made available the stallion Mulgrave Supreme, originally destined to be sold to the US. He was so successful that by 1977 there were 15 stallions, most of them his progeny.

CONSTITUTION The Cleveland remains an important cross with the Thoroughbred to produce jumpers, hunters, and, of course, superb carriage horses. It transmits to all of these size, bone, a hardy constitution, stamina, and strength. Clevelands are among the longest-lived breeds, and they are particularly fertile.

ROYAL FAVORITES Clevelands have always featured at Britain's Royal Mews, and great encouragement was given to the breed by the Duke of Edinburgh's successes with teams of Clevelands and part-bred Clevelands in international competition driving.

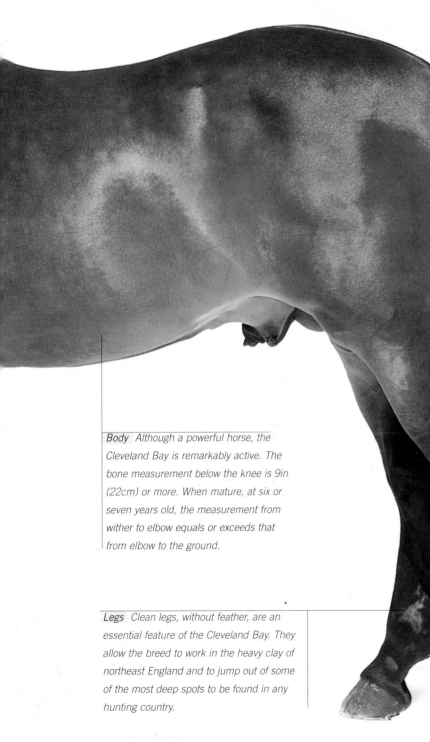

Body Although a powerful horse, the Cleveland Bay is remarkably active. The bone measurement below the knee is 9in (22cm) or more. When mature, at six or seven years old, the measurement from wither to elbow equals or exceeds that from elbow to the ground.

Legs Clean legs, without feather, are an essential feature of the Cleveland Bay. They allow the breed to work in the heavy clay of northeast England and to jump out of some of the most deep spots to be found in any hunting country.

REAR VIEW Quarters big enough to carry a heavyweight "over a house," with second thighs, hocks, and fetlock joints to match, are common attributes to what is probably as good a heavyweight hunter as any in the world.

Gelderlander

The breeders of the Gelder province in the Netherlands have always been innovative and market savvy. They breed horses for their own use, but also with an eye on demand from their neighbors. One hundred years ago, they began on the Gelderlander. Their aim was to produce a great carriage horse with presence and action, capable of light draft work and suitable as a heavy riding horse.

HISTORY

To obtain such a horse, while retaining the docile temperament, they crossed the dull, rather common, native mares with stallions from Britain, Egypt, Hungary, Germany, Poland, and Russia. Then they interbred the best of the progeny until they obtained a fixed type. Later, they introduced Oldenburg blood and some of the lighter East Friesian Horses. Around 1900, a Hackney was used to add a spark to the breed. Since then, a little use has been made of French Anglo-Normans.

Much later, the Gelderlander was used with its heavier neighbor, the Groningen, as a base for the successful Dutch Warmblood (see pp.68–9). The modern Gelderlander is a high-class carriage horse and has proved to be a reliable show jumper as well.

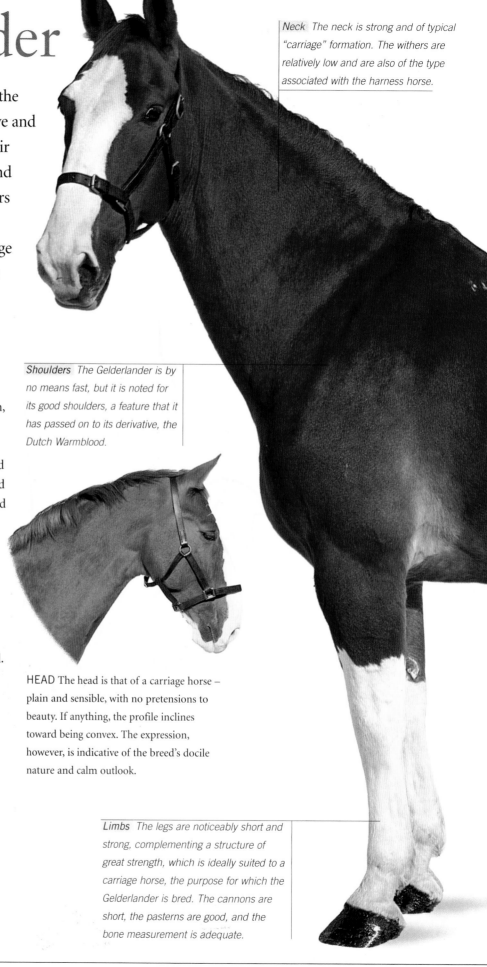

Neck The neck is strong and of typical "carriage" formation. The withers are relatively low and are also of the type associated with the harness horse.

Shoulders The Gelderlander is by no means fast, but it is noted for its good shoulders, a feature that it has passed on to its derivative, the Dutch Warmblood.

HEAD The head is that of a carriage horse – plain and sensible, with no pretensions to beauty. If anything, the profile inclines toward being convex. The expression, however, is indicative of the breed's docile nature and calm outlook.

Limbs The legs are noticeably short and strong, complementing a structure of great strength, which is ideally suited to a carriage horse, the purpose for which the Gelderlander is bred. The cannons are short, the pasterns are good, and the bone measurement is adequate.

FREEDOM OF MOVEMENT Gelderlanders enjoying a canter around the field. Essentially carriage horses, they have the action needed for that usage, but they also have good shoulders and move freely.

WORKING AS A TEAM An impressive team of powerful Gelderlanders, seen at the World Driving Championships. Gelderlanders excel in this field of competition.

Back The back, as is usual and desirable in the carriage horse, is a little longer than in a riding animal. It is strong and there is no suggestion of slackness in the loin.

Quarters The croup is straight with the tail set high, a characteristic inherited by some European warmbloods. The quarters are structured for power, but are not conducive to speed.

HORSE SLEIGH ON ICE A scene of a Dutch horse sleigh-gliding over the ice. Dutch breeders, particularly those of the Gelder, Groningen, and Friesian provinces, took great pains to breed to the market requirements.

Outline The outline of the Gelderlander exemplifies the desirable carriage horse pattern. Strength, a proud bearing, and a lofty, rhythmical action, add to the presence of this attractive horse.

Body Good depth through the girth indicates stamina and endurance. The hind leg is well made and correct in its proportions, as well as being ideally suited for carriage work.

Color The predominant color, and the one most associated with the breed, is chestnut, often with some white on the legs, as shown here, but grays are also found and once – long ago – a skewbald or two.

Feet The feet are good. The old-type Gelderlander would have had more feather on the heel. The modern counterpart has practically none.

The height can be between 15.2 and 16.2hh.

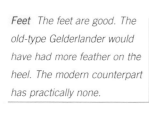

Frederiksborg

In the sixteenth century, Denmark was a principal source of horses for the courts of Europe. Its product was the Frederiksborg, bred at the stud farm founded by King Frederick II in 1562. The stud farm aimed to breed elegant, active horses that would be suited to the disciplines of the manège and with sufficient spirit and quality to be used as military chargers.

ORIGINS

The foundation stock for the Frederiksborg was initially Spanish, which was then, and for centuries after, the foremost riding horse of Europe. Later, imports were made of Neapolitans, close relations of the Spanish Horse. By the nineteenth century, the breed had been outcrossed to eastern and British half-bred stallions. The result was a lively riding horse of impressive appearance and scope and with an excellent, vigorous action. The Frederiksborg was admired throughout Europe for what Count Wrangel in *Die Rasen des Pferdes* (1908–9) described as his "elegant conformation, his lively and kindly temperament and his strong, sweeping, and high action."

The breed was much used to improve other stock, such as the Jutland to increase its activity. One Frederiksborg from the Royal Danish Court Stud, the white Pluto, born in 1765, founded the important Lipizzaner line, which still exists today. In fact, the popularity of the Frederiksborg proved to be its undoing. Exports of the Frederiksborg became so numerous that the old breeding stock was seriously depleted and the stud farm turned to breeding Thoroughbred-type stock in 1839. Private breeders continued to raise Frederiksborgs to use as light draft/carriage horses. Recently, Thoroughbreds have been used with the object of producing competition horses, and it is unlikely that many of the old Frederiksborgs still exist.

HARNESS HORSE The Frederiksborg conformation is predominantly that of a quality harness horse of considerable strength. After the closure of the Court Stud, the Frederiksborg was used increasingly in harness.

Forehand The breed is broad in the chest, relatively short and upright in the neck, and with an intelligent but plain head. The shoulders are powerful but somewhat upright, more suited to harness than riding.

TRAVELING CARRIAGE This typical, Danish traveling carriage of the last century is drawn by a pair of strong, plain horses, which would probably have been related to the Frederiksborg. It seems unlikely, however, that they would have been pure-bred, for they can hardly be described as elegant.

Back The back is strong and the neck runs into the fairly flat withers that are characteristic of the harness horse.

Color The characteristic coloring of the Frederiksborg is chestnut, as here. Other colors are rarely, if ever, seen.

Quarters The quarters are not of a structure associated with speed. The croup is typically level with the tail set high and carried well.

INFLUENCES ON OTHER BREEDS Locally bred mares of Frederiksborg character have formed the base stock for the Danish Warmblood (see pp.74–5). Outcrosses have been made to a number of European warmbloods as well as to the Thoroughbred and half-bred Danish horses.

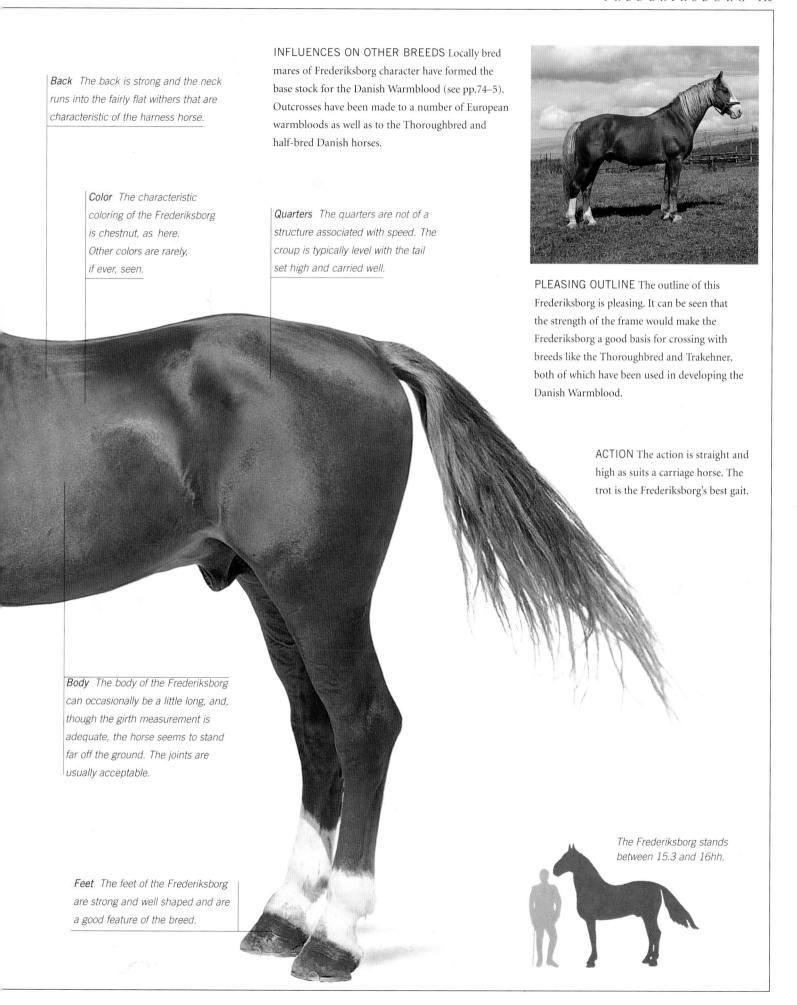

PLEASING OUTLINE The outline of this Frederiksborg is pleasing. It can be seen that the strength of the frame would make the Frederiksborg a good basis for crossing with breeds like the Thoroughbred and Trakehner, both of which have been used in developing the Danish Warmblood.

ACTION The action is straight and high as suits a carriage horse. The trot is the Frederiksborg's best gait.

Body The body of the Frederiksborg can occasionally be a little long, and, though the girth measurement is adequate, the horse seems to stand far off the ground. The joints are usually acceptable.

Feet The feet of the Frederiksborg are strong and well shaped and are a good feature of the breed.

The Frederiksborg stands between 15.3 and 16hh.

Maremmana

The Maremmana is bred in the province of Maremma, Italy. Although there has been a steep decline in the horse population of Italy over the past 50 years, riding horses, often of mixed blood, are still bred in Maremma, the Po valley, Sicily, and Sardinia.

APPEARANCE "Rustic" is a good description for the Maremmana. Like its ancestor, the important but not very pretty Neapolitan, it is average in appearance.

HISTORY

In ancient times, there were probably no horses or ponies indigenous to Italy, the early stock being that brought in from Spain, Persia, and Noricum, a vassal state of the Roman Empire. Nonetheless, Italy and its breeds have been important for over 2,000 years. In the seventeenth century, Italy was foremost among the horse-breeding countries of Europe. Its breeds – the most notable being the Neapolitan – derived from Spanish, Barb, and Arabian stock. In more recent times, Italy has been best known for producing some of the world's greatest Thoroughbreds. As harness racing is a hugely popular sport in Italy, some first-class trotters have also been bred.

Much outcrossing has obscured the background of the Maremmana, which is neither indigenous to Italy nor of a definite type. Nonetheless, in the nineteenth century the local horses would have benefited by crosses with English stock, notably the Norfolk Roadster. There must also be a background of Neapolitan blood. The result was a "rustic" animal. Solid and by no means handsome, it is, however, steady, enduring, and versatile. It is used in agriculture as a light draft horse and was a reliable troop horse for the military and the police. The Maremmana is also chosen as a cattle horse by the local *butteri*, the Italian version of the cowpoke.

Color There is no restriction on color in this horse of mixed background. All solid colors are acceptable, and none is dominant. This horse is bay.

The height is variable but averages around 15.2 –15.3hh.

REAR VIEW The quarters are not built for speed, but they are strong and serviceable, and the hock joints are well defined. In this example, the quarters and the line of the hind leg are better than would usually be found in a Maremmana. In general, they would be expected to be coarse and with the tail set fairly low.

Neck *The neck is proportionate to the body and complements the flattish wither and the corresponding lack of slope in the shoulder.*

Withers *The withers tend to be flat, contributing to some heaviness in the action, but the structure is strong enough.*

Head *The old Maremmana was coarse, and even ugly, around the head. Horses of the type shown here have done much to refine the stolid Maremmana and to correct its more obvious conformational failings.*

TEMPERAMENT Although not bred with great selectivity, the Maremmana is economical to keep, calm and steady in temperament, and good-natured and willing – qualities that suit it well for such purposes as draft work and under saddle.

Limbs *The bone is usually adequate. Improvements have been made in the correctness of the limbs through the use of better quality stallions.*

ITALIAN COWBOY A Maremmana fulfilling its traditional role as the mount of the Italian cowboy, the *buttero*. Because of its endurance and good temper, the breed is a reliable partner in herding and moving cattle, making it a favorite among cattlemen.

Murgese

Italy's preoccupation with the Thoroughbred and the country's excellent trotters have resulted in some neglect of the riding horse and light draft strains. Nonetheless, there are some typical Italian horses that are well suited to the requirements of the areas in which they are bred. As well as the Avelignese and the basic riding types, such as the Salerno, the less attractive San Fratello, and some more acceptable Anglo-Arabians, there is the breed of the Murge, the district near Puglia once noted for its horses.

HISTORY

The Murge is a dry, hilly region that produces animals of good bone and hard feet. In the fifteenth and early sixteenth centuries, the horses of the Murge, the Murgese, were very much in demand for use as cavalry remounts. Since that time, in a manner that seems characteristic of Italian horse-breeding history, the Murgese horse has suffered from a lack of interest.

MODERN HORSES

The old Murgese horse, whatever it may have been, is now extinct, and the new version, which dates from the 1920s, probably bears little resemblance to it. The present Murgese is basically a light draft horse, an inferior kind of Irish Draft. There is a lack of uniformity in the breed, but the best are acceptable and they can be used to fulfill a number of purposes. The Murgese can perform a useful role in agriculture and is probably even more valuable as a base stock for outside crosses. A good kind of riding horse can be produced by putting Murgese mares to a Thoroughbred or good-quality, half-bred stallion. The resulting progeny will not approach the quality of the Irish Draft but will be, nonetheless, a practical animal in the required respects, suitable for light draft work, riding, and as a good all-around horse. The Murgese mares can also be used to breed the strong mules, for agriculture and transportation, so essential to the rural economy of Italy.

Eyes The eyes are placed to the outside of the face.

Limbs The limbs are straight but the knees have a tendency to be too small and rounded.

Bone The bone below the knee is variable as might be expected of a horse of unfixed character. In the Murgese, the pasterns are often a little upright.

HEAD The head is plain and has no outstanding feature, but the expression is honest and genuine. There is some fleshiness in the jowl, and the eyes are placed somewhat to the outside of the face. The whole reveals the presence of a coldblood base, which has yet to be refined by selective outcrossing. The horse is, nonetheless, active and energetic and is said to be even-tempered and economical to keep, and suits the needs of the country well.

ANNUAL COMPETITIONS Breeding of the Murgese is not subject to strict control or breed society regulations. At one time, however, it was usual for an annual competition to be held in the town of Martina Franca to assess the potential of the young stallions.

ACTION The movement of the Murgese is fairly active, but the stride is short and the engagement of the hind legs under the body is limited by the overall conformation. In draft, this is not a serious disadvantage.

Withers The withers are inclined to be overloaded with muscle, inhibiting free movement, but the back is strong and the tendency to undue length has been checked.

Quarters Quarters are not always a good feature of the Murgese, the tail may be low, and some horses lack sufficient muscling through the second thigh.

SALERNO The Salerno evolved at the stud farm at Persano, which was founded, in 1763, by Charles III of Naples and then of Spain. The foundation stock was Neapolitan with a powerful admixture of Andalucian blood. Later crosses to the Arabian, and particularly to the Thoroughbred, produced quality riding horses with a pronounced jumping ability. The Salerno is probably the best of the Italian riding horses and was, at one time, used extensively as a cavalry horse. Generally, it has good conformation. There is much quality about the head, a well-sloped, riding shoulder, and powerfully built quarters, while the limbs are notably correct. The Salerno may be of any solid color and stands at 16hh.

Color Although this horse is black, the principal color is chestnut, like the Avelignese and the Italian Draft, either of which might have had some slight influence on the Murgese.

MOUNTAIN HORSE The Murgese is not a distinctive horse. At its best, it is suitable for use as a light draft animal. It could be ridden, but is better suited as a base for crossing. Because of the rocky environment in which it is bred, it inclines more to a mountain horse type than to the massive draft animal.

Feet The feet of the Murgese should be hard and well formed.

The height of the Murgese is 15–16hh.

Camargue

Indigenous to the Rhone delta in southern France, which is its natural habitat, the Camargue bears a strong resemblance to the Lascaux cave drawings of horses dated around 15,000BC. It is thought that the remains of prehistoric horses, discovered at Solutré, may be those of the breed's ancestors.

INFLUENCES

The indigenous horse was influenced by the Barb (see pp.44–5), brought over by the Moorish invaders. Since then, the isolation of the Camargue has ensured that the *manades*, the wild herds of white horses, have remained untouched by outside influences.

The harsh environment is responsible for the incredible hardiness of the breed, which exists solely on what it can scavenge from the reed beds. The area is extremely inhospitable, hot in summer and covered in a sheet of cold, saltwater the rest of the year. The landscape is dominated by the mistral – a salt-laden wind, which stunts the sparse growth. Yet the local people are fiercely loyal to their heritage and call it "the most noble conquered territory of man." The mounts of the Camargue cowboy (*gardian*) are called "white horses of the sea," and have been immortalized in verse and story over the centuries.

Forehand The neck is generally short, running into fairly straight, upright shoulders, which accentuates the impression of a primitive horse with overtones of the North African Barb. The forehand and the set of the foreleg to shoulder are responsible for the action that is peculiar to the breed.

HEAD The head of the Camargue, with a distinctive head rope made of twined horse hair, hardly accords with romantic legend. Though showing a North African influence, it is usually coarse and heavy and with more than a suggestion of the breed's far-off ancestors of prehistory. Still, the Camargue is an intelligent animal and generous by nature.

RIDING ON THE MARSHES The Moorish influence on the Rhone delta is evident in the saddlery, which is traditional to the *gardian* and the Camargue.

Feet Although the feet are wide to correspond with the marsh environment, they are incredibly hard and strong, so much so that Camargue horses are rarely shod.

TEMPERAMENT The Camargue is an independent horse, fiery and most courageous under saddle. Agile and surefooted, the breed has an innate instinct for working the Camargue's black bulls.

ACTION The action is peculiar to the breed. The walk is active, long-striding, and high-stepping. The trot is rarely employed and is short, stilted, and jarring. The canter and gallop are both amazingly free.

Color Color is the Camargue's greatest visual asset. The coat is white, like sea-foam, and strangely silky.

Tail Both the mane and the tail are luxuriant.

INCREASED TOURISM Today, the wild waste of the Camargue, which has supported the *manades* – the wild herds – for thousands of years, is being drained. However, the new tourist industry is creating a further use for the Camargue region, by allowing tourists to ride around the nature reserve on the "horses of the sea."

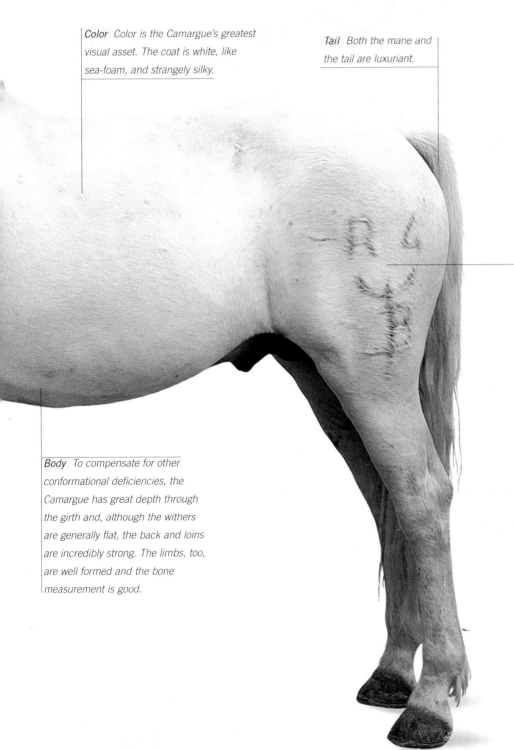

Quarters The croup is often sloped, with the tail set low, but it is invariably muscular and strong. The quarters, displaying the brand mark, are generally powerful, if otherwise unprepossessing.

EXCEPTIONAL LONGEVITY The Camargue develops slowly and is not full grown until it is five to seven years old, but it has great stamina and is exceptionally long-lived.

ANNUAL INSPECTION For most of the year, the Camargue lives out in a near-wild state, each stallion having a big following of mares and young stock. However, the herd is brought in for inspection and branding annually.

Body To compensate for other conformational deficiencies, the Camargue has great depth through the girth and, although the withers are generally flat, the back and loins are incredibly strong. The limbs, too, are well formed and the bone measurement is good.

The height of the Camargue is 13.1–14.1hh.

Furioso

The Furioso is one of many breeds that evolved during the period when the Austro-Hungarian Empire was the dominant force in Europe. The stud farm at Mezőhegyes was founded in 1785 by the Hapsburg emperor, Joseph II. It became the center for breeding the Nonius (see pp.124–5) and then the Furioso.

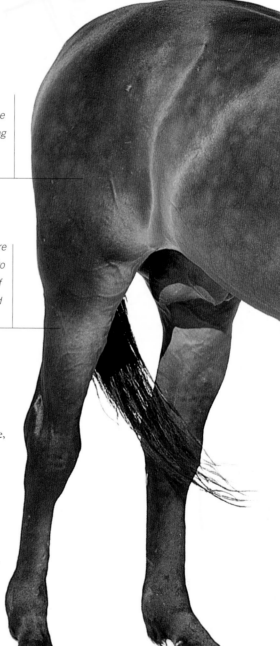

APPEARANCE (LEFT) The pronounced oriental influence in the Hungarian horse is clearly demonstrated by this attractive charger. The Hungarian light horsemen were considered to be among the best in the world.

ORIGINS

The Furioso breed was formed following the importation of two English horses. They were called Furioso and North Star – the breed is also often termed Furioso-North Star. Both stallions were used on Nonius mares whose foundation stallion was Nonius Senior, who in turn was by an English half-bred stallion out of a Norman mare.

Furioso, an English Thoroughbred, was imported by Count Karolyi around 1840. At Mezőhegyes, he produced no less than 95 stallions. These were used at many of the imperial stud farms. North Star was imported three years later. He had a background of Norfolk Roadster; however, he was also a son of Touchstone, winner of the 1834 St. Leger and twice winner of the Ascot Gold Cup. North Star sired many good harness racers as did his great-grandsire, Waxy, the 1793 Derby winner. Later in the evolution of the Furioso breed, more Thoroughbred blood was introduced; most notable was that of Buccaneer, who sired Kisber, the Hungarian-bred winner of the 1876 Derby.

Initially, the two lines of North Star and Furioso were kept separate. In 1885 they were intercrossed and, thereafter, the Furioso strain became predominant.

Quarters Although a good riding horse, the quarters slope down from the croup, betraying the presence of the more plebeian Nonius.

Hind limbs The hind limbs are strong and the hocks are low to the ground, but they are not of the kind associated with speed and scope.

CHARACTER The Furioso is intelligent with a most amenable disposition. Not only is it exceptionally versatile, but it is a good, all-around riding horse, which will go well in harness and is able to compete credibly in all disciplines, including steeplechasing at the standard in central European countries.

The height of the Furioso is around 16hh. or a little above.

Feet Overall, the feet are good, and better than most of the fashionable warmblood breeds.

Shoulders The shoulders and withers are of clear riding type, but the action retains something of the exaggerated coaching lift of the breed's Nonius ancestors.

Head The head is almost that of a Thoroughbred, although the ears are more prominent. The expression is intelligent and kindly. A relatively straight profile is characteristic.

Muzzle The Furioso has a somewhat squared muzzle and large nostrils.

Color Most colors are acceptable, but the Furioso is usually black, dark brown, or dark bay, as here. White markings are the exception.

Limbs The limbs are good and the joints are clean, large, and well defined. If anything, the pasterns are a little too upright – an inheritance from the carriage antecedents.

BRIDLE The traditional bridle on this Furioso reflects the Asian influence of the Magyar horsemen. These were a people of the steppes, descendants of the Huns, who finally settled in the Carpathian basin 1,000 years ago. They inherited a horse culture that began in central Asia 6,000 years ago, and as Hussars of the Hapsburg Empire, they were acknowledged as the supreme light horsemen of all time.

COACHING-HORSE LEGACY Although the Thoroughbred is much in evidence, the legacy of the coaching horse is still present in the Furioso.

AUSTRO-HUNGARIAN DOMINANCE There were no stud farms in the world that exceeded, in size and architectural merit, those custom-built establishments created by the Hapsburg emperors of the Austro-Hungarian dynasty. Even today, the Hungarian stud farms carry large breeding herds under the care of the czikos horsemen of the great puzsta. The Furioso was first bred at Mezőhegyes; today it is bred all the way from Austria to Poland. The Hungarian Furioso is now centered on the Apajpuszta Stud, between the Danube and Tisza rivers.

Nonius

By the end of the nineteenth century, Hungary had a horse population of over two million, and it sold cavalry remounts throughout Europe. It also had some of the world's greatest stud farms, including Mezöhegyes, founded by Emperor Joseph II in 1785.

Withers The withers are well defined and the shoulder is sufficiently sloped.

HISTORY

The stud farm of Mezöhegyes was the center for the breeding of the Nonius and the related Furioso (see pp.122–3). The Nonius was founded on the stallion, Nonius Senior. He was foaled at Calvados, Normandy, in 1910 and captured by Hungarian cavalry at the Rosières stud farm after Napoleon's defeat at Leipzig in 1813.

According to the records, Nonius Senior was out of a common Norman mare by the English half-bred stallion Orion, who without much doubt carried Norfolk Roadster blood. Nonius Senior was by no means an attractive horse. Standing 16.1½hh., he was described as having a coarse, heavy head with small eyes and long, "mule" ears. His other characteristics were a short neck, long back, narrow pelvis, and low-set tail. Despite his conformation, Nonius Senior was a prolific sire and quickly found to be a successful one. He was used on a wide variety of mares and consistently produced good stock, far superior to himself in both conformation and action. The progeny of Nonius Senior included no fewer than 15 outstanding stallions.

Neck Though not long and elegant, the neck is, nonetheless, well formed and complementary to the overall frame.

CHARACTERISTICS

In the 1860s, more Thoroughbred blood was introduced to improve the conformation, and the breed was subdivided into two types – large and small. The large type is a carriage or light farm horse; the small type, carrying more Arabian blood, is an all-around horse, which performs well under saddle and in harness. Put back to Thoroughbreds, Nonius mares produce competition horses of scope and quality and with jumping ability.

FOAL This big-limbed Nonius foal will not be mature until he is six years old, but he will be commensurately long-lived. Today, Nonius breeding in Hungary is centered at the Hortobagy stud farm, while in the Czech Republic, where the Nonius is also bred in quite large numbers, the center is at Topolcianky.

Back The outline, and particularly the strong back, is that of a good middleweight hunter or of an enduring, active, carriage horse.

Quarters The quarters are always strong, although they are sometimes inclined to slope away from the croup. Nonetheless, they are suitable for both riding and driving.

HEAD The head, despite the Thoroughbred influence, is that of an honest, half-bred horse. The calm, honest outlook of the Nonius reflects its willing nature and equable temperament, which is an important feature of this tough, genuine all-around performer.

Color The breed's coat color is predominantly bay, but there are also dark browns, as here, blacks, and some chestnut shades.

CAREFUL BREEDING The distinctive Nonius type was obtained by mating the carefully selected offspring of Nonius Senior out of Arabians, Lipizzaners, Norman and English half-breds, back to their prepotent sire. Nonius Senior died in 1832, but by 1870 his registered descendants numbered 2,800 stallions and 3,200 mares. Thoroughbred blood was used as a refining agent and to correct faults of conformation.

Body The Nonius is a very sound horse with good, short limbs, well-made feet, and obvious strength in all the proportions. Joints are correct, bone is more than sufficient, and there is good depth through the girth.

The large type are 15.3–16.2hh., and the small type are around 15.3hh.

ACTION Speed is not a notable feature of the breed, but it is adequate enough for all-around, riding purposes and for harness work. The paces, however, are all marked by great activity and freedom.

Knabstrup

Denmark was once famous for its Frederiksborg horses, which were bred at the Royal Danish Stud, and for the eye-catching spotted Knabstrup. In their old form, both have almost disappeared. The early Knabstrups were white with brown or black spots of varying size, occurring all over the head, body, and legs. The modern Knabstrup now looks more like an American Appaloosa (see pp.186–7) than otherwise.

ORIGINS

The Knabstrup breed dates from the Napoleonic Wars and is based on a spotted mare of Spanish ancestry, Flaebehoppen. Spotted strains were common in Spanish Horses up to the nineteenth century. Flaebehoppen was bought from a Spanish officer by a butcher named Flaebe (hence Flaebehoppen – Flaebe's horse), who in turn sold her to Judge Lunn, who may be said to have founded the breed.

Flaebehoppen was noted for speed and endurance, and Judge Lunn bred her to Frederiksborg stallions at his Knabstrup estate in Denmark. She founded a line of spotted horses, not so substantial as the Frederiksborg, but much in demand for their color and ability. Her grandson, Mikkel, is recognized as a foundation sire.

CONFORMATION

In terms of conformation, Knabstrups were raw-boned. They were, nonetheless, constitutionally tough, sound, tractable, and quick to learn, and so were in great demand as circus horses. Injudicious breeding for color resulted in the breed's deterioration late in the last century. The present-day Knabstrupers, however far removed from the original, are much improved. They have substance, more quality, and a greater range of colors.

The height of the Knabstrup is 15.2–15.3hh.

REAR VIEW The sparse mane and tail of the Knabstrup seems to accompany spotted coat patterns, being a characteristic of the Appaloosa and also found in the old and the modern Knabstrup. The best of the breed have good, well-rounded quarters with substantial muscular development. The older type was probably more "ragged" across the hips.

HEAVENLY HORSES For the Heavenly Horses of Ferghana, spotted horses not unlike the Spanish-based Knabstrup, the Emperor Wu Ti of China was prepared to wage war for upward of a quarter of a century, in the second century BC. Such horses, much revered in the ancient world, were frequently buried with their royal masters.

CONFORMATIONAL IMPROVEMENTS
This modern Knabstrup stallion is a more substantial animal with better conformation than that of the Knabstrups of 50 years ago. During that period of the breed's history, a typical Knabstrup would not have displayed the quality of this attractive horse.

Topline The line of the back from the wither appears to be peculiar to the Knabstrup and to some Appaloosa strains.

Mane The mane is sparse. Here it is braided.

Head The kindly head of the Knabstrup reflects the breed's intelligence. Almost all spotted strains are easily managed, cooperative, and quick to learn. These qualities, together with the striking color, ensured the breed's popularity as a circus horse.

Color The original coloration of the Knabstrup was white, with brown or black spots covering the whole body. The roan coloring, as here, is a more recent introduction.

Limbs The spotted coloring extends down the legs to the feet. The conformational defects in the limbs produced during the period of the breed's deterioration have now been largely corrected.

Feet The horn of the feet often has vertical stripes.

OLD KNABSTRUP The old Knabstrup was strong and had more of a harness conformation, particularly in respect of the shoulder and the short neck. It was reputed to be a tough and enduring horse, and the foundation mare, Flaebehoppen, was said to be a good performer and easily trained. The Knabstrup was, nonetheless, coarse in many respects and undistinguished other than in its color.

Akhal-Teke

The Akhal-Teke is one of the most distinctive and unusual horses in the world, and also one of the oldest. It is bred around the oases of the Turkmenistan Desert, north of Iran, and centered in Ashkabad. Horses were bred and raced here 3,000 years ago, and the present-day Akhal-Teke is almost exactly like the Horse Type 3 (see Origins, pp.10–11). There is also some resemblance to the Arabian racing strain, the *Munaghi*.

KUBAN COSSACK (Left) The Kuban Cossacks – incredibly skillful riders, and as enduring as their horses – were often mounted on Akhal-Tekes. Well adapted to climatic extremes, the Akhal-Teke's legendary stamina was well suited to these indomitable horsemen.

HISTORY

There is nothing quite like this horse. Its endurance and its resistance to heat are phenomenal. In 1935, Akhal-Tekes completed a ride from Ashkabad to Moscow, a distance of 2,580 miles (4,152km), in 84 days. The ride included some 600 miles (966km) of desert, much of it crossed virtually without water.

Racing is endemic to the Turkoman people. They used to feed their charges a high-protein diet of dry lucerne, when available, pellets of mutton fat, eggs, barley, and *quatlame*, a fried dough cake. The horses were wrapped in heavy felt to protect them from the cold, desert nights and from the heat of the midday sun. Today, the Akhal-Teke is a racehorse, a long-distance performer, and the Russian sports horse in the dressage and jumping disciplines.

Quarters The quarters are narrow and mean and would be a nightmare in a show class, but they are spare and sinewy, and the thighs are long and muscular.

Coat The coat is exceptionally fine, and the thin skin is in character with a horse of desert origin.

Tail A feature of the breed is a short, silky tail and a sparse, short forelock and mane, here hogged.

Hind legs The long hind legs are usually sickle-shaped and cow-hocked. The hocks are carried high off the ground.

COLOR Colors found in the Akhal-Teke include chestnut (main picture), black, and gray, but the most striking is the dun with its golden-metallic bloom (above), which is amazingly beautiful in the sunlight. A silvery color also occurs.

Neck *The long, thin neck is set very high and almost vertically to the body, the head joining it at an angle of 45 degrees. Because of the long neck and the angle of the head, the line from the mouth is often higher than the withers, a feature peculiar to the breed.*

Head *The head is fine, and the big eyes give an impression of boldness. The nostrils are wide, the profile straight, and there is width between the large, beautifully shaped ears.*

MARES AT PASTURE Akhal-Teke mares are now kept at pasture during the day and stabled at night, in contrast to the old ways. The traditional practices of weaning foals at two months old and racing yearlings have also been discontinued, along with the outcrossing to the Thoroughbred, a practice that diluted the essential character of the breed.

CONFORMATION The Akhal-Teke incorporates every kind of conventional conformational failing. The body is tubelike, the back long, the rib cage shallow, and the loin may appear slack. Nonetheless, this is one of the world's most enduring and exceptional horses.

ACTION The action, like the breed, is unique: the horse "slides" over the ground in a flowing movement without swinging the body.

CHARACTER The Akhal-Teke can be rather obstinate and bad-tempered and cannot be said to have an easy temperament.

Forelegs *The forelegs are usually set too close together but they are otherwise straight, and the forearm long.*

Feet *The feet are small but regular and they are hard and very durable.*

The average height is 15.2hh. Mares may be smaller.

Budenny

The Budenny is typical of the move begun in the USSR during the 1920s to create new breeds – a process that involved complex experiments in crossbreeding. Originally intended as a cavalry horse, today it is a specialized riding horse that is good enough to compete at show jumping and dressage, as well as race over fences.

BREEDING

The Budenny breed is based on Chernomor (similar to the Don but lighter and smaller), and Don mares crossed with Thoroughbred stallions. Kazakh and Kirgiz crosses were also involved, though less successfully. The progeny was reared carefully on a generous diet, and performance tested at two and four years of age.

Of the 657 mares used in the original experiment to produce the Budenny, 359 were Anglo-Don (a Thoroughbred cross), 261 Anglo-Don x Chernomor, and 37 Anglo-Chernomor. These mares were put to Anglo-Don stallions. When Thoroughbred characteristics were insufficiently pronounced in mares, they were recrossed with Thoroughbred stallions.

THE TERSK (Right) Another Russian creation, the Tersk, was developed between 1921 and 1950 at the Tersk and Stavropol stud farms in the Northern Caucasus. The Tersk is founded on the Strelets Arabian – a part-bred produced by crossing Arabian stallions with Orlov and Orlov-Rastopchin mares. Thoroughbreds were also involved in the Strelets makeup to a lesser degree. By the early 1920s, the Strelets had nearly died out. What stock remained was transferred to Tersk, where the new breed was created. The Tersk, a very beautiful horse, retains the Arabian appearance and movement.

HEAD Overall, the neck and head are of good proportion, with the head having a straight or slightly concave profile. It is a handsome, quality head that shows the Thoroughbred influence.

Neck and shoulders The long, straight neck runs into high withers and is joined to a reasonably sloped shoulder. The shoulder, however, lacks the length of that of the Thoroughbred.

Skin The head is "dry": veins show clearly through the fine, supple skin.

Limbs The limbs are fine and light, though there are some failings in the size and quality of joints.

Foreleg An original fault in the breed was for the forelegs to be spread, resulting in a clumsy action. Don/Kazakh crosses suffered from this failing.

Bone Pasterns are usually properly sloped. Bone is inclined to be light in comparison with the body, but the medium-size feet are quite well formed.

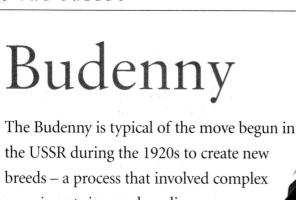

ENDURANCE The Budenny is rigorously tested on the racecourse and over long distances. A Budenny has won the Czechoslovakian Pardubice Chase (Gran Pardubice). Another Budenny stallion, Zanos, covered 192 miles (309km) under saddle in 24 hours, being ridden for 20 hours of that time.

Body A lightly built horse with a comparatively heavy body. The Budenny has a back that is straight, short, and inclined to be wide and flat: The loins are somewhat long; and the croup is long and usually straight.

Measurements The essential measurements aimed for are: length of barrel 5ft 4in (163cm); girth 6ft 3in (190cm); and bone below the knee an optimistic 8in (20cm).

LOKAI (Above) The Lokai is a breed of mixed ancestry that originated in southern Tajikistan, a republic of the former Soviet Union on the western side of the Pamir mountain range. For many centuries the horses of central Asia were crossed with the primitive steppe stock. From the sixteenth century onward, the Lokai people improved this base stock with crosses to Akhal-Teke, Karabair, and even Arabian blood. As a pack- and saddle horse, the surefooted Lokai is indispensable for work in the highlands, where altitudes vary between 10,000 and 20,000 feet (2,000 and 4,000m). Tajik riders use the tough, swift-moving Lokai in the fierce national game of kokpar (fighting over the goat) at which the small horses (no more than 14.3hh.) excel.

TEMPERAMENT The breed is said to be calm and sensible, as well as possessing stamina and endurance.

Color Eighty percent of Budenny horses are chestnut, often having a golden sheen, which is a throwback to the Dons and Chernomors. Bay and brown horses are found otherwise. This horse is black.

Hind leg Although the Budenny has inherited some of the better qualities of the Thoroughbred, the conformational defects inherent in the base stock are more or less apparent. Perhaps the poorest conformational feature is in the weak structure of the hind leg.

On average, the Budenny stands 16hh.

Kabardin

The Kabardin, the breed of the northern Caucasus, is derived from the horses of the steppe people crossed with Karabakh, Persian, and Turkmen, strains. This mountain horse, well known since the sixteenth century, is capable of working in difficult terrain and is undeterred by snow and fast rivers. It is a tractable and obedient animal, and is both hardy and infinitely enduring.

WORK HORSE (Left) Although the Kabardin is considered primarily to be a saddle horse, it can also be used for every kind of work in harness, as shown in this seventeenth-century etching.

MODERN TYPE

Following the Russian Revolution, the breed was much improved by the Kabardin-Balkar and Karachaev-Cherkess stud farms. These stud farms created a stronger type for riding and agricultural work. The Kabardin is the principal breed of the Kabardin-Balkar Republic and is used to improve native stock in Armenia, Azerbaijan, Dagestan, Georgia, and Osetia.

The best Kabardins are raised at the Malo-Karachaev and Malkin stud farms. They live out, but are given extra feed in the winter, and they are performance-tested on the racecourse.

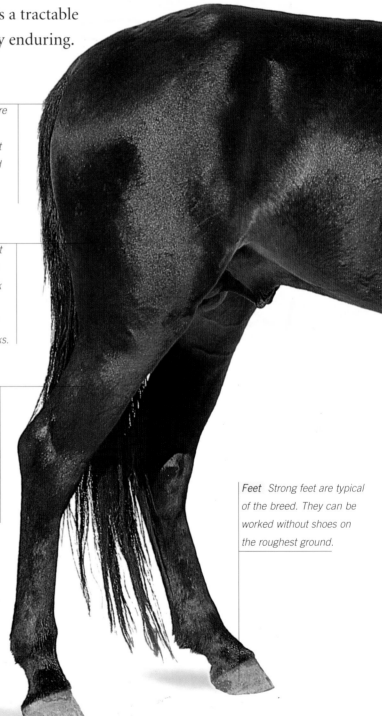

Tail A typical feature of the Kabardin is the usually luxuriant growth of mane and tail, often found in mountain breeds.

Color Predominant colors found in the breed are bay, dark bay, and black, as here, without other distinguishing marks.

Hind legs Mountain horses, as a rule, do not have hind legs that are perfect. The Kabardin is no exception, the hind legs usually being sickle-shaped.

Feet Strong feet are typical of the breed. They can be worked without shoes on the roughest ground.

MOUNTAIN HOME The Kabardin is at home in the mountains and has developed characteristics that are suited to the terrain and the rigors of the climate. It is surefooted and agile, and it has an uncanny ability to find its way in mist and darkness.

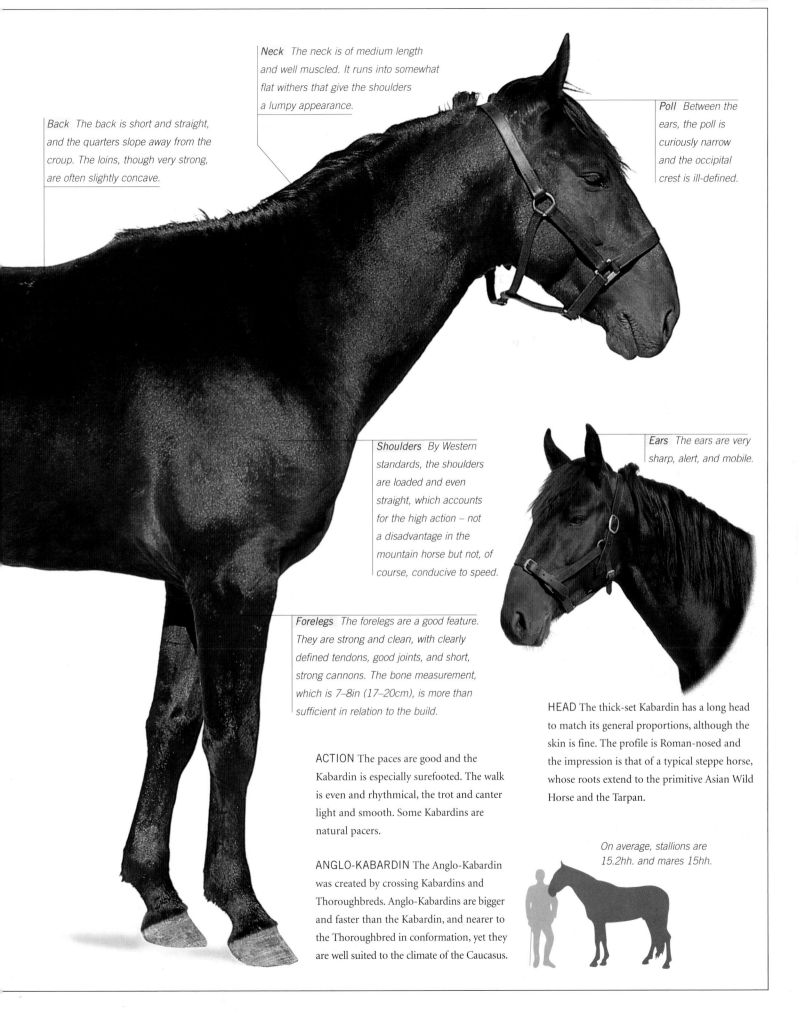

Neck *The neck is of medium length and well muscled. It runs into somewhat flat withers that give the shoulders a lumpy appearance.*

Poll *Between the ears, the poll is curiously narrow and the occipital crest is ill-defined.*

Back *The back is short and straight, and the quarters slope away from the croup. The loins, though very strong, are often slightly concave.*

Shoulders *By Western standards, the shoulders are loaded and even straight, which accounts for the high action – not a disadvantage in the mountain horse but not, of course, conducive to speed.*

Ears *The ears are very sharp, alert, and mobile.*

Forelegs *The forelegs are a good feature. They are strong and clean, with clearly defined tendons, good joints, and short, strong cannons. The bone measurement, which is 7–8in (17–20cm), is more than sufficient in relation to the build.*

HEAD The thick-set Kabardin has a long head to match its general proportions, although the skin is fine. The profile is Roman-nosed and the impression is that of a typical steppe horse, whose roots extend to the primitive Asian Wild Horse and the Tarpan.

ACTION The paces are good and the Kabardin is especially surefooted. The walk is even and rhythmical, the trot and canter light and smooth. Some Kabardins are natural pacers.

ANGLO-KABARDIN The Anglo-Kabardin was created by crossing Kabardins and Thoroughbreds. Anglo-Kabardins are bigger and faster than the Kabardin, and nearer to the Thoroughbred in conformation, yet they are well suited to the climate of the Caucasus.

On average, stallions are 15.2hh. and mares 15hh.

Don

The Don, traditionally associated with the Don Cossacks, evolved in the eighteenth and nineteenth centuries. Its foundations were the steppe horses of the nomadic tribes. Early influences were the Mongolian Nagai and breeds such as the Karabakh, the Persian Arabian, and the Turkmen.

HISTORY

Don horses were hardly pampered. They lived in herds on the steppe pastures where they fended for themselves, scraping away the snow in winter to get at the frozen grass beneath. The Don is not a prepossessing specimen, but it is incredibly tough and adapts easily to every kind of climatic hardship.

The breed and its riders became famous between 1812 and 1814 when 60,000 Cossacks, mounted on Dons, helped to repel Napoleon's forces from Russia. Dons were then improved using Orlovs (see pp.136–7), Thoroughbreds, and Strelets Arabians, high-class part-breds from the Strelets Stud. No other blood has been introduced since the early twentieth century, when the breed emerged as a solid army remount that could be put in harness and required minimum attention.

Neck The neck is of medium length and usually straight.

Head The head is of medium size with a straight profile. The short, constricted poll makes flexion difficult.

Color This Don is light bay, although the predominant colors are chestnut and brown, often with a golden sheen.

Forelegs The forelegs are usually well muscled, but there is a tendency toward calf knees, that is, an inward curve below the knee.

KARABAKH (Left) The Karabakh, a principal influence on the Don, was established as long ago as the fourth century; it originates in the mountains of Karabakh in Azerbaijan. The best are bred at the Akdam Stud where they are crossed with Arabian stallions. The Karabakh stands at about 14hh., and it has a calm temperament and good action. Like many of the eastern Russian breeds, it usually has the metallic, golden-dun coloring. It is performance-tested on the racecourse and is used in games like *chavgan* – a form of polo – and *surpanakh* – a type of mounted basketball.

Body The modern Don is a large framed horse with a strong constitution to match. Its faults include short, straight shoulders that limit the length of stride, but the chest is well developed and the ribs long and well sprung.

BUDENNY STUD The Don is raced, mainly in long-distance events, and the present-day horse is larger and of better conformation than formerly. Some of the best are bred at the Budenny Stud, where the Budenny Horse was developed as the result of crossing Don mares with Thoroughbred stallions.

Back The back is straight and wide, the withers low, and the loin straight.

Quarters The croup is rounded and the quarters tend to slope away, the tail being occasionally low-set.

BRINGING IN THE HARVEST (Above) Don horses are good-natured, calm, and easily managed, and they are able to work in harness and in light, agricultural draft. Energetic workers, with a high level of endurance, they do not demand any special attention. The early Don was inclined to be wiry, but later developments have produced a heavier horse.

Hindlegs The hindlegs have a tendency to be sickle-hocked and, in the old types, the pelvic corner was so placed that it restricted the freedom of movement.

ACTION Because of the conformational deficiencies that, in addition to the straight shoulder and faulty forelegs, include somewhat upright pasterns, the action of the Don is sometimes restricted and rough. It is regular but neither elegant, elastic nor over-comfortable.

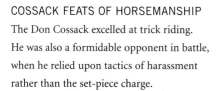

COSSACK FEATS OF HORSEMANSHIP
The Don Cossack excelled at trick riding. He was also a formidable opponent in battle, when he relied upon tactics of harassment rather than the set-piece charge.

The Don stands at about 15.3hh. but is sometimes larger.

Orlov Trotter

The Orlov Trotter is one of the oldest and most popular breeds in Russia. At the end of the eighteenth century, the white Arabian stallion Smetanka was used at the Orlov Stud with Dutch, Mecklenburg, and Danish mares. He left only five progeny, but among them was Polkan I, out of a Danish mare that carried much Spanish blood.

DROSHKY (Above) A Russian Droshky, presented to British Queen Victoria's husband, Prince Albert. It is drawn by an Orlov wearing a Russian harness that includes the arch, or *douga*.

FOUNDATION STALLION

Polkan I was the sire of the Orlov breed's foundation stallion, a gray called Bars I, out of a substantial, free-moving Dutch mare. Bars I was foaled in 1784 and was used extensively at the new stud farm of Khrenov. It was at Khrenov that from 1788 Count Orlov and his stud manager, V.I. Shishkin, continued to work on the evolution of the Orlov. Bars I was mated with Arabian, Danish, and Dutch mares as well as English half-breds and Arabian/Mecklenburg crosses. Thereafter, the policy was to inbreed to Bars and his sons to establish the desired type. The pedigrees of all purebred Orlov Trotters show a strong connection with the foundation stallion.

Training and a regular program of trotting races were carried out in Moscow from 1834 onward. Orlov and Shishkin did a great deal to encourage improvement in the breed and to increase the performance levels.

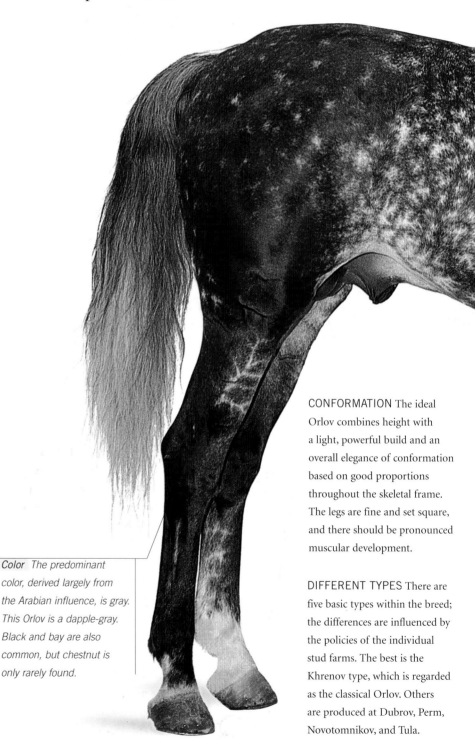

CONFORMATION The ideal Orlov combines height with a light, powerful build and an overall elegance of conformation based on good proportions throughout the skeletal frame. The legs are fine and set square, and there should be pronounced muscular development.

Color The predominant color, derived largely from the Arabian influence, is gray. This Orlov is a dapple-gray. Black and bay are also common, but chestnut is only rarely found.

DIFFERENT TYPES There are five basic types within the breed; the differences are influenced by the policies of the individual stud farms. The best is the Khrenov type, which is regarded as the classical Orlov. Others are produced at Dubrov, Perm, Novotomnikov, and Tula.

TROIKA The troika is a Russian method of harnessing three horses side-by-side. The center horse works at a fast trot. The out-spanners are bent outward by tight side reins. They must canter or gallop to keep up with the center horse.

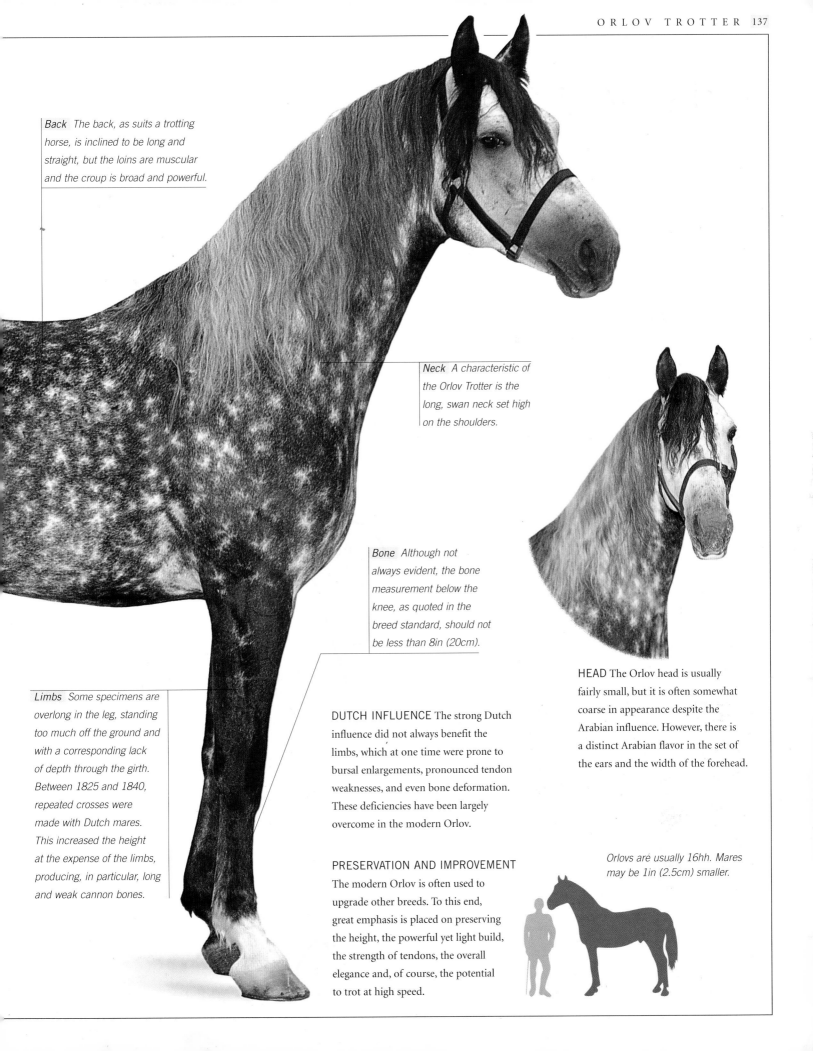

Back The back, as suits a trotting horse, is inclined to be long and straight, but the loins are muscular and the croup is broad and powerful.

Neck A characteristic of the Orlov Trotter is the long, swan neck set high on the shoulders.

Bone Although not always evident, the bone measurement below the knee, as quoted in the breed standard, should not be less than 8in (20cm).

Limbs Some specimens are overlong in the leg, standing too much off the ground and with a corresponding lack of depth through the girth. Between 1825 and 1840, repeated crosses were made with Dutch mares. This increased the height at the expense of the limbs, producing, in particular, long and weak cannon bones.

HEAD The Orlov head is usually fairly small, but it is often somewhat coarse in appearance despite the Arabian influence. However, there is a distinct Arabian flavor in the set of the ears and the width of the forehead.

DUTCH INFLUENCE The strong Dutch influence did not always benefit the limbs, which at one time were prone to bursal enlargements, pronounced tendon weaknesses, and even bone deformation. These deficiencies have been largely overcome in the modern Orlov.

PRESERVATION AND IMPROVEMENT
The modern Orlov is often used to upgrade other breeds. To this end, great emphasis is placed on preserving the height, the powerful yet light build, the strength of tendons, the overall elegance and, of course, the potential to trot at high speed.

Orlovs are usually 16hh. Mares may be 1in (2.5cm) smaller.

Bashkir

The Bashkir, or Bashkirsky, evolved centuries ago in Bashkiria, around the southern foothills of the Urals. There it is bred as a pack, draft, and riding animal and to provide meat, milk, and clothing. In a seven- to eight-month lactation period, one mare yields 400–425 gallons (1,500–1,600 liters). Moreover, the peculiarly thick, curly coat of the Bashkir can be spun into cloth.

CHARACTERISTICS

The hardy Bashkir is kept outside and can survive winter temperatures of -22 to -40°F (-30 to -40°C), and find food under 3ft (1m) of snow. A pair of Bashkirs are said to be able to draw a sleigh 75–85 miles (120–140km) in 24 hours without being fed.

TYPES

Two types have developed within the habitat, the Mountain and the Steppe Bashkir. The former has been crossed with Dons and Budennys, and the latter, a harness type, with both trotters and Ardennais stallions. The Bashkir "Curly" is an American term descriptive of its curly coat.

The pony pictured here is one of the 1,100 or so Bashkirs registered in the US. It has been claimed that they arrived on the American continent across the land bridge that is now the Bering Strait. However, that takes no account of the fact that the species *Equus* was extinct on the American continent after the Ice Age, which swept away the land bridge across the Bering Strait, and the horse was not reintroduced until the arrival of the Spanish conquistadores some 10,000 years later.

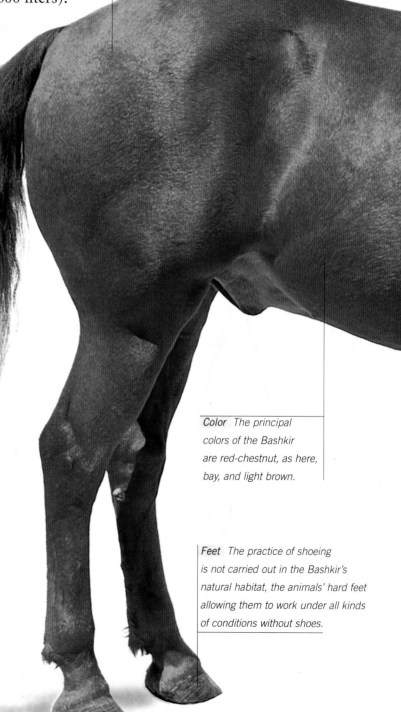

Coat A principal feature of the Bashkir, which is described as being docile and intelligent, is the very thick, curly winter coat that enables it to survive in subzero temperatures.

Color The principal colors of the Bashkir are red-chestnut, as here, bay, and light brown.

Feet The practice of shoeing is not carried out in the Bashkir's natural habitat, the animals' hard feet allowing them to work under all kinds of conditions without shoes.

The height of the Bashkir is 14hh.

Mane As might be expected, the Bashkir's mane and tail should be exceptionally thick.

Head The head of the Russian Bashkir is massive and set on a short, fleshy neck that runs into flat withers. The American version has been improved in these respects, and in recent years selective crosses have produced a better quality animal in its homeland.

Body The Bashkir is described in the official standard as being small with a wide body and a flat, straightish back. The measurement around the girth for stallions is 71in (180cm).

Limbs The limbs of this solid little horse are comparatively short, and the official Russian breed standard quotes a remarkable bone measurement of 8in (20cm) below the knee.

THE AMERICAN BASHKIR In the US, Bashkir-type ponies are found in the northwest. They are reputed to have been popular with the Native Americans, who used them in the same way as the Bashkiri people. It is claimed that the ponies were first seen running wild in the 1800s.

LIVING IN LUXURY The breed is able to fend for itself in the most severe climatic conditions and is, as a consequence, among the most hardy in the world. This American Bashkir is indulging in the luxury of a Kentucky paddock.

Kathiawari

The Kathiawari, bred principally in the Kathiawar Peninsula, is found throughout Maharashtra, Gujerat, and south Rajasthan, India. It is closely related to the Marwari but is a little smaller. Highly regarded in its native area it is used extensively in police work.

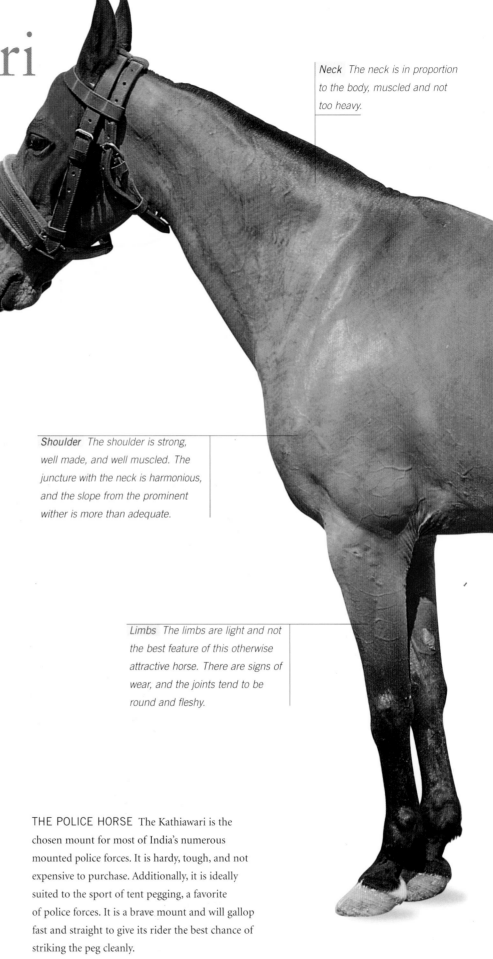

Neck The neck is in proportion to the body, muscled and not too heavy.

Shoulder The shoulder is strong, well made, and well muscled. The juncture with the neck is harmonious, and the slope from the prominent wither is more than adequate.

Limbs The limbs are light and not the best feature of this otherwise attractive horse. There are signs of wear, and the joints tend to be round and fleshy.

ORIGINS

There was a horse stock of mixed type in the provinces of the western coast well before the time of the Moghul emperors of the sixteenth century. It came from the north, with breeds such as the Baluchi and Kabuli, which were related to the steppe and desert horses to the west and northwest. Later in time there were substantial Arabian infusions coming from the Gulf and Cape province of South Africa. The horses were bred selectively by the princely houses, and twenty-eight strains still survive.

The highly mobile curved ears are a notable breed characteristic, and the best of the Kathiawaris are attractive, game little horses. Like all desert horses they are resistant to the heat, and they are tough and enduring. They have an innate ability to perform the *revaal*, the swift, lateral pacing gait.

The Kathiawari Horse Breeders' Association operates a register, and there is a government stallion station in Junagadh, Gujerat.

The Kathiawari stands between 14.2 and 15hh.

THE POLICE HORSE The Kathiawari is the chosen mount for most of India's numerous mounted police forces. It is hardy, tough, and not expensive to purchase. Additionally, it is ideally suited to the sport of tent pegging, a favorite of police forces. It is a brave mount and will gallop fast and straight to give its rider the best chance of striking the peg cleanly.

Back The back is strong with muscled loin, and of just the right length. There is a pleasing line from the wither to the croup.

CLASSIC HEAD This head study of a well-bred Kathiawari is typical of the best of the breed. The fine, extravagantly curved ears are sufficiently mobile to move easily through 360 degrees and are a much-prized feature. The halter, too, is notable.

Body The body is deep through the girth, compact and powerful, with a well-sprung rib cage. The overall impression is of a robust little horse, chunky in its outline.

Hind leg The hind leg is short of muscle in the second thigh and tends to be sickle-hocked. This is, in fact, a weak hind leg in comparison to the rest of the structure; nonetheless it appears to suit its owner well enough.

Marwari

The state of Rajasthan, in western India, is a land of horsemen where horse-breeding is still centered on Marwar (Jodhpur) whose traditional rulers, the Rathores, embraced the ideal of the Rajput warrior and whose Marwari horses enjoyed a reputation equal to their own.

ORIGINS

The probable origin of the Marwari horses is in the areas to the northwest of India: Uzbekistan, Kazakhstan, and, almost certainly, Turkmenistan, home of desert horses of the caliber of the distinctive Akhal-Teke (see pp.128–9). Arabian-type strains, found in Iran, probably had an influence, and Arabian horses were certainly imported to neighboring Gujerat in the nineteenth century from the Gulf and the Cape of South Africa.

A much-prized characteristic of the Marwari are the distinctive, curving ears, which are to be found on horses all down India's western coast well into Maharashtra.

Horses were essential to the Rajput warriors, and from the twelfth century the Rathores bred selectively to produce tough, enduring horses that would thrive in a desert environment. The breed has a natural pacing gait, known as *revaal*, which is a feature of many Asian strains.

There is an active breed association that promotes the horse with energy and considerable skill.

Mane Both mane and tail are fine, and the coat is silky to the touch.

Shoulder The shoulder slopes from prominent withers and is deceptive in its length. It allows plenty of room in front of the saddle and is a structure of some strength.

Forearm The forearm is well enough muscled and the legs appear hard and clean with firm, flat joints. The breed is noted for its dense, hard-wearing feet.

The Marwari stands between 14.3 and 15.2hh.

A MARWARI MARE This mare belongs to a select bloodline. The head is particularly fine and very typical. Colored, or part-colored coat patterns are popular in the wide range of Marwari coat colors. Bay, brown, shades of chestnut, and occasionally palomino occur.

Back *The back, behind the well-formed wither, is strong, and the loins muscular. It is ideally formed to carry a saddle well.*

Croup *There is pronounced slope from croup to tail, but the overall impression is one of wiry strength with a disposition to speed. Hip to hock is of good length.*

HAUTE ECOLE A tradition of circus or Haute Ecole riding exists in Rajput horse culture that might have been seen in the circuses of antiquity. Recognizable Haute Ecole leaps form part of the repertoire of the trained Marwari horse, and advanced movements are to be seen at the performances given at fairs and special events.

Hind leg *The hind leg fails a little in the thigh and in the muscling of the gaskin. The hock joint is, nonetheless, big, well formed, and with no tendency toward being lymphatic. Marwaris may sometimes tend to be cow-hocked.*

Body *The body is deep enough with sufficient length to allow for a degree of speed in the movement. It is in correct proportion to the length of the back.*

Hind limbs *The hind limbs are not too long in the shank, and the pasterns are correctly sloped and of the right length. The limbs are said to be hard-wearing.*

HAIR WHORLS Great importance is attached to hair whorls on the horse's body. Many are regarded as auspicious, but buyers will avoid assiduously those that they associate with ill fortune. Proportion is assessed on the basis of finger's width. The length of the face varies between 28 and 40 fingers. Four times the length of face is equal to the length from the poll to the horse's dock.

Australian Stock Horse

The first horses were imported into the settled districts of New South Wales some 200 years ago. First they came from South Africa, and then increasingly from Europe, with the favored breeds being Thoroughbreds and Arabians. The stock bred locally soon became known as Walers, after their province, a name that persisted until recently.

HISTORY

During and after World War I, the Walers were recognized as being the finest cavalry horses in the world because they were sound, had stamina, and could carry weight – no other horse performed as well. Despite their excellent merits, many Walers never returned to Australia, being destroyed at the end of the war by the order of the Australian government. What is now called the Australian Stock Horse – essentially an Anglo-Arabian type topped up with Percheron, Quarter Horse, and even a little pony blood – was based on the Waler.

The Australian Stock Horse is used widely on cattle stations, chiefly because of its endurance. Though not fast, it is a good all-around worker with great stamina. The Australian Stock Horse Society works to promote and standardize the breed, but as yet, it remains of no set type and its appearance varies enormously. Therefore, the horse has no standard of conformation, although the Thoroughbred type is favored.

Head *The head inclines toward the Thoroughbred but there is often a suggestion of the more chunky, thicker, and squarer Quarter Horse influence.*

Shoulders and chest *The adequate slope to the shoulders and the deep chest are those of a good, all-around saddle horse.*

The height of the Australian Stock Horse is 15–16.2hh.

RIDING HORSES The Australians have always been very successful in producing admirable riding horses that not only stand up to hard work but are capable of doing every job on the vast sheep stations of the country. They are tough, hard, and yet have plenty of quality about them.

A PERFECT CAVALRY HORSE If there were still a call for a cavalry horse today, the Australian Stock Horse would be in great demand because of its ability to carry weight, its capacity for endurance, its innate hardiness, as well as its amenable temperament.

EARLY TRANSPORTATION (Above) Cobb and Co. operated coaches over 6,000 miles in New South Wales and Queensland during the 1880s. The horses they used were Walers, often driven in seven-horse teams to the famous Concord coaches.

Color The Australian Stock Horse is usually bay, but other colors occur, although gray is rare. This horse is black.

AUSTRALIA'S BRUMBIES After the great Australian Gold Rush in the early 1850s, numerous horses – the imported forebears of the Walers and Stock Horses – were turned loose in the bush. Over the years, these horses ran wild and the herds grew ever larger while the animals degenerated in type and quality. These Brumbies, the Australian equivalent of the American Mustang, became so numerous that in the 1960s it was necessary to begin an extensive culling operation. The methods employed, however, were often inhumane and so unacceptable that Australia earned worldwide condemnation. In this picture, a Brumby exercises no little ingenuity in digging for water in a dried riverbed in the harsh Northern Territory.

Body The best specimens of Australian Stock Horse, if lacking consistency of type, are well-made, proportionate animals. The old-time Waler was often described as resembling the best type of Anglo-Arabian. The same description suits many of the modern Australian Stock Horses, although there is also evidence of the Quarter Horse in its features.

ACTION To gallop through the bush after sheep or cattle requires a horse with good balance, and a well-proportioned neck and shoulder.

ENDURANCE The Australian Stock Horse, like its predecessors, is capable of great feats of endurance, although it is nowhere near as fast as the Thoroughbred. In 1917, the Australian horsemen of Allenby's Mounted Corps marched 170 miles (274km) in four days in temperatures of 100°F (37.8°C). Even today, station hands cover long distances under the heat of the Australian sun.

Limbs Australian-bred horses have always been noted for their excellent limbs and feet, as well as for their enduring qualities and level tempers.

Cattle Driving

Around the cattle industry begun by the Spanish settlers in the New World, and around the men and horses, grew the legend and mythology of the American West. It was created first by novelists, and then assiduously cultivated and romanticized by the Hollywood film industry to become one of the great phenomena of our times.

FEEDING AMERICA

The Western became the modern morality play, in which good must always triumph over evil, and its appeal has not diminished with time. The reality was less romantic and by no means heroic. It was a hard life and demanded exceptional skills of the Western cowboy and the horses, which were essential to his very survival.

Initially, the end product of the early ranching enterprises in Mexico and Argentina was leather, but the increasing populations of the East, and the industrialization taking place in both Europe and the Americas, caused the emphasis to switch to the production of beef to feed the new societies. As a result, cattle ranching spread swiftly into the Western states.

Cattle ranching and the long trails to the railheads over harsh, difficult country involved the use of many horses trained in the techniques of cattle herding, as well as tough, resourceful men with special skills.

THE COWBOY

In the early days the principal mount of the cowboy was the Mustang, or wild crosses of the original Spanish stock. They were small, not beautiful, and wild, but they were also wiry, tough, and agile. After the Civil War (1861–5), the Quarter Horse was more in evidence. Without doubt the breed had developed into the world's finest cattle horse with an innate ability to work the often unpredictable herds.

The cowboy rode his horse at a jog and a comfortable lope and chose his string of horses with care. The elite of the remuda (the herd of broken ranch horses) was the Quarter Horse, which would "cut" a designated steer from the herd. Then there was the roping horse, providing the platform from which the rider threw his lariat and performing his work just as instinctively. Finally, there was the night horse, steady and able to work in the dark.

Western equipment evolved to meet the needs of the work. For example, the comfortable, hard-wearing Western saddle had its roping horn – a work platform meeting the needs of the range rider.

The cowboy wore a broad-brimmed Stetson hat and low-hipped denims (or Levis, named, like the hat, after their maker). He wore large, heavy spurs that jangled, making the cattle aware of his presence, and stout leather chaps (*chaparajos*) as protection against the thorny scrub. On the open range the chaps were often made of sheepskin. Most cowboys had strong leather gloves to save the hands from rope burns.

LONGHORNS (Above) A cattle drive in the Big Belt Mountains with a herd of Texas longhorns, a breed of cattle that could be unpredictable and dangerous if alarmed. A team of six to eight men or more were needed on a drive such as this, as well as a *remuda* of trained horses.

PUSHING THE HERD (Above top) Cowboys push the herd forward quietly and slowly along the trail. On the longer cattle trails it was important to keep the animals in good condition and to move them quickly. Any unforeseen delays increased the risk of the cattle losing weight and not fetching the best price at the market.

BRAZIL (Left) Brazilian cowboys on a cattle drive concentrating on keeping the herd together. The cowboy wears a pair of chaps made from sheepskin, while his companions wear ponchos and traditional hats.

Morgan

The Morgan is used for hunting, jumping, dressage, and for competing in the more artificial Park classes, either under saddle or between the shafts. It is also used for Western and pleasure riding, driving, and trail riding. It owes its existence to a phenomenal stallion of unprecedented prepotency, Justin Morgan, the undisputed sire of the first American breed.

MORGAN COLT This stylized depiction of a Morgan colt would meet the Morgan Horse Association's breed standards in some respects, but not in others!

HISTORY

Justin Morgan, a dark bay, was a horse of no more than 14hh. He was born in either 1789 or 1793 at West Springfield, Massachussetts, and was originally called Figure. He came into the possession of the schoolmaster Justin Morgan, after whom he was named, in 1795, and he died in 1821. He was worked incredibly hard in the plow, at woodland clearance, and in draft, but through all his lifetime of hard work and exploitation, he was never beaten in hauling matches or in races, either under saddle or in harness.

All Morgans trace to Justin Morgan through his most famous sons: Sherman, Woodbury, and Bullrush. The breed played a large part in the evolution of the Standardbred, the Saddlebred, and the Tennessee Walker, and it was the chosen remount for the US Army until mechanization.

Tail The show Morgan is always exhibited with a long, flowing tail that reaches to the ground when the horse is not in movement.

Quarters The official standard of the American Morgan Horse Association stipulates perfect quarters and hind legs – and they usually are very good.

Limbs The Morgan's cannon bones are short and, though the limbs are slender, there is plenty of bone and the joints are particularly well formed. The pasterns are strong, of medium length, and not too sloping.

SHOW HORSE The modern Morgan, shod to produce an elevated action, is a popular show horse in the US. Although tractable and versatile, the Morgan moves with great fire and spirit.

ORIGIN OF JUSTIN MORGAN The breeding of Justin Morgan, the foundation stallion, has never been established. There are suggestions that an early Thoroughbred, True Briton, was the sire. Others attribute the horse to a Friesian import, and the Welsh claim him as the progeny of a Welsh Cob, which is not impossible.

Neck *The neck must be well crested, of medium length, and very clean through the throat. The withers are clearly defined but slightly higher than the point of the hip.*

Shoulders *Sloped well from the wither, the shoulders are of particular strength. The neck joins low at the point of the shoulder.*

Mane *The mane and forelock are full, and the hair is soft and silky, never harsh.*

Ears *The ears are pointed and set wide apart.*

Body *The body is distinctive. The back is short, broad, and muscled, the barrel large and round, the chest wide and deep and the whole close-coupled.*

Color *Morgan colors are bay, as here, black, brown, and chestnut. There are no grays or part-colors.*

HEAD The Morgan has a medium-sized head that is clean-cut and tapers from jaw to muzzle. The profile is straight or just slightly dished, but never Roman-nosed. The muzzle is fine, of medium size, and with small, firm lips and large nostrils. The eyes are large and bright.

ACTION The walk is long, straight, and elastic; the trot is very free, straight, well balanced, and collected; the canter is smooth and easy, straight and in balance.

The height is from 14.1–15.2hh. Some may be a little over or under.

TEMPERAMENT The Morgan is a spirited and courageous horse, but easily handled and intelligent. It is also a hard, versatile horse, very powerful, well proportioned in all respects, and with great stamina.

Feet *All four feet are round, of medium size, and of smooth, dense horn.*

Galiceno

The Galiceno pony belongs to Mexico, taking its name from the Spanish province of Galicia where it was first developed. Galicia was an area famed for its smooth-gaited horses distinguished by their swift running walk. They were prized for their comfortable traveling gait throughout sixteenth-century Europe, and this characteristic is still retained in the modern Galiceno. Though only 14hh., the Galiceno is more horse than pony in character and proportion.

THE BACKGROUND

There was Galiceno stock among the earliest horses brought by the Spanish from Hispaniola (Haiti) in the sixteenth century. Almost certainly they were much influenced by the hardy Sorraia and Garranos indigenous to the Iberian Peninsula. Both these ancient breeds, stemming from primitive stock like the Tarpan (see pp.10–11), contributed directly to the evolution of the great Spanish Horse.

THE PRESENT DAY

Some of the present-day Galiceno in Mexico are probably as close to the original Sorraia type as can be found, particularly with respect to the dun coloration. They inherit the tough constitution of the Iberian stock and are popular for ranch work and competition.

ALL-AROUNDER As well as being an attractive everyday riding horse, with the bonus of the special gait, the tractable and intelligent Galiceno has a tough constitution. It is also worked in harness in the cultivation of the land and for general farm usage.

COAT COLOR The coloring of this attractive horse reflects that of the early Spanish stock. Duns and palominos are found along with bay, brown, and some chestnut. The dun coloration, with black mane and tail and dorsal list, sometimes shows zebra bars on the lower limbs, a legacy of the Sorraia connection.

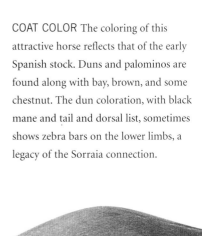

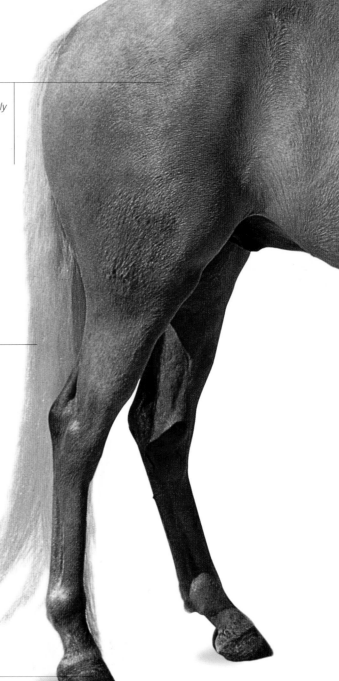

Quarters The formation of the quarters is not particularly notable, but there are no major deficiencies and it is serviceable enough.

Tail The fine-haired, well-set tail follows the conventional palomino coloring: it is virtually pure white.

Feet The horn is hard, and foot troubles are rare.

Back The withers tend to be round, but the back is well made. Length between the last rib and the haunch is perhaps a bit long.

Neck The neck is a little short but is conducive to the specialized gait.

Head This is a neat quality head with an alert expression, neat, sharp ears, and generous width between the large, kindly eyes.

Forehand The shoulder, the lowish wither, and the rather short neck are what might be expected from a horse noted for its smooth, running walk. The juncture with the foreleg is notably good. There is depth through the girth and the chest is wide and deep.

Forearm The notably good forearm is of sufficient length and has adequate muscle development. The knee is flat and big enough, set straight with forearm and cannon.

HORSE OR PONY? While the Galiceno standing at 14hh. is termed a pony, the proportions and character of the breed – and even the appearance of the head – are compatible with those of a small horse. The overall conformation makes for a responsive and agile animal.

A COUNTRY HORSE The Galiceno is very much a horse of the country. Hard and tough, it adapts easily to climatic conditions, and its hard feet and inherent soundness enable it to work well on the hard, sun-baked ground. The special running gait is very comfortable for the rider and covers a lot of ground swiftly.

Lower limb These are nice, short cannons with sufficient bone in relation to the size of the animal. The joints are clean and the slope of the pastern very correct.

The Galiceno stands at 14hh.

Criollo

Criollo means "of Spanish descent" and covers a number of South American horses. There is the Crioulo Braziliero, and the tough Llanero cattle horse of Venezuela, which is not dissimilar to the Argentine Criollo, with which it shares a common background.

THE GAUCHO'S HORSE

The Argentine Criollo, not much known outside its native country, is one of the world's most important breeds. It descends from early Spanish stock in which there was a strong Barb element. There is also evidence of some Sorraia blood (see pp.150–1). It is the mount of the legendary *gauchos*, among the last of the world's horse people, and is as tough, sound, and enduring as any horse in the world, capable of carrying heavy weights over long distances and the most difficult terrain.

The Criollo can withstand the most severe climatic conditions, inadequate feed, and a minimal fluid intake. In short, it has the ability to survive in near-impossible conditions.

SELECTIVE BREEDING

Its breed society, which was formed in 1918, encourages selective breeding by the most rigorous endurance tests.

Criollos are used for all military purposes and, when crossed with the Thoroughbred, provide the base for the Argentinian polo pony, the best in the world.

Neck The elegant, muscular neck is indicative of supreme balance and speed.

Headcollar The nosepiece of the gaucho *headcollar* affords almost complete control.

Shoulder A long, sloping shoulder with well-defined withers is a notable feature and important in the varied use made of the horse. It is particularly important with regard to its galloping ability.

Limbs The splendid short limbs have prominent joints and a short cannon.

The Criollo stands between 14 and 15hh.

HEADGEAR The *gaucho* bridle (above) and headcollar (main picture) are expertly made from braided rawhide and are entirely practical for work on the range. The bridle's origin lies with the Persian bridles of remarkably similar construction dating from the third century BC, and a similar form of headgear is used by the Ukranian Cossack.

COLOR The coat color of the Criollo is varied but shades of dun predominate. There are also blue and strawberry roans, chestnuts, skewbalds, and piebalds. The most prized color is *grulla* or *gateado*, a brown- or mouse-dun shade.

Quarter A good, well-formed, and muscular quarter with impressive length from hip to hock joint. It promises agility and balance combined with speed.

Back Strong, compact, and with a muscled loin. The back joins shoulder and quarters harmoniously and could scarcely be bettered.

SELECTION TESTS The rigorous selection tests imposed by the breed society are in every way a test of endurance. One selection march involved a route of over 470 miles (756km) and had to be completed in 15 days carrying a weight of 242lb (110kg) without supplementary feed being given.

Thigh The quarter comes down in to a long, well-developed second thigh that gives great strength to the whole structure.

Body The body is reflective of overall excellence. Ribs are nicely rounded, and there is adequate depth through the girth.

Hocks The joints are clean, excellent, and held close to the ground. The feet are uniformly good and hard-wearing.

FOUR-SQUARE The Criollo is stockily built, standing no more than 15hh. The neck is short but elegant, and the profile is usually convex. Modern Criollos move conventionally but some retain the lateral ambling gait of the Spanish horses.

MANCHA AND GATO The most famous journey undertaken by Criollos was made by Professor Aime Tschiffely with Mancha and Gato, then aged 15 and 16 respectively. Starting in 1925, Tschiffely rode 10,000 miles (16,090km) from Buenos Aires to Washington, DC, in two-and-a-half years, traveling over some of the most difficult and dangerous country in the world.

American Crème

The US has a genius for creating breeds that highlight a particular facet of the species *Equus*, and the American horse population is commensurately large and varied. The American Crème is a case in point. Zoologically it is a color type, like the palomino (see pp.184–5), and does not fulfill the criteria that constitute breed status.

Color *Albino breed descriptions gave specific measurements for the frame and its proportions. Crèmes are more concerned with color and this example cannot be regarded as characteristic of the type in its proportions.*

AMPLE LATITUDE

The breed controversy apart, the Crème has a close relationship with the American Albino, whose governing body, the American Albino Horse Club, was founded in 1937. By 1970 it had changed its name to the American White Horse Club and had separated the registry into Whites and Crèmes. The Albino Association had published specific and detailed breed descriptions and standards for both stock horse and Arabian types. The American Crème can be of many types including Morgan, Thoroughbred, Arabian, and Quarter Horse, but there were four main color classifications as well as subsequent combinations. The classifications were: A. Body ivory, mane lighter white, eyes blue, skin pink; B. Body crème, darker mane, dark eyes; C. Body and mane pale crème, eyes blue, skin pink; D. Body and mane sooty crème, eyes blue, skin pink.

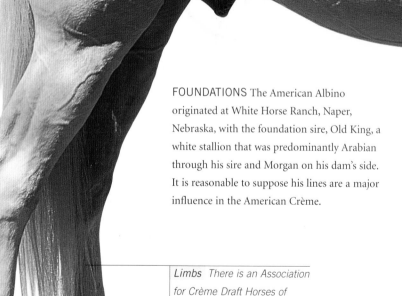

FOUNDATIONS The American Albino originated at White Horse Ranch, Naper, Nebraska, with the foundation sire, Old King, a white stallion that was predominantly Arabian through his sire and Morgan on his dam's side. It is reasonable to suppose his lines are a major influence in the American Crème.

ARABIAN TYPE This is an Arabian type of crème-colored horse. However, color rather than type is the prime requisite for registration, and this is produced consistently. Crème and Albino horses are popular circus animals. The Lone Ranger's Silver was a famous Albino.

Limbs *There is an Association for Crème Draft Horses of medium to heavy type, but these limbs are of pronounced riding type.*

Outline This conformation inclines to that of the stock horse and is unremarkable. Nonetheless, there is ample depth through the girth and an appearance of overall strength.

Muzzle The muzzle is coarse and, because of the lack of pigment, could be susceptible to sunburn.

Neck In this instance, the neck, though short, is commendably muscled, although the parotid gland at the jowl is unduly prominent.

Limbs The limbs are acceptable although not exceptional, while the joints are insufficiently defined. The fetlocks are particularly puffy.

HEAD A stock-horse head, serviceable, workmanlike, and not unattractive. To the practical horseman, however, the color (or lack of it) in the pigment is suspect as it can indicate inherent weaknesses with respect to sensitivity to sunlight as well as possible impairments or defects in vision.

The American Crème stands 15.2hh. on average.

Feet The feet are of dark-colored horn when one might have expected them to be white, a characteristic of the Albino.

Quarter Horse

The American Quarter Horse is the first all-American breed. A distinctive type, it was bred in Virginia and the Seaboard Settlements very early in the seventeenth century. Fans of the breed claim that it is "the most popular horse in the world." To support that claim, the American Quarter Horse Association's register has millions of entries.

HISTORY

The first significant import of English horses to Virginia was in 1611, well before the establishment of the Thoroughbred in England. Therefore, they would have had a background of native, Eastern, and Spanish blood. Crossed with the stock of Spanish origin already in America, they became the foundation for the Quarter Horse, which quickly evolved into a compact horse with massively muscled quarters.

The settlers used them for farm work, herding cattle, hauling lumber, in light harness, and under saddle. The sports-loving English settlers also raced them on quarter-mile courses – hence the name Quarter Horse. This also explains why the breed developed an explosive ability to sprint over short distances. In the West, the Quarter Horse made another name for itself as the perfect cow pony.

Quarters Heavy, muscular quarters of depth and width are characteristic of this chunky horse.

ACTION The Quarter Horse became the perfect cow pony because of its speed, inherent balance, and agility, and it developed an uncanny instinct for working cattle virtually independent of its rider. It was said that "he could turn on a dime and toss you back nine cents change."

HALTER CLASS This entry in a halter class typifies the Quarter Horse conformation, revealing clearly the hugely muscled quarters that are characteristic of the breed. The symmetrical structure and the proportion of the component parts ensure a perfect balance.

Withers *The excellent saddle back of the Quarter Horse is due to the well-defined withers that extend back beyond the top of the shoulder to hold the saddle firmly in place.*

Neck *The neck needs to be fairly long and flexible as the Quarter Horse works with his neck extended and his head down. An arched or crested neck would be undesirable.*

Muzzle *The muzzle is small, and the mouth is shallow and firm with the teeth meeting exactly.*

Color *The usual Quarter Horse color is chestnut, but any solid color is acceptable.*

Joints *The cannons are short with the hock set low to the ground. There is no play in the joint other than directly forward.*

Feet *The hoof is oblong and proportionately sized. The slope is the same as that of the pastern, about 45 degrees.*

ALL-AROUND PLEASURE HORSE The Quarter Horse excels as a trail-riding mount. It also makes a good, sagacious, and tireless hunter and is as prominent in the show ring as it is in the traditional rodeo classes. It is a natural jumper and a proven performer in dressage competitions, while Quarter Horse racing is now a firmly established and popular sport, carrying high prize money.

The Quarter Horse stands between 14.3 and 16hh.

Western Riding

Western riding continues to reflect the horse culture and equipment brought to the Americas 400 years ago by the early Spanish settlers. However, its subsequent development as a recognized style has produced a wholly original form of horsemanship that is in every way as skillful as any other practiced in the modern world.

DEDICATION AND DEVOTION

At its highest level Western riding is on a par with that of Europe's classical schools and just as demanding of dedication and devotion to the basic training principles.

Both Western and European disciplines have the same objectives: lightness, obedience, relaxation, and a supple, fluid balance. They differ in purpose, method, and emphasis.

In Europe the purpose is largely competitive, an element by no means absent in Western riding. In the latter, collection is imposed through a mixture of driving aids ("cues" in Western parlance) and the restraining aids applied largely through contact by the hand through the double bridle, and supported by the body weight.

The Western system has at its base the practical objective of producing an all-around working horse against the background of handling cattle, often at speed and with the greatest need for efficiency and skill. The Western horse is no less balanced than its European counterpart but the outline is very different. Instead of an impression of elevation and collection, the horse moves in a lower, more extended outline that still calls for the hocks to be well engaged. Moreover, the horse is ridden almost entirely on one hand with little more than a "floating" rein – which is not, indeed, inconsistent with the classical ideal.

The definitive Western paces are the jog and the smooth lope. Basic requirements are the rein-back (backup), the turns on the forehand and quarters, as well as the ability to move sideways effortlessly.

Advanced work involves flying changes of leg, the roll-back (a turn through 180 degrees); the spin (the Western equivalent of the pirouette), carried out at speed; and, last but not least, the potentially damaging sliding halt, made from an accelerating gallop and involving a slide of up to 30ft (9m) on the hind legs.

LONG AND LOW (Above) A Quarter Horse competing in a trail riding class. The horse crosses the poles in a relaxed fashion but in balance, and in the long, low outline required. The rider maintains contact with the horse's mouth through the weight of a looped rein held lightly in one hand.

THE PROOF (Above top) In the system of Western horsemanship, the rodeo sport of barrel racing is "the proof of the pudding." Raising a cloud of dust the horse rounds the barrel with minimal rein contact at breakneck speed while retaining perfect balance.

HALT! (Left and inset) The spectacular sliding stop epitomizes Western riding, although it is not always regarded as its most attractive feature. Nonetheless, to execute the movement while riding with one hand calls for consummate skill.

Standardbred

In the US, harness racing attracts a following of over 30 million people. In many European countries, and in Scandinavia and Russia, it is more popular than Thoroughbred racing. The supreme harness racer is, without doubt, the American Standardbred, many of which can go one mile (1.6km) in around 1.55 minutes. A few are even faster.

ANCESTOR (Above) The incomparable Norfolk Roadster was a far-off ancestor of the Standardbred. In its day, it regularly carried 170lb (77kg) riders at speeds of 15–16mph (24–27km/h).

HISTORY

The term Standardbred, first used in 1879, refers to the speed standard required for entry into the breed register. Separate harness races are held for conventional, diagonal trotters, and for pacers that employ the lateral gait (see pp.162–3). The pacer, faster and less likely to break the gait, is preferred in the US. In Europe, trotters are more numerous.

The Standardbred was founded on Messenger, a Thoroughbred imported from England in 1788. He did not race in harness but, like all early Thoroughbreds, had trotting connections with the old Norfolk Roadster. The foundation sire of the breed is Messenger's inbred descendant, Hambletonian 10, foaled in 1849. He, too, never raced in harness, but he had a peculiarity of conformation that contributed to his success as a sire of harness racers. He measured 15.3¼hh. at the croup, and 15.1¼hh. at the wither, a structure that gives enormous propulsive thrust to the quarters.

Quarters Quarters are exceptionally powerful so as to deliver the maximum possible forward thrust at the pacing gait.

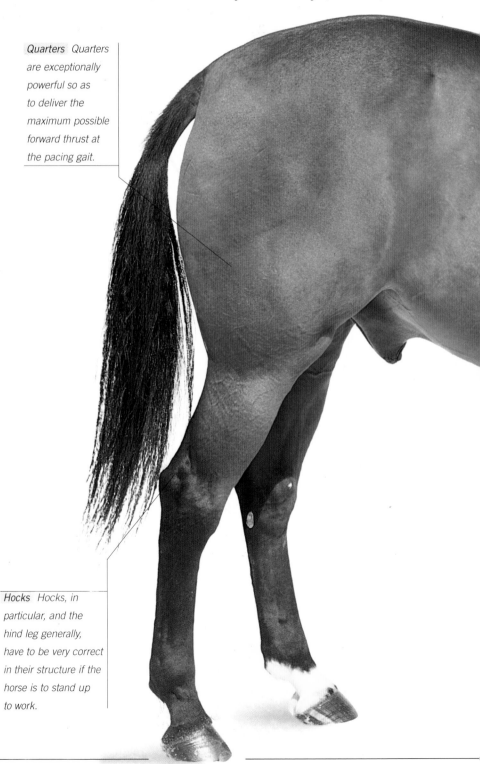

RED MILE RACEWAY The popular sport of harness racing at the famous Red Mile Raceway in Lexington, Kentucky. There are over 70 major tracks in the US, all staging at least 50 meetings a year. All tracks are left-handed, and evening racing under floodlights is the rule.

Hocks Hocks, in particular, and the hind leg generally, have to be very correct in their structure if the horse is to stand up to work.

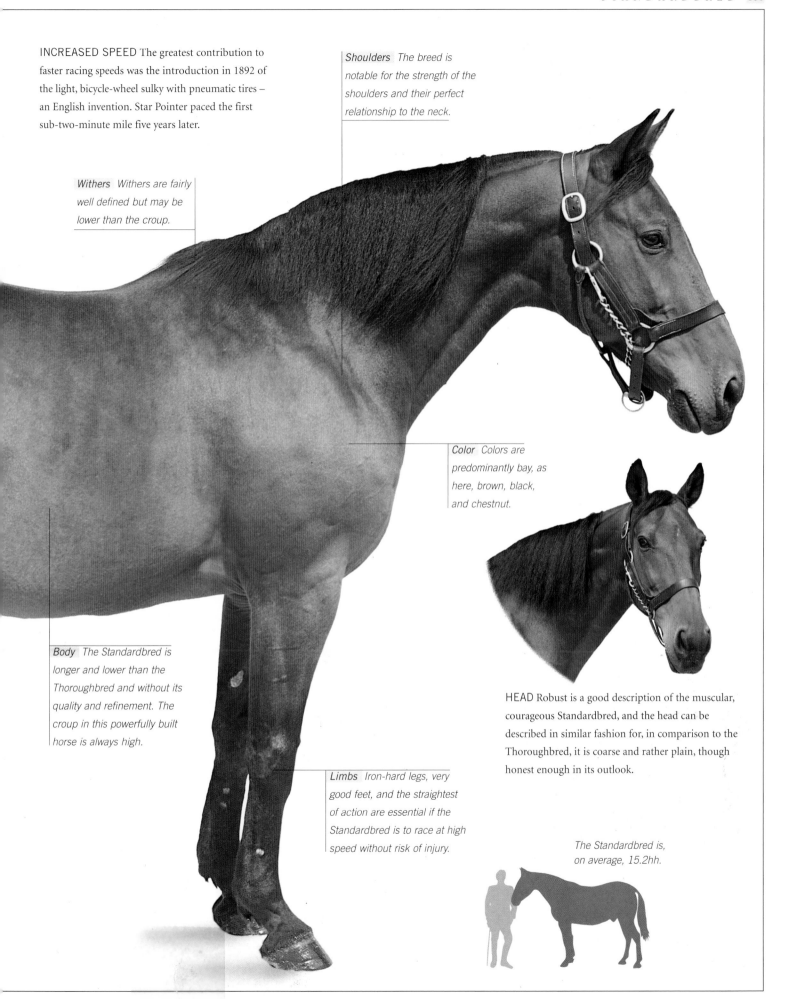

INCREASED SPEED The greatest contribution to faster racing speeds was the introduction in 1892 of the light, bicycle-wheel sulky with pneumatic tires – an English invention. Star Pointer paced the first sub-two-minute mile five years later.

Shoulders The breed is notable for the strength of the shoulders and their perfect relationship to the neck.

Withers Withers are fairly well defined but may be lower than the croup.

Color Colors are predominantly bay, as here, brown, black, and chestnut.

Body The Standardbred is longer and lower than the Thoroughbred and without its quality and refinement. The croup in this powerfully built horse is always high.

Limbs Iron-hard legs, very good feet, and the straightest of action are essential if the Standardbred is to race at high speed without risk of injury.

HEAD Robust is a good description of the muscular, courageous Standardbred, and the head can be described in similar fashion for, in comparison to the Thoroughbred, it is coarse and rather plain, though honest enough in its outlook.

The Standardbred is, on average, 15.2hh.

Harness Racing

The sport of harness racing has its roots in the Greek and Roman circuses of the pre-Christian era. The modern sport is well established in the US, Europe, and Australasia, and it attracts a following that in some countries exceeds that of Thoroughbred racing and offers equivalent prize money.

RACING CENTERS

The US is the world's leading harness-racing nation, with over 70 major raceways where evening racing on standard, left-handed tracks is the norm. The leading raceway is Meadowlands in East Rutherford, New Jersey, which stages some of the world's most valuable races, including the Hambletonian, which is the first of the Triple Crown races for trotting horses, the others being the Yonkers Trot at Yonkers Raceway, New York, and the Kentucky Futurity at Red Mile. The Triple Crown for pacers comprises the Cane Futurity (Yonkers), the Little Brown Jug (Delaware), and the Messenger Stakes at Roosevelt, Long Island. Pacers and trotters are not raced against each other.

PACERS AND TROTTERS

In the US it is the pacing horse rather than the trotter that predominates (see Standardbred, pp.160–1). The pacer moves the legs in lateral pairs, while the conventional trotter moves its legs diagonally. The former is preferred by the betting fraternity because it is less likely to break into a gallop, a failing which obliges it to be checked and moved to the outside of the field, thus losing any chance of winning.

To assist the pacing gait and to prevent "breaking" (moving into canter) the pacing horse is fitted with hobbles, a harness designed to connect the fore and hind legs above the knee and hock, respectively.

The US is, indeed, the home for much of the specialized equipment demanded by the sport. Harness racers need to wear leg boots to protect against a foot striking into a leg at speeds of up to 40mph (65km/h). Heavy "antishadow" nosebands of sheepskin are often fitted as well as sophisticated bitting arrangements designed to control the horse and also to ensure that he runs straight.

EUROPE AND AUSTRALASIA

In Europe, Scandinavia, and Russia, harness racing is more popular than flat racing, and the trotting horse is more numerous than the pacer.

At France's most important track, the Hippodrome de Vincennes, some 1,000 races are staged annually, including the famous Prix de Cornulier, for ridden trotters (see French Trotter, pp.102–3).

The sport in Australia and New Zealand is almost a national pastime. It was New Zealand that produced one of the greatest harness racers of all time, Cardigan Bay, who raced successfully in both Australasia and the US and was the first Standardbred to win one million dollars.

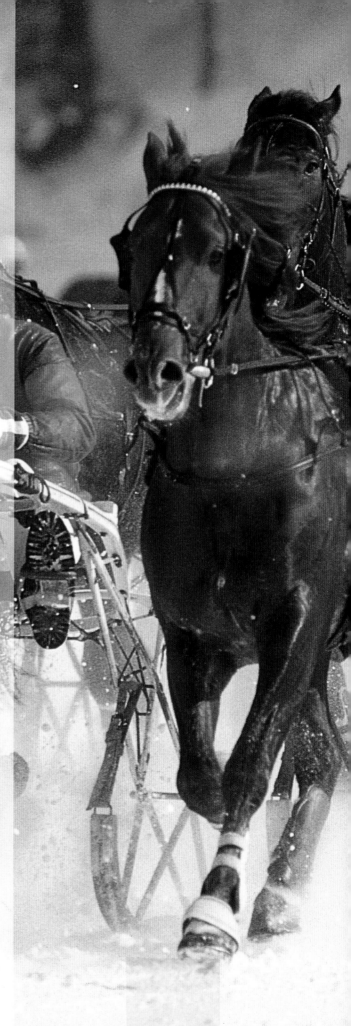

SITTING EASY (Above) The harness-race "jockey" sits in a bike-wheel racing sulky, invented in 1892 and perfected by an engineer called Joe King in the mid-1970s. King's efforts resulted in a phenomenal rise in the recorded number of two-minute miles from a total of 685 in 1974 to 1,849 only two years later.

HARNESS GATE (Above top) The racing sulky aside, the mobile starting gate is the most important invention in the sport. Made up of two retractable wings attached to a truck that accelerates away from the field, it ensures a fair start to the race.

ON THE SNOW (Left) In St. Moritz, Switzerland, racing is on prepared snow tracks. Most races are for conventional trotters and the horses are specially shod. The racing sulky is equipped with lightweight sleigh runners.

Saddlebred

The Saddlebred, originally called the Kentucky Saddler, evolved in the southern states of the US in the nineteenth century. It was a practical horse, as well as one of great elegance. It could perform a variety of farm tasks; it could carry a man in great comfort over rough terrain throughout a long, working day; and it could also double up as a sharp carriage horse.

ORIGINS

The Saddlebred developed from the Canadian Pacer and the Narragansett Pacer (the work horse of plantation owners of Rhode Island), two naturally gaited breeds. Morgan and Thoroughbred blood was also introduced to produce a distinctive and impressive horse.

The modern Saddlebred, either three- or five-gaited, is generally regarded as a brilliant, if artificial, show horse, somewhat like the English Hackney (see pp.98–9). It is still shown in harness and, with its feet trimmed normally, is used as a pleasure and trail-riding horse. It can also work cattle, jump, and compete in dressage tests. Despite its versatility, however, the American Saddlebred Association still describes it as "America's most misunderstood breed" because of the artificial way in which it is produced and its show-ring image of a nicked, high-set tail, overlong feet and the use of somewhat dubious training aids.

FIRE, SPEED, AND BEAUTY The specialized action is a legacy of the old, Spanish-based pacers and amblers. The Saddlebred's fire, speed, and beauty of form derive from the Thoroughbred.

THREE-GAITERS AND FIVE-GAITERS
A three-gaited Saddlebred performs at walk, trot, and canter. Each gait is performed with high action and in a slow, collected manner. The five-gaiter has two additional paces, the "slow gait," a four-beat prancing movement, and the full-speed, brilliant "rack," a high, four-beat gait free from any pacing movement.

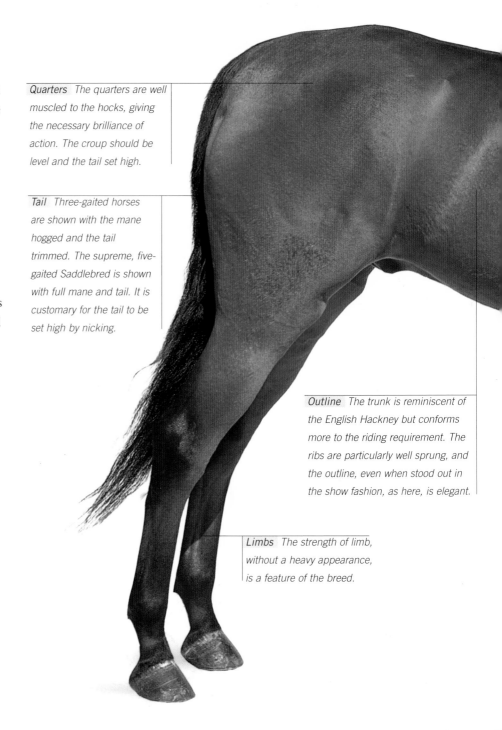

Quarters The quarters are well muscled to the hocks, giving the necessary brilliance of action. The croup should be level and the tail set high.

Tail Three-gaited horses are shown with the mane hogged and the tail trimmed. The supreme, five-gaited Saddlebred is shown with full mane and tail. It is customary for the tail to be set high by nicking.

Outline The trunk is reminiscent of the English Hackney but conforms more to the riding requirement. The ribs are particularly well sprung, and the outline, even when stood out in the show fashion, as here, is elegant.

Limbs The strength of limb, without a heavy appearance, is a feature of the breed.

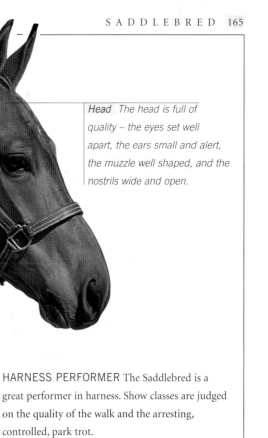

Neck *The neck is long and arched with no fleshiness in the jowl. It is set in the prominent withers, which give an especially high head carriage – one of the breed's features.*

Withers *The withers are clean, sharp, and much higher than in the pure harness horse. The back is notably short and strong.*

Head *The head is full of quality – the eyes set well apart, the ears small and alert, the muzzle well shaped, and the nostrils wide and open.*

HARNESS PERFORMER The Saddlebred is a great performer in harness. Show classes are judged on the quality of the walk and the arresting, controlled, park trot.

Shoulders *The Saddlebred has a particularly good, sloped shoulder. The scapula blades at the wither are placed fairly close together to give a wonderfully free action.*

ELEGANCE AT LARGE A champion Saddlebred at liberty, moving with great, natural elegance and freedom. The high carriage of head and tail is typical, adding to the stately presence of this uniquely attractive horse.

Color *The range of permitted coat colors is surprisingly wide. Bay, as here, and chestnut are the most common colors, but blacks, grays, and palominos occur, as well as the occasional roan. The coat hair is noticeably silky and fine.*

FEET To enhance the action, the feet are grown unnaturally long and shod with heavy shoes. The pasterns are long and sloping to provide a comfortable, springy ride, which is exceptionally smooth.

The height is between 15 and 16hh., although sometimes it is a little more.

Missouri Fox Trotter

The Missouri Fox Trotter is one of the trio of North American gaited horses (the other two being the Saddlebred and the Tennessee Walker). It was established in about 1820, having evolved in the Ozark Mountains of Missouri and Arkansas, as the early settlers interbred Morgans, Thoroughbreds, and horses of predominantly Spanish Barb ancestry.

HISTORY

The early settlers aimed to produce a fixed type of enduring, utility horse that would carry a rider comfortably at a steady speed over long distances and rough terrain. Following later infusions of Saddlebred and Tennessee Walker blood, they created a compact, plain horse of amiable disposition that moved surefootedly in a very smooth, peculiarly broken gait.

THE FAMOUS FOX TROT GAIT

The horse actually walks actively from the shoulder in front and trots behind, the hind feet stepping on to the track of the forefeet and then sliding forward. This sliding action serves to minimize the concussive effect and the rider is carried along while scarcely being aware of the movement. The horse can maintain this gait for long distances at a regular 5–8mph (8–13km/h) and over short distances will reach 10mph (16km/h). In it the horse is expected to move with style and animation, in perfect rhythm and with a degree of collection, accompanied by an up and down movement of the head, similar to that of the Tennessee Walker (see pp.168–9). The slightly elevated tail bobs rhythmically all the while.

Colors All colors occur, including part colors. However, shades of chestnut, as here, are the most common, with some red-roans being found.

Limbs The body is well muscled throughout; deep, and relatively compact. The limbs are muscular. The hind legs appear more heavily built than the forelegs.

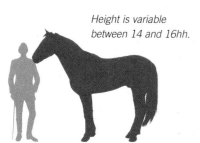

Height is variable between 14 and 16hh.

MODERN FOX TROTTER The modern Missouri Fox Trotter is an all-around pleasure and show horse. Although the stud book for the breed did not open until 1948, today there are well over 15,000 registered Fox Trotters. The breed is usually ridden in Western gear.

Outline *The Fox Trotter has a low outline in comparison to the high, showy Walkers and Saddlebreds, and its action is also much lower.*

Head *The head is neat enough with pointed, well-shaped ears, tapered muzzle, large eyes, and an alert expression.*

ACTION The walk is in strict four-beat time with distinct overstriding of the hind feet. The canter is halfway between the fast, long-rein lope of the cow pony and the high, slow gait of the Walkers and Saddlebreds. The Trotter does not have the high action of the Saddlebred and Walker. The Breed Society prohibits the use of artificial training aids to accentuate the natural gait.

Chest *The chest is wide and deep and the walking movement comes from the sloped, powerful shoulder without exaggerated knee action.*

Joints *Joints are usually flat and large, even though the bone sometimes seems to be insufficient.*

TRAIL AND SHOW RING The Fox Trotter, because of his inherent surefootedness and easy gaits, is the ideal trail horse in rough, inhospitable country. All the horse shows in the Ozarks feature show classes for the breed, when horses are shown at the Fox Trot, which is judged at 40 percent of the total marks awarded. The four-beat walk and the canter each make up 20 percent of the overall marks.

Feet *The breed is noted for its good feet and is especially surefooted.*

Tennessee Walker

The Tennessee Walker is one of the unique American group of gaited horses, all of which have their roots in early Spanish stock. Its origins, like those of the Saddlebred and the Missouri Fox Trotter (see pp.164–7), are in the southern states. The Walker evolved in nineteenth-century Tennessee as a practical horse that could carry its owner in comfort for hours while inspecting crops on the plantations.

HISTORY

The breed traces back to the old Narragansett Pacer of Rhode Island. It evolved as an amalgam of Standardbred, Thoroughbred, Morgan, and Saddlebred blood. The foundation sire is recognized as the Standardbred Black Allan, who came from a line of trotters (not pacers) out of a Morgan mare. As a harness racer, Black Allan was a failure because of his peculiar walking pace, a characteristic that has now won his descendants wide acclaim.

The Walker is noted for three exceptional gaits: the flat walk, the famous, running walk (the predominant feature), and the high, smooth, rocking-chair canter. All are said to be "bounce-free." In addition, the breed has a most amiable disposition and has the reputation of being the most reassuring horse for a novice or nervous rider.

READY FOR THE RING The Tennessee Walker turned out for showing. The nicked tail is in accordance with American convention. Very long hooves assist the action which is, nonetheless, largely inbred and cannot be taught successfully to other horses. Boots are used for protection.

Quarters The horse's tail is grown long and is usually nicked and high set. The quarters are strong and, in movement, the hind legs are brought well under the body.

PROMOTION The Tennessee Walking Horse Breeders Association was formed at Lewisburg, Tennessee, in 1935. It promotes its breed by promising that if you "ride one today, you'll own one tomorrow."

Limbs The limbs are powerful, though not outstanding in terms of conformational correctness.

TEMPERAMENT The outstanding feature of the Tennessee Walker is its temperament. Steady and reliable, it can be ridden by a beginner with absolute confidence. This, as well as the easy comfort of the movement, makes it a popular family mount. It is claimed to be the most naturally good-tempered of all horses and the most comfortable in the world.

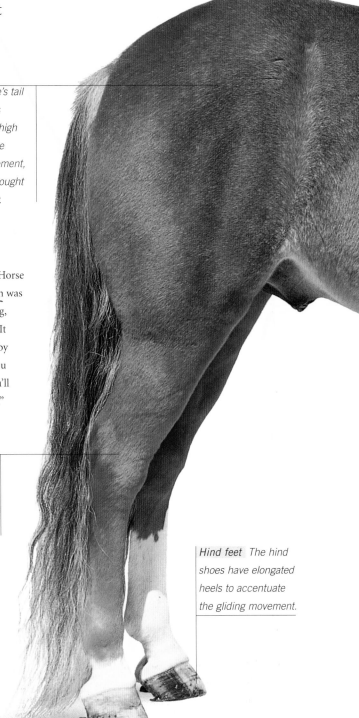

Hind feet The hind shoes have elongated heels to accentuate the gliding movement.

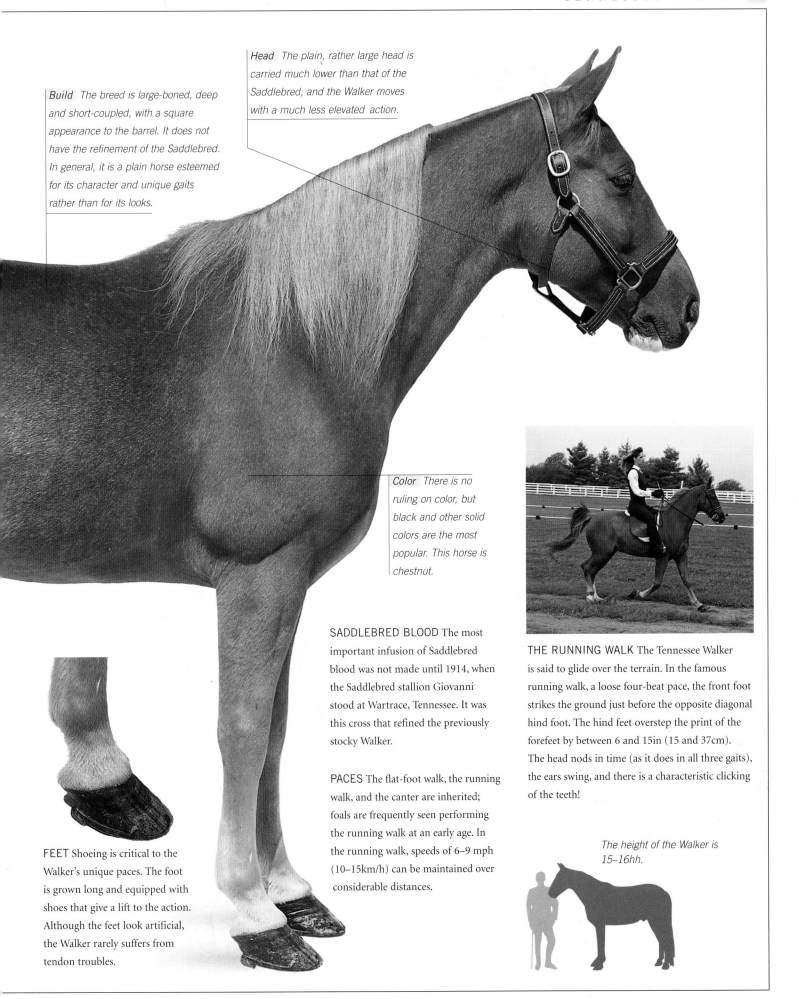

Head The plain, rather large head is carried much lower than that of the Saddlebred, and the Walker moves with a much less elevated action.

Build The breed is large-boned, deep and short-coupled, with a square appearance to the barrel. It does not have the refinement of the Saddlebred. In general, it is a plain horse esteemed for its character and unique gaits rather than for its looks.

Color There is no ruling on color, but black and other solid colors are the most popular. This horse is chestnut.

SADDLEBRED BLOOD The most important infusion of Saddlebred blood was not made until 1914, when the Saddlebred stallion Giovanni stood at Wartrace, Tennessee. It was this cross that refined the previously stocky Walker.

PACES The flat-foot walk, the running walk, and the canter are inherited; foals are frequently seen performing the running walk at an early age. In the running walk, speeds of 6–9 mph (10–15km/h) can be maintained over considerable distances.

THE RUNNING WALK The Tennessee Walker is said to glide over the terrain. In the famous running walk, a loose four-beat pace, the front foot strikes the ground just before the opposite diagonal hind foot. The hind feet overstep the print of the forefeet by between 6 and 15in (15 and 37cm). The head nods in time (as it does in all three gaits), the ears swing, and there is a characteristic clicking of the teeth!

FEET Shoeing is critical to the Walker's unique paces. The foot is grown long and equipped with shoes that give a lift to the action. Although the feet look artificial, the Walker rarely suffers from tendon troubles.

The height of the Walker is 15–16hh.

Peruvian Paso

Both the Peruvian Paso (*paso* meaning "step") and the Paso Fino of Puerto Rico and Colombia, originate with the horses brought to the South American continent by the sixteenth-century Spanish conquistadores. Both of these breeds are extremely popular in the US.

COMMON ANCESTRY

The Paso breeds share a common ancestry in a blending of Spanish Jennet, the supreme pacing mount of the Old World, the Spanish Barb, and the Andalucian, and have been developed by skilled selective breeding. Characteristically, hind legs and pasterns are long, and the joints are capable of unusual flexion. Bone and feet are exemplary and, like all Criollo-related stock, the lungs and heart are big in relation to overall size.

UNIQUE GAITS

The horses are renowned for their unique, specialized lateral gaits, which are natural to both breeds and unlike the lateral movements of any other gaited breeds. Both horses are said to be so smooth in their action that a rider could carry a full glass of water without it being spilled, although the precise nature of the gait distinguishes the Peruvian Paso from the Paso Fino. The Peruvian Paso (also called the Peruvian Stepping Horse) moves in a four-beat lateral gait, called the *paso*. The Paso Fino has three, carefully preserved, named gaits.

CONFORMATION The Paso is not a big horse nor does it have the characteristics of a galloper. It is a compact, muscular animal, broad and deep through the body and standing on short, strong limbs.

Tail A long, abundant tail of fine hair is well placed in rounded quarters. The skin is covered with fine, shiny hair.

Hock joints In order to perform any of the three gaits over long periods of time, the hock joints must be large and particularly well constructed.

Hind leg There is exceptional strength in the construction of the hind leg, which is carried well under the body when the animal is in movement.

Feet The feet of the Paso are strong and hard, and the horse is naturally surefooted and agile.

The Peruvian Paso and Paso Fino stand between 14 and 15hh.

Color Bay and chestnut, as here, are possibly the most common colors, but every other coat coloring occurs, including part colors.

THE PASO Essentially, the *paso* is a four-beat, lateral gait in which the forelegs arc out to the side, rather like a swimmer's arms. This dishing action is called *termino*. The hind legs take very long, straight strides, overstepping the tracks of the forefeet, while the quarters are held low with the hocks well under the body. The back is held straight, absorbing concussion. The *paso* can be maintained for long periods over rough country and can reach speeds of up to 13mph (21km/h) without causing discomfort to the rider.

Neck The arched, muscular neck is fairly short and in proportion to the frame. It sits well into the wither and the broad, deep chest.

Shoulders The shoulder is obviously strong and just sufficiently sloped to produce the required elevation in the forelegs. The Paso is able to canter, but rarely does so, preferring its natural gait.

Limbs Sound limbs are essential in any riding horse, and those of the Paso are excellent, with exceptionally strong pasterns to meet the requirements of its unique gait.

THE PASO FINO'S GAITS The *paso fino* is the slow, collected, elevated display gait; *paso corto* is the more extended but unhurried traveling gait; *paso largo* is very fast. The Paso Fino can reputedly reach speeds of 16mph (26km/h) without causing discomfort to the rider.

Mustang

The term "mustang" derives from the Spanish *mesteña*, which means a group or a herd of horses, and is applied to the "wild" horses of Western America. The Mustangs were the mounts of Native American and white man alike. The Mustang was also the foundation for a large number of the American breeds. It retained many of the Spanish characteristics, especially with respect to color.

ORIGINS

When the Spanish conquistadores landed on the American continent, the horse had been extinct in that huge land for some 10,000 years. The Spanish introduced both horses and cattle to the New World. These cattle were the foundation stock for the great cattle industry that was to develop extensively during the nineteenth century.

Once the Spanish had become established, after the destruction of the Aztecs and other native peoples, numbers of Spanish Horses escaped or were turned loose and became feral. The Spanish Horses, which we now describe as Andalucian or Iberian (see pp.50–7), were from the finest strains and were regarded as the foremost breed in Europe. They formed the nucleus of the great herds of wild horses that spread upward from Mexico into the United States and the Western plains.

At the beginning of the twentieth century, an estimated one million wild horses roamed the Western states. By 1970, their numbers had been drastically reduced as a result of whole-sale massacre to supply the meat market. The Mustang is now protected by law and there are numerous groups and associations concerned with the preservation of the wild horses.

The height varies between 13.2 and 15hh.

Outline The outline of this horse reflects the degree of cumulative degeneration suffered by the feral Mustang stock. However, its Spanish antecedents remain apparent.

Quarters The quarters of this typically feral specimen are poorly formed as a result of the environment and the relatively sparse feed it sustains.

Mane and tail The full black mane and tail, the usual accompaniment to a dun coat color, is a characteristic of many Spanish/Barb-based stock.

HARDNESS Wild Mustangs are far from being conformationally acceptable in modern terms. They retain, nonetheless, the hardiness of constitution that characterized their Spanish forebears.

Color J. Frank Dobie, author of The Mustangs (1952) gives the colors as being: "bay and sorrel, brown and grullo (dark gray), roan, dun and gray, with here and there black, white, and paint." All the equine colors, in fact. This Mustang is a dun.

Neck The neck is short and lacking in muscular development while being poorly set on the shoulder and the flat, loaded wither.

Profile Some of the Spanish/ Barb profile is retained and the head shows quality. The older mustang type was much less attractive and prone to heaviness and coarseness in the head.

Forehand The chest lacks depth and width, and the shoulder is unacceptably straight, while the forearm is set rather too closely in to the body.

Limbs The knees tend to roundness instead of being big and flat. The cannon is better and the feet will be strong and hard, a legacy of Spanish antecedents.

NEW STRAINS Determined efforts are now being made to preserve the best of what is left of the wild horse population – and with some success, as this group of attractive animals shows. Mustang support groups are now instituting breeding programs based on selective breeding, and a breed standard has been formulated to encourage the best of the Spanish/Barb strains.

Morab

The Arabian, the "fountainhead" of the equine breeds, is acknowledged as the predominant upgrading influence in the breed structure of the world's horses. Crossed with the Thoroughbred it produced the Anglo-Arabian. The American equivalent, using the Morgan in place of the Thoroughbred, might be seen as the Morab.

BREED STATUS?

In comparison with the Anglo-Arabian, which meets conventional breed criteria and has been established definitively over 160 years, the Morab is of very recent origin, although the Arabian-Morgan cross has been known and appreciated for over a century.

In fact, the Morab Horse Association (MHA) has claimed full breed status for horses of the Arabian/Morgan cross as well as its defined permutations – a view unlikely to be accepted outside the US. However, the Association does operate a well-organized registry system and there is no doubt that the registered Morab is a very attractive horse, even if it lacks a basic consistency of type.

There is also a breed standard, although whether it is generally acknowledged by all Morab groups is unlikely. On the whole it consists of generalizations applicable to any well-bred horse. It does, however, state that "the shape of the hindquarters and pelvic angle is the most apparent difference between the Morab and other breeds."

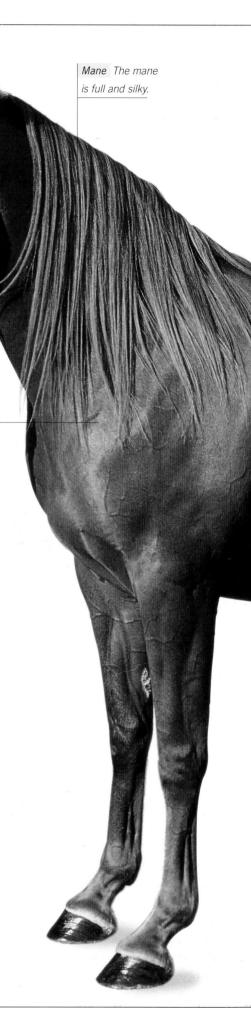

Mane The mane is full and silky.

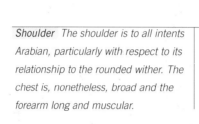

Shoulder The shoulder is to all intents Arabian, particularly with respect to its relationship to the rounded wither. The chest is, nonetheless, broad and the forearm long and muscular.

FRAGMENTATION This is a beautiful Morab head, but to which breed organization do the owners of the horse belong? As well as the fledgling MHA there are two more. The situation detracts from the credibility of breed status and reflects the fragmentation of the "breed" enthusiasts.

The Morab stands between 14.3hh and 15.3hh.

OUTLINE The outline is inconsistent in its proportions and hardly accords with the MHA's less than definitive standards. There are good individual features, the head and the powerful forearms, for instance, but the overall impression is disappointing.

Back The lack of a defined wither detracts somewhat from the otherwise acceptable back structure, which has strength through the loins and sufficient breadth.

Croup The croup is straight, like that of the Arabian. The tail is set high in the quarter with width across the hips.

THE NAME This splendid horse represents the best of Morab breeding. The word Morab was coined long before a breed society by the newspaper magnate, William Randolph Hearst, who used two Arabian stallions on his Morgan mares to create work horses to meet the demands of rough and varied terrain on his California ranch.

Body The body is correct enough if inclined to length. There is good rib swell but some lack of depth through the girth.

Hind leg This reflects something of the traditional conformational failing of the Arabian, now eliminated in the modern breed. Despite careful conditioning it is not the best feature of this Morab, although there is no suggestion of cow- or bowed hocks.

BEST OF BOTH WORLDS The aim of Morab breeders is to combine the superlative Arabian qualities with those of America's own top-class horse, the Morgan. Morgan blood is the underpinning influence in the evolution of the American breeds and, like the Arabian, exceptionally prepotent. The MHA seeks acceptance of a 25 percent/75 percent (Morgan/Arabian) breed standard for registerable Morabs.

Lower limbs The limbs are not incorrect but the hock is placed somewhat too far off the ground for perfection. Feet are uniformly good (this is also a feature of the Arabian), and the joints are acceptable.

Rocky Mountain

The Rocky Mountain horse (formerly referred to most often as
a pony) is an example of the American genius for innovation.
It has yet to develop the fixed characteristics of a "breed,"
but entry to the registry, opened in 1986, is continual
and increasing.

Outline The outline of the
Rocky Mountain horse is
pleasingly rounded and the
proportions uniformly good.

ORIGINS

Its origins are, like those of many American horses, in the
early Spanish imports and the subsequent Mustang stock.
The credit for this distinctive animal, however, belongs to
Sam Tuttle of Stout Springs, Kentucky, who ran the riding
concession at Natural Bridge State Resort Park. Mr. Tuttle had
a stallion, Old Tobe, who was a favorite with the riders and
ideally suited to the rugged foothills of the Appalachians. Old
Tobe, still active at 37, was a prepotent sire who passed
on his good temperament, surefootedness, and
natural, ambling gait, which was a legacy of
his Spanish forebears.

The Rocky Mountain horse is judged
largely on the quality of its gait, which
produces speeds of between 7mph (11km/h)
for comfortable traveling and 16mph
(26km/h) on good going and for shorter
distances. All these horses are hardy and
well able to tolerate cold, mountain winters.

GAIT The usual and natural gait of the Rocky
Mountain horse is an easy, very comfortable amble
– a lateral gait rather than the conventional trot.
This gait was common among the early Spanish
Horses, and it has been greatly appreciated for
easy travel since the Middle Ages.

REAR VIEW The full, flaxen tail and
mane is a distinctive feature of the
Rocky Mountain horse, and is the
perfect complement to the unusual, rich-
chocolate coat. This tone of brown is
a very rare equine coloring.

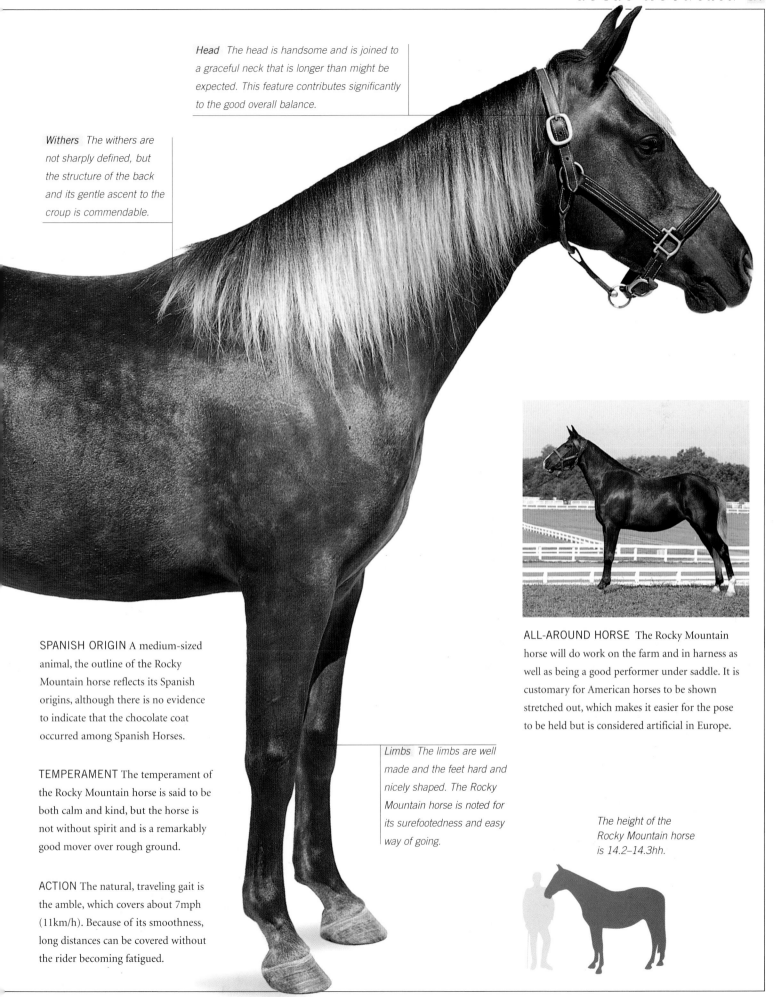

Head The head is handsome and is joined to a graceful neck that is longer than might be expected. This feature contributes significantly to the good overall balance.

Withers The withers are not sharply defined, but the structure of the back and its gentle ascent to the croup is commendable.

SPANISH ORIGIN A medium-sized animal, the outline of the Rocky Mountain horse reflects its Spanish origins, although there is no evidence to indicate that the chocolate coat occurred among Spanish Horses.

TEMPERAMENT The temperament of the Rocky Mountain horse is said to be both calm and kind, but the horse is not without spirit and is a remarkably good mover over rough ground.

ACTION The natural, traveling gait is the amble, which covers about 7mph (11km/h). Because of its smoothness, long distances can be covered without the rider becoming fatigued.

Limbs The limbs are well made and the feet hard and nicely shaped. The Rocky Mountain horse is noted for its surefootedness and easy way of going.

ALL-AROUND HORSE The Rocky Mountain horse will do work on the farm and in harness as well as being a good performer under saddle. It is customary for American horses to be shown stretched out, which makes it easier for the pose to be held but is considered artificial in Europe.

The height of the Rocky Mountain horse is 14.2–14.3hh.

Polo Pony

Although not a breed in strict terms, the modern pony is more fixed in character than many of the warmblood breeds.

Neck *For the sake of balance, a fairly long, well-muscled neck that is in no way heavy is an absolute essential for a polo pony.*

HISTORY

After 1916, the height limit was abolished and today's ponies (never "horses") stand between 5ft and 5ft 3in (15–15.3hh.) and are largely dominated by the Argentinian pony, although good small Thoroughbred ponies are still bred elsewhere. The Argentinian pony is the result of crossing the best Thoroughbred blood with the tough, native Criollo stock (see pp.152–3) and then putting the Thoroughbred back to the progeny.

The Argentinian has the advantage of a unique horse culture supported by a virtually unlimited supply of horses and the traditional skills of the *gaucho* horseman, for whom polo has become a way of life.

The lean, wiry, and distinctive Argentinian pony is pronouncedly Thoroughbred in character with exceptional hocks and quarters, strong limbs, and excellent feet. It is fast, agile, very courageous and with enviable reserves of stamina. It has an innate "ball-sense," following the ball in the same way as a cow pony works cattle.

BEFORE THE MATCH Preparations for the game include braiding the pony's tail in a polo bang so that the stick does not get caught up in it; use of protective boots on all four legs; and meticulous inspection of saddlery to prevent accidents during play.

HEAD A hogged mane is customary on the polo pony to avoid interference with the stick. Otherwise, the head is similar to that of a Thoroughbred. The polo pony is lively, intelligent, and full of character. The Argentinian ponies appear to have an inbred talent for the game, instinctively following the run of play.

Feet *Feet need to be hard and strong, since polo grounds are often hard and the game is played at full gallop.*

QUALITY Although the polo pony is Thoroughbred in appearance, it has a typical, wiry quality of its own.

Body Prominent withers with good, strong shoulders are an essential attribute if the pony is to be sufficiently handy. The back needs to be short and the ribs well sprung.

Quarters Good quarters are an obvious requirement – the pony must be able to gallop flat out, pull up in a second, and turn on a dime.

CRIOLLO The Criollo (see pp. 152-3), the native horse of Argentina, is derived from early Spanish stock and is probably as tough and sound as any other horse in the world. It is the cow pony of the legendary *gauchos* and, when crossed with the Thoroughbred, became the base for the Argentinian polo pony. Although not necessarily a beautiful horse, it is unsurpassed in many ways. It has plenty of bone, very strong joints, and wonderful feet. It is rarely unsound on any of these counts.

ESSENTIAL CHARACTERISTICS The requirements of a polo pony are speed, stamina (for his work is done at the gallop), courage, and very good balance. In addition, the temperament must be bold and lively without being excitable.

Color The polo pony can be any color. his one is bay.

Limbs Limbs and joints must be strong and correctly made for the pony to endure the rigorous game, and to be able to accelerate, turn, and stop quickly. Short cannons and good bone characterize the top-class pony. An unduly long, low stride is not, however, an essential attribute.

The ideal height of the Argentinian polo pony is around 15.1hh.

MORNING WALK Polo ponies getting their morning exercise on the exercise track at the Kentucky Horse Park. The park, with some of the best grounds in the US, regularly stages high-goal polo. The American game maintains consistently high standards.

Polo

Polo is one of the world's oldest and fastest games. Originating in the East it was played in Persia, China, and neighboring areas some 2,500 years ago. The British discovered the game in nineteenth-century India and were responsible for its subsequent introduction to the Western world.

HOCKEY ON HORSEBACK

The cradle of the modern game is in the Cachar Valley of Manipur, the small state between Assam and Myanmar, where polo, played on quick Manipur ponies (about 12.2hh.), was the national sport. The Manipuris, adapting the Tibetan game, called it by the Tibetan word, *pulu*.

The first European club was formed in Manipur by Captain Robert Stewart, the Superintendant of Cachar, and Lt. Joseph Sherer of the Bengal Army, in 1859. Sherer, later to become a Major General, is known as "the father of modern polo."

By 1870 the game was played throughout British India. In 1869, the first match was played in Britain by the 10TH Hussars at Aldershot. At that time it was called "hockey on horse-back" and when, in 1870, the Hussars played the 9TH Lancers, each side fielded eight players.

The game quickly became part of the fashionable "London Season" and was based at Hurlingham, the Hurlingham Club becoming responsible for formulating the modern rules.

Americans took up the sport enthusiastically in 1878, a year after the British took the game to Argentina. The American and Argentinian teams quickly became preeminent in the sport which, since 1886, has been played by teams of four on a low-boarded ground measuring 300 x 200yds (275m x 180m). The "ponies" – and they are always called ponies – are between 15–15.3hh. The object is to hit the 3in (8cm) ball through the opponents' goal with a mallet made of cane. Each player is handicapped from –2 to +10 goals. A match, which lasts just under the hour, is divided into *chukkas* lasting seven-and-a-half minutes each.

A TEAM GAME

Polo is a team game and calls for sympathy and complete coordination between the players. The forwards are No. 1 and No. 2, the latter playing midfield and being the stronger player of the two. No. 1 has to mark the opposing No. 4, No. 2 the opposition's No. 3. No. 3 is the pivotal position, normally played by the captain, from which the game can be controlled.

No. 3 has to get the ball up to his forwards, while being ready to intercept attacks made on his own goal, and he also has to mark the opposing No. 2. No. 4 is at the back. His job is the defense of his own goal. Good marking, which involves good riding off and pushing the opponent off the line of the ball, is integral to the game. The good player rides the opponent first, then the ball.

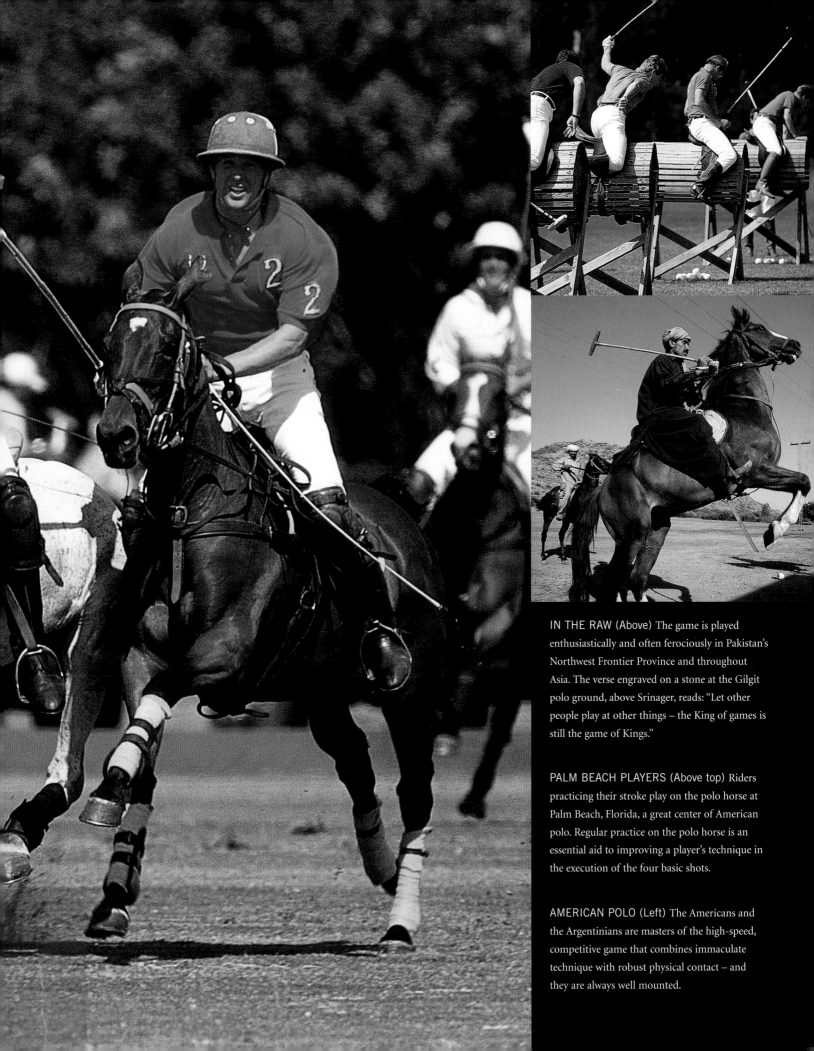

IN THE RAW (Above) The game is played enthusiastically and often ferociously in Pakistan's Northwest Frontier Province and throughout Asia. The verse engraved on a stone at the Gilgit polo ground, above Srinager, reads: "Let other people play at other things – the King of games is still the game of Kings."

PALM BEACH PLAYERS (Above top) Riders practicing their stroke play on the polo horse at Palm Beach, Florida, a great center of American polo. Regular practice on the polo horse is an essential aid to improving a player's technique in the execution of the four basic shots.

AMERICAN POLO (Left) The Americans and the Argentinians are masters of the high-speed, competitive game that combines immaculate technique with robust physical contact – and they are always well mounted.

Pinto

The Pinto descends from the Spanish Horses exported to the Americas in the sixteenth century (see also Mustang, pp.172–3). The Pinto, also called the Paint Horse or Calico, is, academically, a color type and only in the US does it have breed status.

TYPES

The Pinto Horse Association of America maintains a register for horses, ponies, and miniatures. This is divided into stock type, mainly Quarter Horse background; hunter, largely Thoroughbred; pleasure, Arabian or Morgan; and saddle, based on Saddlebred, Hackney, or Tennessee Walker. The Paint Horse Association registers stock-type horses with the emphasis on bloodlines rather than color.

COLORING

The Pinto was much valued for its unusual color, but also for its hardy character, by the Plains Indians of the nineteenth century (particularly the Sioux and Crow), and it was also popular with the cowhands.

The coat patterns fall into two types, Tobiano, a dominant coloring; and Overo, which is recessive (see Markings and Coat Colors, pp.28–9). The Tobiano is white with large patches of solid color; the Overo has a solid coat color with irregular patches of white. The modern Pinto with registration papers is usually a well-made attractive horse, even though there is no fixed type.

Since the Pinto is not a breed in the accepted sense, there is no uniformity of height.

Topline A particularly pleasing topline, both graceful and symmetrical, is an attractive feature of this Pinto.

CAMOUFLAGE Spots, stripes, barred legs or splashes of color on a dark or light background are nature's own system of camouflage. Primitive horses had these broken colorings as a defense against predators. The first horse, Eohippus, of 60 million years ago, most probably had a similarly blotched coat. The Native Americans were quick to appreciate this advantage.

Color This Pinto is Ovaro, its color being chestnut with white.

HEAD This is a good, sensible head of the kind that could be found frequently among the very best Native American ponies. While there are some Thoroughbred-type Pintos, most are all-around animals that are not unlike those agile specimens so beloved by Native Americans.

Limbs Modern Pintos have good limbs. They are bred carefully, particular attention being paid to the correctness of the lower limbs and feet.

Outline This Pinto inclines toward the stock-horse type and has the associated conformation. This is a good example of that kind of animal for it is a powerful horse, very strong in the quarters and well proportioned.

ACTION The majority of Pintos of the type illustrated here are noted for their easy, comfortable paces that can be maintained over long distances, a most important requirement in days gone by.

TOBIANO The Tobiano coat pattern has a white base overlaid with large patches of color. Usually the legs are white, and white crosses over the back and rump. European horsemen are less meticulous in their color definitions than their American counterparts. The general term "part"- or "odd"-colored is applied loosely to coats of two colors, other than the spotted pattern. Patches of black and white are termed "piebald"; white plus another color is known as "skewbald."

Tail The sparse tail of the Pinto is also a characteristic of the Appaloosa (see pp.120–1). Tails like this were encouraged by selective breeding because they did not get entangled with undergrowth in rough and wooded country.

COWBOY The cowboy, who was not averse to ornamentation in his dress and equipment, favored the colorful Pinto, which set him apart from his more soberly mounted fellows.

TWO SOCIETIES The "colored" horse in the US comes under the joint aegis of the Pinto Horse Association and the Paint Horse Association, a situation that can be confusing but is not without precedence. Essentially the smaller Paint Horse Association registers stock-type horses with Thoroughbred, Quarter Horse, and Paint bloodlines, the criteria for entry being more concerned with bloodlines than color. Most Paints are Pintos, but not every Pinto qualifies as a Paint.

Palomino

The striking, golden coat color known as palomino occurs in early artifacts of Europe and Asia and is prominent in Japanese and Chinese art prior to the Ch'in period (221–206BC). The color is found in many horse and pony breeds. For that reason, the palomino is a color type and not a breed.

BREEDING

In the US, however, where the palomino is bred extensively, it has acquired virtual breed status through the efforts of the Palomino Horse Association Inc., a body formed in 1936 "for the perpetuation and improvement of the Palomino horse through the recording of bloodlines and issuing of certificates of registration to qualifying horses." The association defines the desirable characteristics of the palomino in its official standard, allowing the height to be 14.1 to 16hh.

The Spaniards introduced the palomino color to the Americas in the horses they brought with them, and it is now found in many American breeds and types. It occurs frequently in the Quarter Horse and the Saddlebred, but it does not appear in purebred Arabians or Thoroughbreds.

Palominos are much in demand in Western riding activities and not only as showy "parade" horses. They can be seen at horse shows, they are used for pleasure and trail rides and, of course, palomino Quarter Horses are attractive and exciting to watch in rodeos.

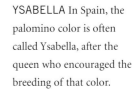

YSABELLA In Spain, the palomino color is often called Ysabella, after the queen who encouraged the breeding of that color.

CONFORMATION The conformation is that of the predominant cross, and may incline toward the stock-horse type or the finer parade type, as here.

REGISTRATION The American register asks for progeny to have one registered parent and the other to be of Quarter Horse, Arabian, or Thoroughbred bloodlines.

HEAD The head, whether the horse inclines toward the Quarter Horse or, conversely, to the Arabian or Thoroughbred, must be one of quality. No horse is considered for registration that "shows coarse, draft horse, Shetland, or Paint breeding." Eyes should be dark or hazel and both of the same color. White markings on the face are limited to a blaze, snip, or star.

The height of the palomino is 14.1–16hh.

JUDGING REQUIREMENTS Color is obviously a prime requirement in the palomino, but judges will not countenance poor conformation on that account.

ARABIAN CROSSES Although purebred Arabians are never palomino, they are often used as a cross to produce that color (see Color and Fluid Movement, right).

Color The body color is defined as being the gold of a newly minted coin and may be no more than three shades lighter or darker. Mane and tail are shining white and must not contain more than 15 percent dark hair. Smudge marks on the coat are not desirable.

COLOR AND FLUID MOVEMENT The combination of color and fluid movement in the palomino is irresistibly attractive. The most appreciated cross to produce palomino coloring, and the one that gives the richest color, is chestnut x palomino. It is also possible to use chestnut to cream or albino.

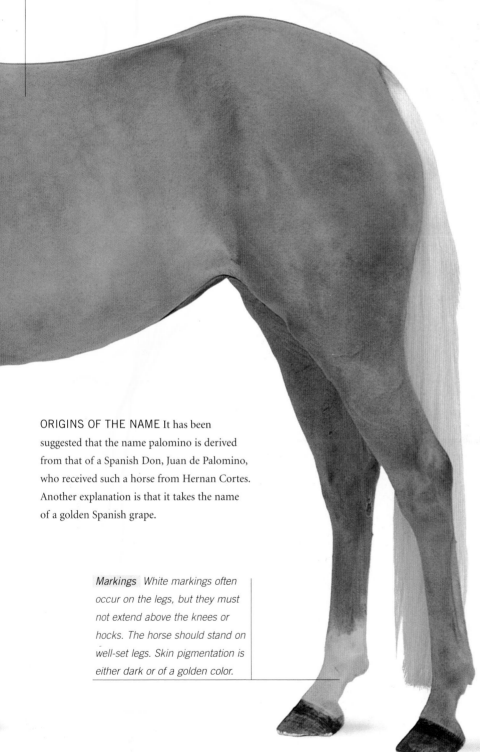

ORIGINS OF THE NAME It has been suggested that the name palomino is derived from that of a Spanish Don, Juan de Palomino, who received such a horse from Hernan Cortes. Another explanation is that it takes the name of a golden Spanish grape.

Markings White markings often occur on the legs, but they must not extend above the knees or hocks. The horse should stand on well-set legs. Skin pigmentation is either dark or of a golden color.

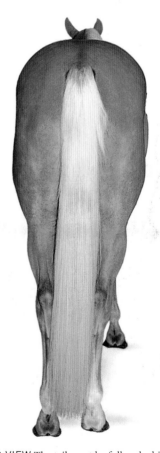

REAR VIEW The tail must be full and white and there should be no suspicion of a dorsal stripe on the back, as found in the dun coloration. Zebra marks on the legs, the unmistakable sign of primitive origin, are similarly unacceptable.

Appaloosa

The Appaloosa is the American version of the spotted horse and is a distinctive and recognized breed in the US. However, the spotted gene in horses is as old as the equine race.

HISTORY

The cave art of Cro-Magnon man, executed as long as 20,000 years ago, depicts horses with spotted coat patterns. Spotted horses, under a variety of names, were known and often highly esteemed throughout Europe and Asia. There was the Knabstrup of Denmark (see pp.126–7), and in France such horses were termed *tigres*. In Britain, where they were once bred in a royal stud farm, they were called Blagdon, or Chubbarie, a Romany name. There is now a thriving British Appaloosa Society, but its product has not yet attained breed status.

The American Appaloosa was developed by the Nez Percé people in the eighteenth century, using as a foundation the Spanish stock imported by the conquistadores, some of which carried the hereditary spotting genes. The Nez Percé lived in northeast Oregon, and their lands included fertile river valleys, principal among which was the Palouse River – Appaloosa is a corruption of that name. They were skillful horse breeders and practiced a strict, selective policy. The result was a practical work horse with the advantage of color.

In 1876, the tribe and its horses were virtually wiped out as US troops seized tribal lands. In 1938 the breed was revived when the Appaloosa Horse Club was formed in Moscow, Idaho.

Mane The mane s characteristically sparse and short.

Eyes A breed requirement of the Appaloosa is the white sclera encircling the eye.

Skin The skin on the nose and, more particularly, around the nostrils is often noticeably mottled with an irregular spotting of black and white. The same marking occurs around the genitalia.

COAT PATTERNS This horse's coat inclines toward a blanket pattern. There are five Appaloosa coat patterns: leopard – white over loin and hips with dark egg-shaped spots; snowflake – spotting all over the body but usually dominant over hips; blanket – white over the hips without dark spots in the white; marble – mottled all over the body; frost – white specks with a dark background.

The height of the Appaloosa is 14.2–15.2hh.

DIVERGENCE OF TYPES There is a certain divergence in type in the Appaloosa in the US and Europe. The best, however, should have the appearance of a well-bred cow pony, compact and with good limbs.

Quarters In the US, Appaloosas have been crossed with the Quarter Horse, and many Appaloosas have acquired that breed's exaggerated development in the quarters. This, of course, is not the case in European Appaloosas, as here.

ATHLETIC AND AGILE (Above) The Appaloosa is used as a stock and pleasure horse, as a parade horse, and for jumping and racing. Not only is it athletic and agile, it is also a willing performer.

Tail The classic Appaloosa tail is thin, short, and sparse. The Nez Percé saw this as a practical feature, for it prevented the tail from being caught on sharp-thorned, close-growing shrubs and thickets.

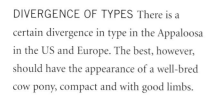

APPALOOSA HORSE CLUB The Appaloosa Horse Club was formed in 1938 from a few descendants of the original Nez Percé horses. Its object was the preservation of the breed. Now its breed registry is the third largest in the world, with over 65,000 registrations.

TEMPERAMENT The Nez Percé people bred their horses as practical, hardy, and versatile mounts for war and hunting. They were also very concerned to breed horses that were sensible and had a tractable temperament. Finally, the Appaloosa had to possess endless stamina and endurance.

Feet The feet are notably good and hard, and are often distinguished by black and white vertical stripes. The Nez Percé Appaloosas were never shod.

Shire

The Shire horse is considered by many to be the supreme heavy draft breed. It was called "Shire" because it was bred in Britain's Midland shires of Lincoln, Leicester, Stafford, and Derby.

ORIGINS

The breed descends from England's medieval war horse, the Great Horse. The Great Horse became known as the English Black, a name bestowed by Oliver Cromwell, in the short period when England was a commonwealth. The principal influence in the evolution of the massive, modern Shire was the heavy Flemish or Flanders Horse. During the sixteenth and early seventeenth centuries, Dutch contractors draining the English fenlands brought with them their strong horses. These crossed with the English stock. The Friesian (see pp.104–5), is another influence, which gave the English Blacks a better movement. During the reign of Charles II, the King's Household Cavalry were still mounted on the old English Black.

FOUNDATION

The foundation stallion of the Shire breed is recognized as the Packington Blind Horse, who stood at Ashby-de-la-Zouche between 1755 and 1770. He is in the first stud book published in 1878. It was not until 1884 that the name Shire came into use, when the Shire Horse Society replaced the English Cart Horse Society.

The height of the Shire is 16.2–17hh.

STRENGTH The massively built Shire weighs between 2,240–2,688lb (1,016–1,220kg). At Britain's Wembley Exhibition in 1924 a pair of Shires pulling against a dynameter (an instrument for measuring power) exceeded the maximum reading. It was estimated that they had exerted a pull capable of moving 50 tons (112,000lb/50,800kg).

Limbs The limbs are clean and hard, the measurement of flat bone being 11–12in (28–30cm). There is heavy feather, but it should be straight and silky.

HEAD The head is of medium size, the nose is slightly Roman, i.e. convex, and the forehead is wide between the eyes. The eyes should be large and docile in expression, indicating the kind disposition of this breed of "gentle giants." For a draft horse, the neck is relatively long, running back into a deep, oblique shoulder, wide enough to carry a collar.

Girth The average girth measurement of a Shire stallion is 6–8ft (180–240cm) and is combined with a broad, powerful chest. These are factors that denote a good, healthy constitution.

Body The short back, thick, powerful musculature (particularly over the loins), and the wide, sweeping quarters exemplify the "strength structure," combined with weight, that are essential in the draft horse.

Color The most popular Shire color is the traditional black of the breed's forebears, with white feathering. Bay, as in this case, and brown are acceptable, and there are numerous grays.

PLOWING MATCHES The Shire may no longer play a significant role in agriculture, but plowing matches are still numerous and very popular. Shires can also be seen on city streets hauling heavy brewers' drays. The brewing companies are the breed's most loyal supporters.

WAR HORSES In medieval England, the English Great Horse was developed to be strong enough to carry a knight wearing plate armor and bearing heavy weapons, and still be agile in combat. The knight mounted his horse only just before battle was joined, otherwise it was led from the right by his squire. Hence the name Destrier for a war horse (from the Latin *dextrarius* – the right side).

REAR VIEW The most important parts of the draft horse are the feet and hocks. The feet must be open, very solid, and perfectly shaped with length in the pasterns. The hocks have to be broad and flat, set at the correct angle for optimum leverage and carried close together. The action is straight in front and behind.

Suffolk Punch

The Suffolk Punch of East Anglia is the oldest of Britain's heavy horse breeds and, perhaps, the most endearing. The English dictionary defines Punch as a short-legged and barrel-bodied variety of English horse, "a short, fat fellow," and that fits its subject exactly. The unique feature of this pure-breed is that every Suffolk traces its descent from one stallion, Thomas Crisp's Horse of Ufford (Orford), which was foaled in 1768. He was a "chesnut" horse, as are all Suffolks. (The word chestnut is spelled without the first "t" in Suffolk records.)

ON THE FARM In this etching, a pair of eighteenth-century Suffolks perform a routine farm chore. Because of their activity and great strength, Suffolks can be used in every kind of heavy draft role.

ORIGINS

The Suffolk's early origins are obscure, but it is inconceivable to think that the trotting Roadsters, developed in East Anglia from the sixteenth century onward, as well as the heavier Flanders mares, did not play their part in its evolution. Both possessed much the same coloring now regarded as characteristic of the Suffolk, and Flanders Horses were robust trotters.

The Suffolk Punch was developed as a farm horse. It is a clean-legged horse (without feather) and so is admirably suited to heavy clay lands. It also possesses enormous pulling power, and in the past was much in demand for heavy draft work in towns and cities.

Maturing early and enjoying a long life, the Suffolk is an economical horse. Despite its unquestionable stamina and power, it thrives on less feed than is needed by other heavy breeds. On typical East Anglian farms, they were fed at 4.30 a.m. Two hours later they went to the fields and could work, with short rests, until 2.30 p.m. Other heavy breeds would have had to stop mid-morning for another feed with additional time needed to allow for digestion.

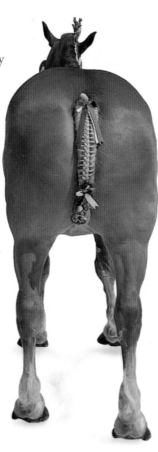

REAR VIEW The quarters are obviously of great strength, but the hind legs must be placed sufficiently close to allow the horse to walk a 9in (23cm) furrow, otherwise, when going between rows of sugar beet, "he'll kick out more than he'll hoe." The long tail is, by tradition, braided for work.

Suffolks stand at 16–16.3hh.

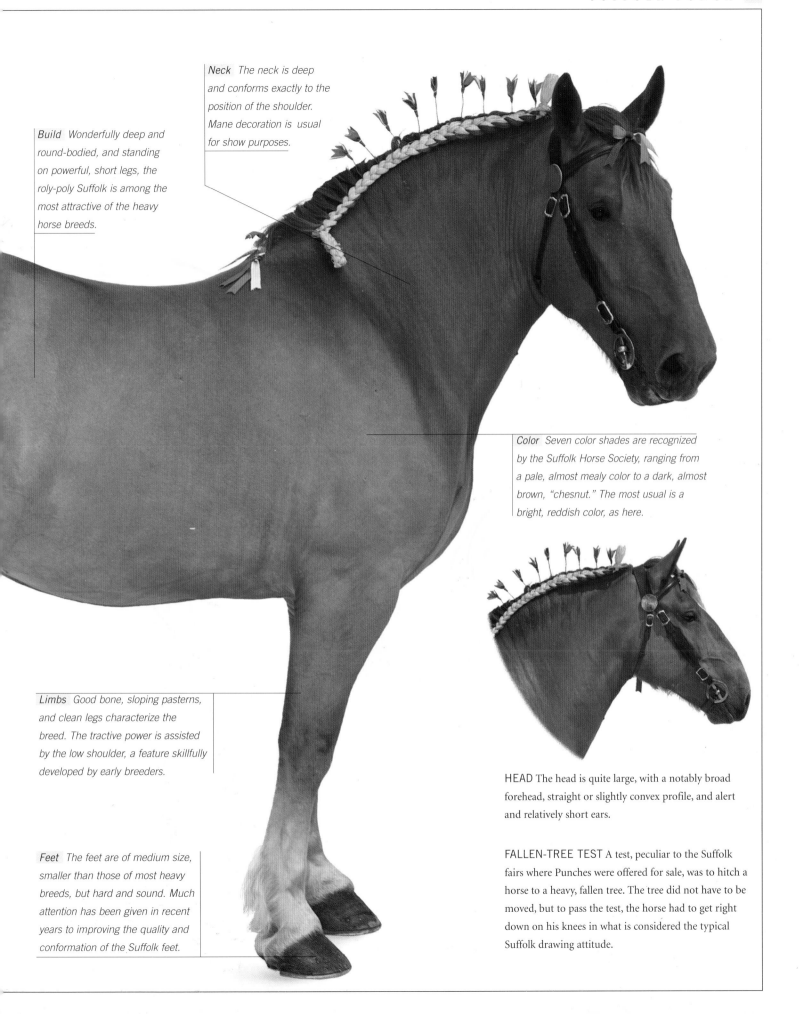

Neck The neck is deep and conforms exactly to the position of the shoulder. Mane decoration is usual for show purposes.

Build Wonderfully deep and round-bodied, and standing on powerful, short legs, the roly-poly Suffolk is among the most attractive of the heavy horse breeds.

Color Seven color shades are recognized by the Suffolk Horse Society, ranging from a pale, almost mealy color to a dark, almost brown, "chesnut." The most usual is a bright, reddish color, as here.

Limbs Good bone, sloping pasterns, and clean legs characterize the breed. The tractive power is assisted by the low shoulder, a feature skillfully developed by early breeders.

Feet The feet are of medium size, smaller than those of most heavy breeds, but hard and sound. Much attention has been given in recent years to improving the quality and conformation of the Suffolk feet.

HEAD The head is quite large, with a notably broad forehead, straight or slightly convex profile, and alert and relatively short ears.

FALLEN-TREE TEST A test, peculiar to the Suffolk fairs where Punches were offered for sale, was to hitch a horse to a heavy, fallen tree. The tree did not have to be moved, but to pass the test, the horse had to get right down on his knees in what is considered the typical Suffolk drawing attitude.

Clydesdale

The Clydesdale is a breed of no great antiquity in terms of equine history, as it has developed over little more than the past 150 years. However, with the exception of the Percheron (see pp.194–5), it is probably the most successful of the heavy breeds in respect of its export throughout the world. It is found as far afield as Germany, Russia, Japan, and South Africa, as well as in the US, Canada, Australia, and New Zealand.

WORLDWIDE POPULARITY

Clydesdales have been exported all over the world. In 1990, a Clydesdale colt standing 18.2hh. was sold to Japan for the price of $35,000 (£20,000) from the Fairways Heavy Horse Centre in Perth, Scotland. The previous record was £9,500, paid in 1911.

ORIGINS

The breed has its foundation in Flemish Horses imported into the Clyde Valley, Scotland, in the eighteenth century. There is also a strong Shire influence. Two Clydesdale breeders of the nineteenth century, Lawrence Drew and his friend David Riddell, believed the Clydesdale and the Shire to be two branches of a single breed.

The Clydesdale Horse Society was formed in 1877, and the first volume of its stud book listed no fewer than 1,000 stallions. The American Clydesdale Society was founded in the following year and the breed was soon established in the US and Canada.

TAIL Elaborately decorated tails are a feature of the heavy show horse. A best-decorated horse class is always held at Britain's Royal Highland Show.

CHARACTERISTICS

The Clydesdale is less massively proportioned than the Shire and has none of the Suffolk's roly-poly appeal, but of the three it is the best mover, having very active paces. It is described by the Clydesdale Horse Society as having "a flamboyant style, a flashy, spirited bearing and a high-stepping action that makes him a singularly elegant animal among draft horses."

Average height is about 16.2hh., but stallions may be up to or over 17hh.

Hocks Cow hocks, the hind legs placed close together, are a breed characteristic. They are not judged as a conformational fault.

Feet The lower limbs carry heavy, silky feather, and the feet, although somewhat flat, are well formed and hard-wearing.

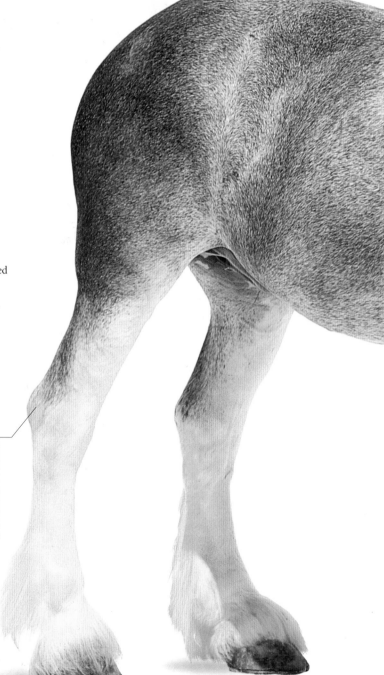

Neck The Clydesdale neck is proportionately longer than that of the Shire.

HEAD The head of the Clydesdale is more elegant than that of most of the heavy horse breeds. Unlike the Shire head, in which the profile is decidedly convex, the Clydesdale profile is straight, giving the impression of quality.

Shoulders The shoulder is sloped and the withers, higher than the croup in the interests of improved traction, are quite sharply defined.

Color The predominant Clydesdale colors are bay and brown, but grays, blacks, and roans, such as this blue roan, are also found. Heavy white markings often occur on the face, legs, and on the underside of the body generally.

BUILDING AUSTRALIA Clydesdale horses were used to work the prairies of Canada and the US, often in teams of seven horses to the three-furrow plow. They also earned the title of "the breed that built Australia."

DRAFT WORK The Clydesdale, weighing 2,240lb (1,016kg) or more but having great activity as well as an extremely tractable disposition, is ideally suited for urban draft. It is said that "the glamour of the Clyde turns an ordinary beer delivery into a public event…".

REAR VIEW Although a big horse, the modern Clydesdale is lighter and even more active than those bred in the past. The leg often appears long, but the Clydesdale is rarely other than deep through the girth. The hock joints are very strong, although cow hocks are common.

Percheron

The Percheron is a handsome, clean-legged, free-moving, heavy horse that originated in Le Perche in Normandy, France. Together with the Boulonnais (see pp.202–3), it is the most elegant of the heavy-horse breeds, and like them, it owes much to Oriental blood. A nineteenth-century authority described it as "an Arabian influenced by climate and the agricultural work for which it has been used for centuries." He may have had an excess of enthusiasm for the breed, but there is no doubting the strength of the eastern influence.

PULLING POWER (Above) The Percheron holds the unofficial pulling record of 3,410lb (1,547kg). It is exceptionally biddable and will do any kind of work.

HISTORY

Some admirers of the breed say that it was forebears of the Percheron that carried the knights of Charles Martel to victory over the Muslims at Poitiers in AD732 and that, as a result, the Barb or Arabian horses of the enemy became available to French breeders. Certainly, eastern blood was introduced after the First Crusade in 1096–9, and by 1760 the stud farm at Le Pin made Arabian sires available to Percheron breeders.

The most influential Percheron lines are dominated by Arabian outcrosses represented by Godolphin and Gallipoly. Gallipoly sired the most famous of Percheron stallions, Jean le Blanc, who was foaled in 1830.

In its long history, the Percheron has been a war horse, coach horse, farm horse, and heavy artillery horse, and has even been used under saddle. The modern Percheron is immensely powerful as well as being hardy and versatile. Among the heavy breeds it has a distinctive and stylish action, which is long, free, and low.

TAIL The Percheron's full tail is usually put up in a kind of "polo bang" when the horse is worked in harness.

The Percheron is between 16.2 and 17hh., but many are 15.2 to 16.2hh. The world's biggest horse was the Percheron Dr. Le Gear. He stood 21hh. and weighed 3,024lb/(1,372kg).

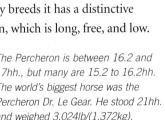

Quarters The Percheron is noted for the excellence of the powerful hindquarters, which are sloped and unusually long for a draft breed.

Feet The feet are of hard, blue horn, and of medium size, with no feather at the heels. They are a notable feature of this exceptionally popular breed.

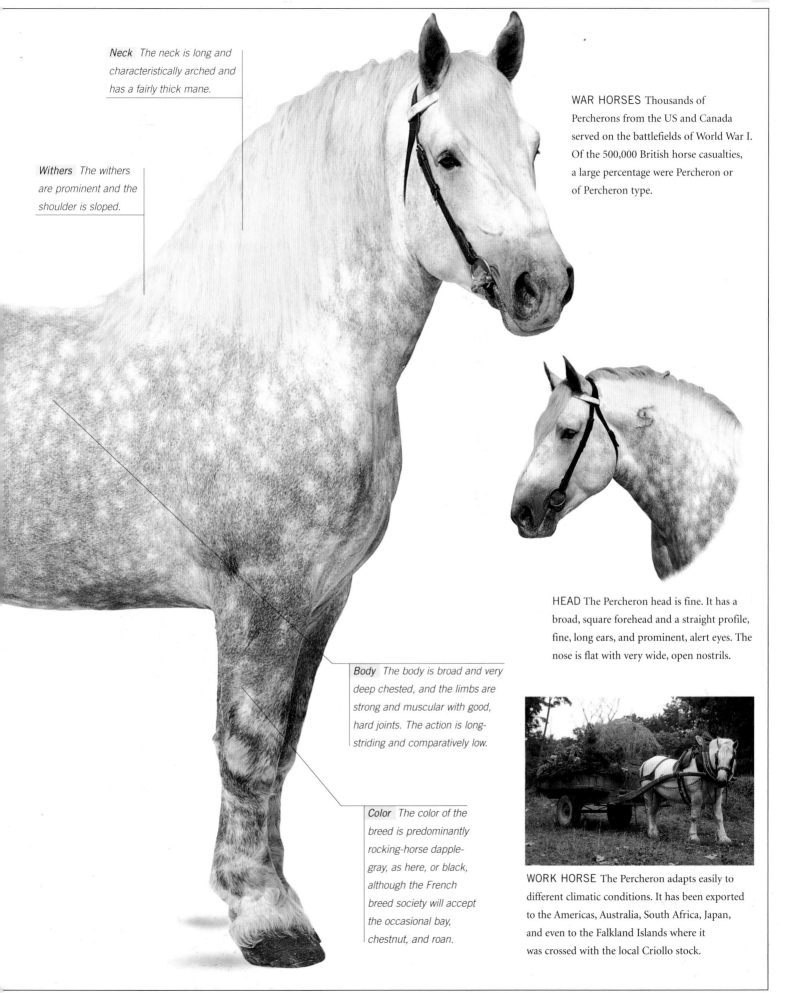

Neck The neck is long and characteristically arched and has a fairly thick mane.

Withers The withers are prominent and the shoulder is sloped.

WAR HORSES Thousands of Percherons from the US and Canada served on the battlefields of World War I. Of the 500,000 British horse casualties, a large percentage were Percheron or of Percheron type.

HEAD The Percheron head is fine. It has a broad, square forehead and a straight profile, fine, long ears, and prominent, alert eyes. The nose is flat with very wide, open nostrils.

Body The body is broad and very deep chested, and the limbs are strong and muscular with good, hard joints. The action is long-striding and comparatively low.

Color The color of the breed is predominantly rocking-horse dapple-gray, as here, or black, although the French breed society will accept the occasional bay, chestnut, and roan.

WORK HORSE The Percheron adapts easily to different climatic conditions. It has been exported to the Americas, Australia, South Africa, Japan, and even to the Falkland Islands where it was crossed with the local Criollo stock.

THE FARM HORSE (Above) The clean-legged Suffolk Punch of East Anglia, UK, (see pp.190–1) is an all-around farm horse that is admirably suited to the system of arable farming practiced in the local area. It is an "economic" horse, able to work and thrive on smaller rations than those needed by the other breeds.

THE BREWER'S DRAY (Above top) The gleaming turnouts of the brewery companies, employing magnificent Shire teams (see pp.188–9), are a popular feature of the show ring and excellent promotion for one of the greatest heavy horse breeds.

CULTIVATION (Right) A team of working horses harnessed in tandem to a disk roller. In the past, farm horses worked a grueling eight-hour day, between 6:30 a.m. and 2:30 p.m., with two breaks for feeding.

Draft Horses

Up to the end of the nineteenth century, and into the beginning of the twentieth, the world's economy was dependent upon horse power, while less than a hundred years ago the US horse population exceeded 25 million. Even now the horse remains an essential element in the less developed countries of eastern Europe.

A VARIETY OF USES

Today, the heavy draft horse is largely confined to farm parks – the Kentucky Horse Park, for instance, maintains the Belgian Heavy Draft Horse (see pp.208–9) as a popular working feature. The great breweries, almost by tradition, use heavy horses in a promotional role to draw the brewers' drays on city deliveries, while the show ring remains a store window for the numerous enthusiasts of the draft breeds. In Europe, on the other hand, many heavy breeds are reared specifically for the meat trade.

It was not always so. The British Industrial Revolution (between 1789–1832) relied upon the efforts of thousands of horses to service the burgeoning manufacturing industry. The canal system and the vast railroads required huge numbers of horses.

Even as late as 1938, the London, Midland and Scottish Company (LMS) still employed 8,500 horses in London alone. A century earlier there were 22,000 horses pulling the trolleys and omnibuses of London, and in 1880 New York City had a population of between 150–175,000 horses engaged in every sort of draft.

THE HORSE IN AGRICULTURE

Modern society is more likely to picture the heavy horse breeds as agricultural animals set in a romanticized, pastoral background.

In fact, it was not until the eighteenth century that the horse finally supplanted oxen in the cultivation of the land and, in reality, the golden age of horse-power farming was as short-lived as that of coaching. Indeed, oxen were still being used in Europe after World War I, and they continue to be used in the Middle East and Asia. Nonetheless, the contribution of the horse, supported by the invention of increasingly sophisticated farm machinery, was enormous and hugely significant in the expansion of agricultural practice.

THE UNITED STATES

The employment of the horse and the development of millions of acres of western prairie land in the US was nothing short of phenomenal. Huge combine-harvesters were drawn by 40-horse teams under the control of six men, and so good was the machinery and the method of harnessing that one man could drive a 36-horse team to a set of harrows or drills.

Ardennais

The heavy horse of the Ardennes region of France and Belgium, the Ardennais, has to be regarded as the doyen of the European heavy breeds. Its ancestors were known 2,000 years ago and probably descended from the snub-nosed, prehistoric horse whose remains were found at Solutré.

HISTORY

Before the nineteenth century, the Ardennais was less massive than it is now, and was ridden and used in light draft. At the beginning of the nineteenth century, crosses were made to the Arabian and Thoroughbred, as well as to the Percheron and Boulonnais, although not always with great success. Three types emerged: the small, old-type Ardennais of about 15hh., now not so much in evidence; the Ardennais du Nord, or Trait du Nord, as shown here, a bigger horse derived from outcrosses to the Belgian Draft (see pp.208–9); and the Auxois, a larger version of the original Ardennais and very powerful.

The climate in which the Ardennais is reared is harsh, and as a result these massively framed horses are very hardy. They are also exceptionally calm and very easily handled. They are still in use as heavy draft horses, but for the most part, are raised for their potential on the meat market.

Neck The neck is heavy but also long.

HEAD A straight-profiled head is distinguished by a low, flat forehead and slightly prominent eye sockets. The neck, though heavy, muscular, and arched, is longer than would be expected in so chunky a horse, and it is well set into the powerful shoulders.

AT WORK The Ardennais, more thick-set than any other cart breed, short and close to the ground, is a willing, hard worker. It has stamina and endurance and is easily managed. Its undoubted energy derives from the Oriental outcrosses, its size from the Belgian blood.

Feet The feet are smaller than might be expected, though strong and well formed.

Colors The preferred colors are roan, red-roan, as here, iron-gray, dark chestnut, and bay. Light chestnuts and even palominos are admissible, but not black.

AUXOIS Auxois, the old horse of Burgundy, has been a contemporary of the Ardennais since the Middle Ages. It is largely considered an offshoot of the Ardennais although it has retained its red-roan color. It is less massive in the legs and quarters.

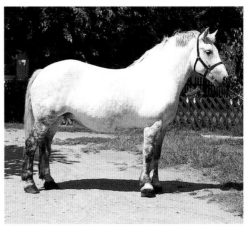

Back The Ardennais is compact with a more than usually short back and exceptionally muscular loins.

Quarters The quarter muscles of the Ardennais are particularly short, thick, and powerful.

MURAKOZER (Above) The Murakozer takes its name from the town of Murakoz in southern Hungary. During the twentieth century, the breed was developed there from native Mur-Insulan mares and was crossed with Ardennais mares, as well as Percherons and Norikers and lighter Hungarian horses of more quality. A swift-moving draft horse, it does not have the Ardennais heavy feather but has inherited something of the latter's heavy frame as well as its equable temperament.

Limbs "Like small oak trees," the limbs are very short and strong, and they carry heavy feather. The small, older type of Ardennais had less feather on the lower limbs and was lighter and quicker.

Body The bone structure of the Ardennais is enormous and is accompanied by musculature of corresponding strength. The girth is naturally deep and the overall impression is of power. The withers, unlike that of most heavy breeds, are on a line with, or even lower, than the croup.

"CART HORSE OF THE NORTH" The popular heavy Ardennais from Lorraine is still called "the cart horse of the north," but there is little evidence now of the lively Ardennes post horse, which brought back Napoleon's wagons from his disastrous Russian campaign.

The height is between 15 and 16hh. The average is about 15.3hh.

Breton

The breeders of Brittany, France, are as skillful as any in Europe. Since the Middle Ages, the area has produced its own distinctive Breton types based on the primitive, little, hairy horse of the Black Mountains. At one time, there were four derivatives of the Breton, two pacers or amblers, a general-purpose ride-and-drive, and a heavier draft. The riding type, the *Cheval de Corlay*, was even raced at local courses.

Outline The outline is attractively short and square, with the body broad, strong, and deep, and the hindquarters showing great power.

TYPES

Today two types are recognized. The Breton heavy draft, a massive, early-maturing horse much sought after in the meat markets, has Ardennais blood. The far more active, almost clean-legged, Breton Postier is a lighter version of the Suffolk Punch (see pp.190–1) and was once the pride of the French Horse Artillery. The Postier has crosses of Boulonnais (see pp.202–3) and Percheron (see pp.194–5), both active, refined animals with the powerful Norfolk Roadster in their ancestry. The Postiers inherit the exceptional energy at trot from the Percheron and Boulonnais, and are ideal for light draft and farm work. Breton Postiers, sharing the same stud book with the heavy drafts since 1926, are selectively bred, and are required to pass performance tests in harness – traditional events at festival days. The Breton Postier is still popular in France, and is exported to North Africa, Japan, Spain, and Italy to be used as an improver of less-developed stock.

TAIL It is customary for the tail of the Breton, like that of the Norman Cob (see pp.108–9), to be docked. It is thought to give the horse a jaunty look and prevents the rein from becoming caught up under the tail.

SUITABLE OUTCROSS
The Breton's hardiness, strength, and stamina, allied to an engaging temperament, make it a suitable outcross for less-developed stock.

AGRICULTURAL EMPLOYMENT A quick, active horse suited for all kinds of agricultural work, the Breton is also employed extensively in the French vineyards of the Midi.

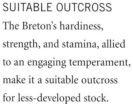

Neck The neck follows the general outline of the body, being short, arched, and thick. It runs into the shoulders, which, although sloping, are shorter than might be expected. Nonetheless, the Breton is active, fast, and free at the walk and trot.

Color The typical coloration is red-roan but chestnuts, as here, bays and grays are also found. Black is not a breed color.

Limbs The limbs are short, strong, and very muscular in the thighs and forearms.

Feet The feet are well shaped, hard, and not too large. The legs are virtually "clean," carrying little or no feather.

HEAD The square head of the Breton has a straight profile and should have large, open nostrils and bright, kindly eyes. The mobile ears are small and set rather low on the head.

The height is 15–16.1hh. The Postier is smaller than the heavy draft.

Boulonnais

The Boulonnais, a native of northwest France, has been acclaimed as the noblest draft horse of them all, and it is, or was, a most beautiful horse. It owes the fineness of its body tissues and its graceful lines to its Oriental background.

ORIGINS

The breed's beginnings are with the ancient heavy horses that were native to northwestern France before the Christian era. When Julius Caesar's Roman legions gathered there for the invasion of Britain in the first century AD, their eastern horses were crossed with the native stock. Much later, during the Crusades, more Arabian blood was introduced, particularly through the agency of Eustache, Comte de Boulogne, and Robert, Comte d'Artois, both skillful and innovative breeders.

The increased use of heavy armor in the fourteenth century enforced the use of northern heavy blood to give greater weight and size, and there were also crossings with Spanish Horses. In the seventeenth century, the breed took on the name Boulonnais and two types emerged. The smaller horse measured less than 16hh. and was known as the *mareyeur* (horse of the tide). It was used to make express fish deliveries from Boulogne to Paris and has almost died out. However, the large Boulonnais, which stands over 16hh., is still bred, if largely for the meat market.

Forehand The neck is thick but gracefully arched. There is more slope to the muscular shoulders than in other draft breeds, and the wither is fairly prominent. The good front, or forehand, is unique among draft breeds.

The Boulonnais stands between 15.3 and 16.3hh. The mareyeur *was 15.1–15.3hh.*

HEAD The head of the Boulonnais is absolutely distinctive and clearly shows the influence of Oriental outcrosses. The profile is straight, the eye-sockets are prominent, the jowl is open and clean, and the forehead is flat and wide. The eye is usually particularly large, the nostrils are open, and the ears are very small, erect, and mobile.

ACTION The action is exceptional in a draft horse, being straight, relatively long, and very swift and energetic. The breed has stamina and can maintain a steady speed over a long period.

Coat *The skin is silky with prominent veining, and the mane is fine and bushy. There is none of the coarseness associated with coldblood breeds.*

Quarters *The Boulonnais's quarters are round and muscular with a characteristic double muscling of the croup. The tail, which is bushy, is set fairly high – much higher than in other draft breeds.*

NORTH SWEDISH HORSE The North Swedish is a compact draft horse used in the forests of Sweden, where half the timber cut is still moved by horses. The stud farm at Wangen has a systematic breeding program that includes hauling tests and regular veterinary inspections of horses in work. Prior to the end of the nineteenth century, the North Swedish was an amalgam of breeds based on ancient native Scandinavian stock. It still bears a strong resemblance to its nearest relation, the Døle Gudbrandsal of Norway (see pp.104–5). The breed stands up to 15.3hh. It is sound and resistant to disease, noted for its longevity and an extraordinarily active gait combined with tremendous pulling power. The main colors are dun, brown, chestnut, and black. Black is accompanied by white socks.

Body *The body is wonderfully compact and deep. The back is broad and straight, the chest wide, and the ribs are as well sprung as those of an Arabian. Combined with the expression of elegance, the whole outline is majestic in appearance.*

Limbs *Boulonnais limbs are strong with prominent muscular projections in both forearm and thighs. Other points are the short, thick cannons, the lack of feathering, and the large, solid joints.*

Color *The coat color is predominantly gray in all its shades, as here, but there are occasionally bays and chestnuts, which were once very sought after.*

Poitevin

The Poitou region of France is famous on three counts: for being the home of the Poitevin horse, or Mulassier, the ugly duckling of the heavy breeds; for the gigantic Poitevin jackass, Baudet de Poitou; and for the mule breeding industry based on these two animals.

MARSH HORSE

The Poitevin, descended from a mix of Dutch, Danish, and Norwegian heavy horses, came to Poitou in the seventeenth century to help drain the marshes of La Vendee and Poitou. Then the mares were put to the Baudet de Poitou to produce the big mules around which an industry was built, the progeny being sold throughout Europe and North America. In countries such as Turkey, Greece, Italy, Spain, and Portugal, they were ideal for working the difficult and inhospitable terrain.

UGLY DUCKLING

The Poitevin, with a primitive background that traces to Europe's old Forest Horse (see pp.10–11), is not an attractive horse, and the conformation leaves almost everything to be desired. Coarse, slow-moving, and with the large, platelike feet of the marsh horse, it is however correspondingly sober in temperament and the ideal partner for the Poitevin jackass, which stands at 16hh. and is a remarkable animal by all standards.

Hair The mane and tail hair is thick, abundant, and very coarse in texture.

Head The head is coarse and heavy, often covered with wiry hair; the ears are thick and not very mobile.

Limbs The limbs are thick and lymphatic, with the lower parts covered in coarse, heavy hair, while the shoulder is strong enough but very upright. Joints are round and often puffy.

Feet The feet are exceptionally large and flat, a characteristic of the old heavy breeds of Europe living in marsh environments. The Poitevin was employed in the drainage of the Poitou marshlands.

The Poitevin stands between 16 and 16.2hh.

Back Usually, the back is long and the withers undefined. But the Poitevin, although slow and ponderous, was strong enough for the heavy drainage work involved on the Poitou marshes.

Quarters The quarters usually slope downward from the croup to a low-set tail. Nonetheless, the hips are broad and roomy. This stallion is of better conformation than the Poitevin mares.

PRIMITIVE COLOR This Poitevin mare with her Baudet de Poitou mule foal has the typical dun coloring of the breed that is indicative of the primitive background. It is often accompanied by zebra stripes around the lower limbs. Apart from producing mules, the mares are put to Poitevin stallions to maintain the breed. Surplus animals can be sold to supply the meat markets.

Hind leg There is some strength in the broad hind leg of this stallion, the proportions being short and thick with a notably strong muscular development.

Body The body is large and long, with flat-sided ribs and the elbow tied in close to the body.

Hock The hock is big, and although it is fleshy and lymphatic the structure is not without strength. Curly tufts of hair grow around knees and hocks.

MULES OF POITOU The Poitevin mules are renowned for their versatility and exceptional strength, and the area enjoyed a good market to countries where mules are essential to the agricultural economy. The mules are constitutionally sound, willing workers, long-lived, and economical to keep. Many have a working life of up to 25 years.

BAUDET DE POITOU The Poitevin jackass, used to sire the Poitevin mules from heavy Mulassier mares, is a big animal, as big as the Poitevin mares. Though coarse in many respects it has a quick sure action of greater length than might be imagined. Carefully bred for size and conformational strength, the jackass is exceptionally hardy.

Jutland

Denmark's heavy horse, the Jutland, has been bred on the Jutland Peninsula from time immemorial. In the twelfth century it was a war horse, capable of carrying an armored knight and enduring the hardships of campaigning.

ORIGINS

The Jutland seems to have been largely responsible for Germany's Schleswig Horse, and infusions of Danish blood were being made into that breed well into the twentieth century.

At some point in the development of the modern Jutland, there were crossings with Cleveland Bays and their derivative the Yorkshire Coach Horse. However, the overwhelming influence is that of Oppenheim LXII, a dark-chestnut Suffolk Punch (see Suffolk Punch, pp.190–1) imported to Denmark in 1860. Even today, there is a very close resemblance between the Suffolk, the Jutland, and the Schleswig. The most important bloodline of the Jutland is that of Oldrup Munkedal, one of the many descendants of Oppenheim LXII.

CHARACTERISTICS

The Jutland's great endurance and its exceptionally tractable nature make it ideal for both draft and agricultural work. Unhappily, this most attractive coldblood has decreased in numbers in recent years as a result of mechanization. However, it is still used for city draft work and is appreciated as a most willing worker. Jutlands are also seen at horse shows and occasionally working on the land.

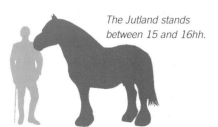

The Jutland stands between 15 and 16hh.

Forehand The neck is short and thick, a typical conformation for the draft horse, and the shoulders are strong and heavily muscled. The chest, even for a draft horse, is exceptionally broad.

HEAD The Jutland head has no pretensions to graceful refinement. It is heavy and very plain, not unlike, one imagines, that of its far-off primitive ancestor, the Forest Horse. Nonetheless, the expression is kindly and reflects the breed's docile and willing temperament. Otherwise, the conformation clearly reveals the connection with the Suffolk Punch. If there was ever Cleveland Bay blood introduced to the breed, it is not apparent.

Body The compact, roly-poly body shows the breed's connection with the Suffolk Punch as clearly as anything else. It is further distinguished by an exceptional depth through the girth.

Back The back is short, wide, and powerful, giving a compact appearance to the body. The withers are relatively flat and broad, which is not unusual in the European coldbloods.

Color Without a doubt, the Jutland's attractive coat color derives from the Suffolk Punch. The breed color is a dark chestnut with flaxen mane and tail, and there are very few exceptions to this general rule.

Quarters Like its Suffolk forebears, the quarters of the Jutland are appealingly round. They are also massive and very muscular.

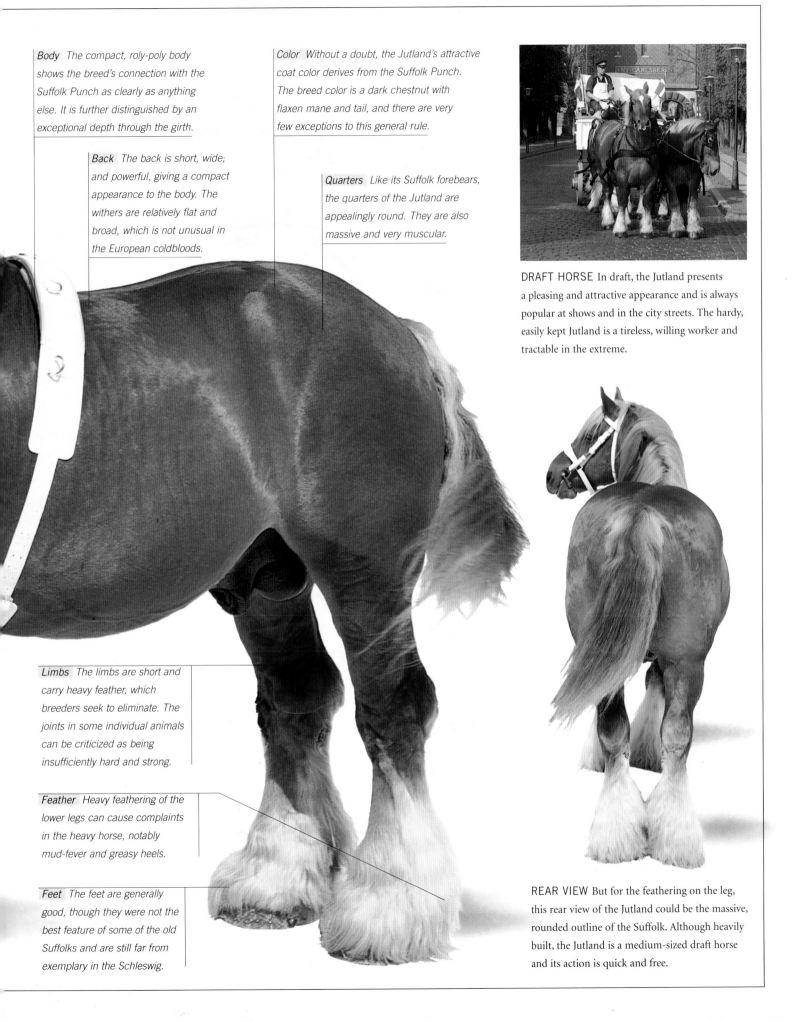

DRAFT HORSE In draft, the Jutland presents a pleasing and attractive appearance and is always popular at shows and in the city streets. The hardy, easily kept Jutland is a tireless, willing worker and tractable in the extreme.

Limbs The limbs are short and carry heavy feather, which breeders seek to eliminate. The joints in some individual animals can be criticized as being insufficiently hard and strong.

Feather Heavy feathering of the lower legs can cause complaints in the heavy horse, notably mud-fever and greasy heels.

Feet The feet are generally good, though they were not the best feature of some of the old Suffolks and are still far from exemplary in the Schleswig.

REAR VIEW But for the feathering on the leg, this rear view of the Jutland could be the massive, rounded outline of the Suffolk. Although heavily built, the Jutland is a medium-sized draft horse and its action is quick and free.

Belgian Draft

The Belgian Draft is also known as the Brabant, taking the name from one of its principal breeding areas. It is one of the world's most important breeds, having contributed to equine development well outside of its native country. The breed is little known in Britain and not sufficiently recognized in the country of its origin, but it is popular in the US, a number being kept at the famous Kentucky Horse Park.

ORIGINS

The breed is is likely to be directly descended from the Ardennais (see pp.198–9) and, therefore, from the primitive foundation of the European heavy-horse breeds – the Forest or Diluvial Horse (*Equus silvaticus*). These horses were known to the Romans and received honorable mention in Julius Caesar's *De Bello Gallico* as most willing and untiring workers.

In the Middle Ages, the Belgian Draft was called the Flanders Horse. As such, it was instrumental in the evolution of the English Great Horse and, later, in the development of the Shire. It was the basis of the Clydesdale (see pp.192–3), it had a large effect upon the Suffolk Punch (see pp.191–2), and it had an influence on the Irish Draft (see pp.106–7).

THREE BLOODLINES By 1870, there were three main Brabant groupings, based on bloodlines rather than conformational differences. The lines are those of Orange I, founder of the massive Gros de la Dendre line; Bayard, founder of the Gris du Hainaut, which produced sorrels and red-roans; and Jean I, who founded the Colosses de la Mehaique.

Quarters   The huge, powerful quarters of the Belgian Draft are distinctively rounded, and the croup is characteristically "double-muscled."

Color   Colors vary from line to line. Bays, duns, and grays occur, but red-roan with black points, sorrels, and chestnuts, as here, predominate.

Feet   Short, very strong legs usually terminate in a good deal of feather. The feet are of medium size and always well formed.

BRABANT Principally bred in Brabant, Belgian Drafts have been distinguished by that name, although they are also referred to as *race de trait Belge*. The breeders of this horse produced exceptional qualities through stringent selection, excluding foreign blood, and occasionally inbreeding.

Back The Belgian Draft is thick-set and compact. The Colosses de la Mehaique line is particularly noted for the great strength of the short back and loins and for its overall power.

Head The head is small in proportion to the body, square and somewhat plain, but the expression is intelligent and kindly.

Neck A short, thick, powerful neck joining withers and shoulders of similar proportions is an ideal combination for every kind of heavy draft purpose.

Body Power is the hallmark of this massive breed, and it is exemplified in the deep-girthed, compact body that goes with the Belgian Draft's traditional strength of constitution.

Limbs The Belgian Draft is noted for the extreme strength and hardness of its short limbs. Soundness of limb was a feature in all the three principal lines.

WORKING THE LAND The Belgian Draft was bred with great care to suit the traditional agricultural skills of the country, its climate, its rich, heavy soil, and the economic and social reliance upon the land. The action of the breed is not "brilliant," but it is practical in relation to its purpose.

Belgian Drafts stand between 16.2 and 17hh.

Italian Heavy Draft

The most popular heavy horse in Italy is the Italian Heavy Draft horse, sometimes called the Italian Agricultural horse. It is bred throughout northern and central Italy, but chiefly around Venice. A feature of the breed is that it matures early, a distinct advantage in a horse that is now produced for its potential in the meat market as well as for its working qualities.

HISTORY

There was a time when Italy imported the massive Belgian Draft – the Brabant – initially to improve their local strains. Thereafter, the more active Boulonnais and Percheron were tried, but none really fulfilled the Italian requirement for a quick-moving horse of smaller proportions. The answer was found eventually in outcrossing heavily to the lighter, clean-legged Breton Postier (see pp.200–1). Because of the Breton's connection with the Norfolk Trotter or Roadster, it was renowned for its speed at trot and was the ideal type for the light draft and farm work required in Italian agriculture. They crossed well with the more common Italian draft mares, and the progeny were powerful animals with kind, docile temperaments. Their speed in action accounts for the Italian breed title, *Tiro Pesante Rapido* – Quick Heavy Draft.

CONFORMATION The Italian Heavy Draft, though not so attractive as the Breton from which it derives, is, nonetheless, a compact, symmetrical animal retaining some of the Breton's good, conformational features.

Forehand Like that of the Breton, the chest is exceptionally deep, and the forelegs are spaced well apart. Some coarseness is apparent, the legacy of the common and less well-made Italian mares.

Limbs The limbs are fairly muscular, but the joints are inclined to roundness, another characteristic of the poor-quality base stock.

BARDIGIANO (Left) The Bardigiano is a mountain-pony strain from the northern Appenine region. It owes something to the heavier mountain strains as well as to the Avelignese, a pony almost identical to the Haflinger (see pp.252–3). A pronounced Oriental influence is also discernible. The Bardigiano is a strong, well-made pony of character, hardy and quick-moving. Despite the unusual mixed background, it appears to be bred with greater care than is usually the case with Italian breeds, other than the Trotter, the Thoroughbred, and the Salerno. It is one of the most attractive of Italy's equines.

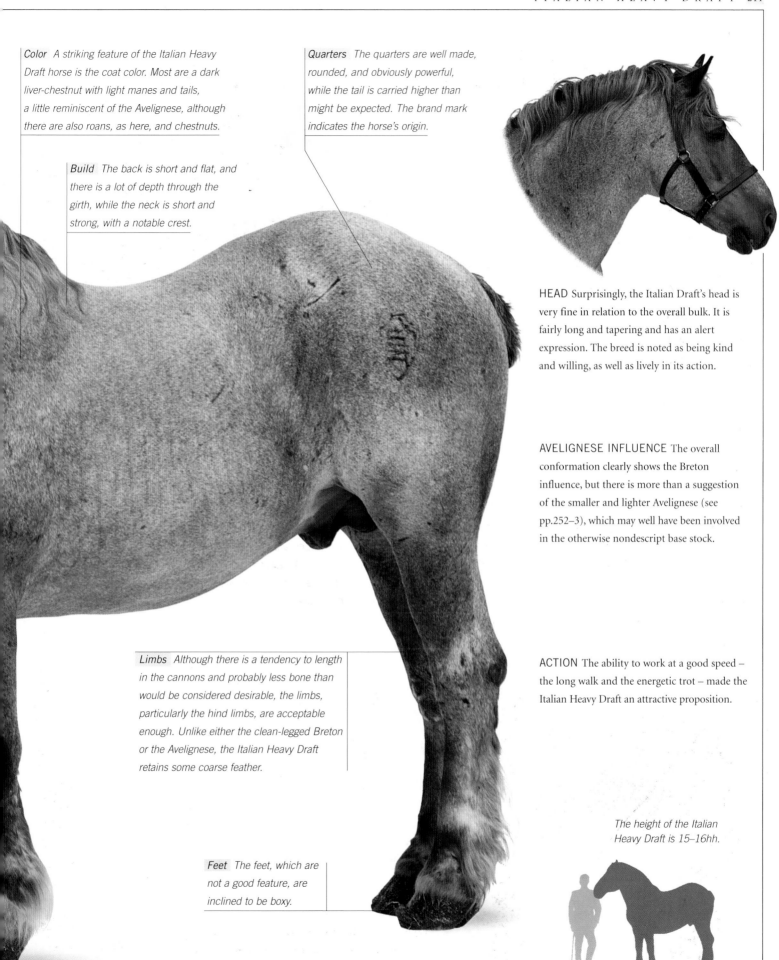

Color *A striking feature of the Italian Heavy Draft horse is the coat color. Most are a dark liver-chestnut with light manes and tails, a little reminiscent of the Avelignese, although there are also roans, as here, and chestnuts.*

Quarters *The quarters are well made, rounded, and obviously powerful, while the tail is carried higher than might be expected. The brand mark indicates the horse's origin.*

Build *The back is short and flat, and there is a lot of depth through the girth, while the neck is short and strong, with a notable crest.*

Limbs *Although there is a tendency to length in the cannons and probably less bone than would be considered desirable, the limbs, particularly the hind limbs, are acceptable enough. Unlike either the clean-legged Breton or the Avelignese, the Italian Heavy Draft retains some coarse feather.*

Feet *The feet, which are not a good feature, are inclined to be boxy.*

HEAD Surprisingly, the Italian Draft's head is very fine in relation to the overall bulk. It is fairly long and tapering and has an alert expression. The breed is noted as being kind and willing, as well as lively in its action.

AVELIGNESE INFLUENCE The overall conformation clearly shows the Breton influence, but there is more than a suggestion of the smaller and lighter Avelignese (see pp.252–3), which may well have been involved in the otherwise nondescript base stock.

ACTION The ability to work at a good speed – the long walk and the energetic trot – made the Italian Heavy Draft an attractive proposition.

The height of the Italian Heavy Draft is 15–16hh.

Noriker

The Noriker has been developed for over 2,000 years and now accounts for 50 percent of the Austrian horse population. The center of Noriker breeding and the greatest influence on the breed has been in the Salzburg area, which, in Roman times, was known as Juvavum and was famous for the horses produced there.

PRINCIPAL STRAINS As well as the spotted Pinzgauer, the Salzburg Stud Book recognizes four principal Noriker strains: Carinthian (Kartner), Steier, Tyrolean (Tiroler), and Bavarian or South German Coldblood. All are renowned for their hardiness, soundness, and willing temperament.

THE SALZBURG BOOK

The name Noriker derives from the state of Noricum, a vassal province of Rome corresponding roughly to modern Austria. The Romans bred a heavy warhorse that they used also as a draft and pack animal.

From the Middle Ages the monasteries were a significant factor in the development of the Noriker. Under the Prince-Archbishop of Salzburg, the Salzburg Stud Book was established and new stud farms created with standards being carefully controlled.

SPOTTED STRAIN

In the eighteenth century, as a result of outcrosses to Spanish blood, a spotted strain became evident in the Pinzgau district which resulted in the term Pinzgauer-Noriker. Today's Noriker continues to include Pinzgauer as well as four other recognized strains. The adaptable, well-built Noriker is ideally suited to work in mountainous terrain and is much used in the forestry industry. Breed standards are strict and include performance-testing of stallions and mares.

A typical Noriker strain is bred at the oldest German state stud farm of Marbach and is referred to as the Black Forest Horse.

Quarters *The quarters are powerful and symmetrical, with the tail well set. There is no heaviness and the overall outline is compact.*

Hind legs *The hind legs are notable for the strong second thigh and are correctly set with the hocks low to the ground.*

The Norika stands between 16 and 17hh.

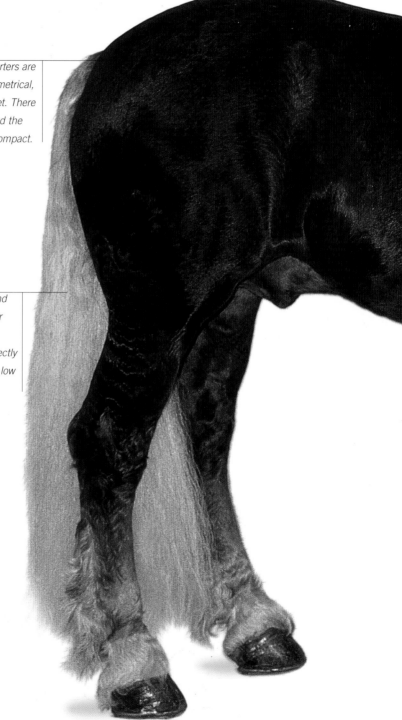

Mane The flaxen mane is the characteristic accompaniment to the rich, liver-chestnut coat color.

Poll There is remarkable breadth over the poll between the ears and also between the large, well-set eyes.

Head The squared head tapering to the muzzle is full of quality and a feature of this attractive horse.

COLOR LINES Distinct color lines are recognized by the breed society, including dapple and brindle coat patterns; black-headed dapple-gray; brown and shades of chestnut. The Marbach horses have the traditional liver-chestnut color with flaxen mane and tail. It is possible to see a resemblance to the Haflinger ponies (see pp.252–3), with which the Noriker has a natural connection.

Shoulder The strong, free, and nicely sloped shoulder, running from defined withers, allows for the economical activity of the movement and the length of the stride.

Limbs Strict breed standards ensure that the joints are large and clean and the forearm well muscled. Cannons are short and have ample bone below the knee.

Feet The feet of this essentially mountain horse are a particular feature. They are necessarily well shaped, hard, very sound, and proportionate to the structure.

VERSATILITY The compact, surefooted Noriker is the ideal agricultural horse for heavy work in mountainous country, and it can be put to good use for timber haulage in the forests. Early in the breed's development the best specimens were bred high in the mountain region of Gross Gluckner. The quick-moving, active Noriker is also an excellent and obliging harness horse.

Exmoor

The Exmoor is the oldest of Britain's mountain and moorland breeds and, apart from "primitives" such as the Tarpan, is probably as old as any breed. It retains features found in its main ancestor, Pony Type 1 (see Origins, pp.10–11) – a particular jaw formation with a seventh molar, for instance, that is present in no other equine.

ORIGINS

The breed takes its name from the high, wild moorland in southwest England, its natural habitat, where it has been largely isolated for centuries. It is this harsh, inhospitable environment that is responsible for the peculiar character of the incredibly strong and hardy Exmoor. Efforts were made to "improve" the breed in the nineteenth century, but without any great success. It is thought that Spanish blood was introduced after 1815 through "a sort of specter horse," who came to be known as Katerfelto, and ran on the moor. He was eventually captured, but it was never discovered from where he had come. He was described as being dun with black points and a pronounced eel-stripe down his back.

There are still herds running on Exmoor whose purity and quality are jealously safeguarded by the Exmoor Pony Society, as well as, of course, others bred off the moor. However, ponies bred away from the moor tend to lose type, and it is necessary for breeders to return to the original stock to maintain the original character.

STRENGTH The Exmoor is enormously strong, well balanced and capable of carrying weight far out of proportion to its size. It has been known to carry a man for a full day's hunting.

Neck Bronze Age harnesses compelled chariot ponies to pull largely from a strap across the neck, resulting in a muscular development on the underside. For generations, the Exmoor, first used in chariots, exhibited this peculiarity.

The Exmoor stands between 12.2 and 12.3hh.

HEAD The Exmoor head is unique. The muzzle is mealy colored; the nostrils are wide; the ears are short, thick, and pointed; the forehead is broad; and the eyes are large and prominent. They are termed toad eyes because they are hooded to provide protection against the weather. The head is a little larger than in other breeds because of the length of the nasal passages, which allow the air to be warmed before inhalation.

BRAND MARKS (Left) Foals passed by the breed inspectors at the annual autumn "gathering" are branded with a star on the near shoulder to indicate that they are pure-bred Exmoors. Beneath the star the herd number is branded, and on the left hindquarter you find the number of the pony within the herd. Therefore, you can always identify ponies by their brand.

Color The Exmoor's color is distinctive. The ponies are bay, brown, or dun with black points. They are mealy colored on the muzzle, around the eyes, on the inside of the flanks and thighs, and on the under-belly. No white markings are permissible.

ACTION The action is straight, smooth, and balanced without any exaggerated knee lift. Exmoors are noted for their ability to gallop and jump.

ON EXMOOR Ponies have run on Exmoor since before the Ice Age, their character being formed by the harshness of the environment. In a sense, the Exmoor herds remain wild. Although they are brought in annually for inspection, they are naturally nervous of encounters with humans. They are also nervous of dogs, possibly because encounters with them arouse atavistic memories of attacks by wolves.

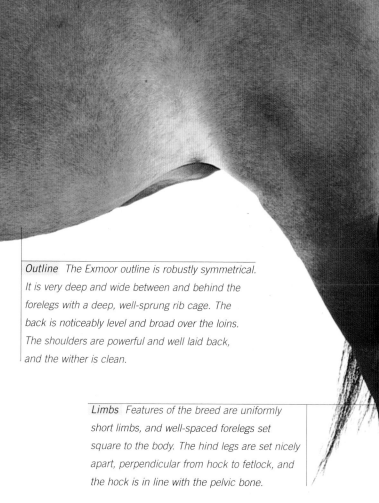

Outline The Exmoor outline is robustly symmetrical. It is very deep and wide between and behind the forelegs with a deep, well-sprung rib cage. The back is noticeably level and broad over the loins. The shoulders are powerful and well laid back, and the wither is clean.

Limbs Features of the breed are uniformly short limbs, and well-spaced forelegs set square to the body. The hind legs are set nicely apart, perpendicular from hock to fetlock, and the hock is in line with the pelvic bone.

Feet and bone Short cannons, good bone, and hard, neat feet are general in the breed.

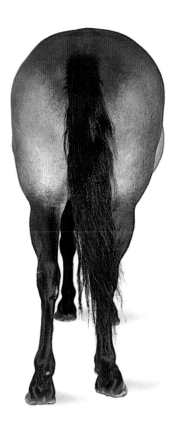

REAR VIEW The Exmoor tail naturally has a thick and fanlike growth at the top. This "ice" tail gives protection against rain and snow. The coat, too, is double textured and waterproof. In winter it grows thick, harsh, and springy. In summer it becomes dense and hard and has a peculiar metallic sheen.

Dartmoor

"There is on Dartmoor a race of ponies much in request in that vicinity, being surefooted and hardy and admirably calculated to scramble over the rough roads and dreary wilds of that mountainous district. The Dartmoor is larger than the Exmoor and, if possible, uglier." So wrote William Youatt, a British authority, in 1820.

CHARACTERISTICS

Fifty years later, comment was made in *The Field* magazine about the ponies' jumping ability: "They can jump as well as the moor sheep, and much after the same fashion." Today, the Dartmoor still performs well over obstacles. However, Youatt would be amazed at the transformation that the original ponies have undergone to produce the modern Dartmoor. It is one of the most elegant riding ponies in the world, far removed from the stock that he observed.

ORIGINS

The breed has its origin on the rough moorland of the Dartmoor Forest, England, intersected by the rivers Dart, Taw, and Tavy. Today, few ponies are bred on the moor.

The Dartmoor has been influenced by several different breeds. There is an early connection with the Old Devon Pack Horse, drawn from both Exmoor and Dartmoor blood, and the Cornish Goonhilly pony. Both are now extinct. Oriental or eastern horses may have been introduced as early as the twelfth century. Among the many breeds used in the nineteenth century were trotting Roadsters, Welsh Ponies and Cobs, Arabians, small Thoroughbreds, and some Exmoors. There was also one disastrous experiment using Shetlands in an attempt to produce pit ponies.

During World War II, Dartmoors came close to extinction. Between 1941 and 1943 only two males and 12 females were registered. The breed was saved largely by the UK Pony and Riding Society (now the National Pony Society).

Neck The Dartmoor neck is strong but with the length associated with a riding pony.

Shoulders The Dartmoor is notable for the excellence of the shoulder, which is wonderfully sloped to give the best sort of riding action, and which ensures that the Dartmoor is a first-class performer.

HEAD The head, set gracefully on the neck, is "pure pony": small, full of quality, and with the characteristic small and very alert ears. The temperament is excellent, and the Dartmoor makes an ideal child's pony, not least because of the easy smoothness of the distinctive action.

Color Dartmoors are bay, as here, black, or brown. Skewbald or piebald are not accepted by the breed society, which also discourages any excessive white markings.

Loin The loin and hind leg are particularly correct. The excellence of the Dartmoor's conformation gives the breed a natural balance.

RIDING PONY CHAMPIONS Along with Welsh Ponies, the Dartmoor dominates the riding pony classes and has contributed greatly to the beautiful British riding pony. It is very popular in Europe, and crosses well with either Thoroughbred or Arabian. The second cross with the Thoroughbred produces class competition horses.

THE LEAT The greatest factors in the development of the Dartmoor were the stallion, the Leat, and his owner, Sylvia Calmady-Hamlyn. She was honorary secretary of the Dartmoor Pony Society for 32 years. The Leat, a part-bred, was 12.2hh., and was described as "a magnificent pony." His sire was the desert-bred Arabian, Dwarka, and his dam the black 13hh. mare Blackdown (by Confident George, out of a Dartmoor mare).

Limbs Limbs and feet are excellent. The cannons are short and the bone measurement under the knee of the forelimbs is more than ample.

ACTION The Dartmoor action is notable among the pony breeds for the lack of knee lift. It is low, long, and economical – "typical hack or riding action."

CONSTITUTION Like all the British native breeds, the Dartmoor is hardy and constitutionally sound.

Height does not exceed 12.2hh.

Welsh Mountain Pony

The Welsh Pony and Cob Society stud book was opened in 1902 and is divided into four sections: two for ponies and two for cobs. The base for the Welsh breeding is the smallest of the purebreds, the Welsh Mountain Pony, which occupies Section A in the stud book. From this foundation emanate the Welsh Pony (Section B), the Welsh Pony of Cob Type (Section C), and the Welsh Cob (Section D).

ORIGINS

The Romans were the first "improvers" of the indigenous Welsh stock. They introduced eastern blood, an outcross that recurs often in the breed's history.

The first recorded influence was that of the Thoroughbred Merlin, a direct descendant of the Darley Arabian, put out on the Ruabon hills in Clwyd in the eighteenth century. Apricot, a Merioneth stallion, also had an influence. He was described as an Arabian-Barb out of a mountain mare. The patriarch of the modern Mountain Pony is acknowledged as being Dyoll Starlight, born in 1894, whose dam was said to have been a "miniature Arabian." After Dyoll Starlight came Coed Coch Glyndwr, whose dam was Starlight's granddaughter.

CHARACTER

The modern Welsh Mountain Pony is arguably the most beautiful of all ponies, but in its evolution it has, nonetheless, retained its characteristic hardiness, strength of constitution, inherent soundness, and the pony sagacity peculiar to the breed. The Mountain Pony is a splendid child's mount, a brilliant performer in harness, and an unsurpassed foundation to produce bigger ponies and horses.

Welsh Mountain Ponies do not stand over 12hh.

Color *Dyoll Starlight was largely responsible for the predominance of grays in Section A ponies, but bays, such as this one, and chestnuts also occur, and there are notable palomino strains.*

MARES AND FOALS The Welsh Mountain Ponies of today owe much to the second great progenitor of the breed, Coed Coch Glyndwr. He was the foundation stallion of the influential Welsh stud farm, Coed Coch, founded in 1924 by Miss M. Brodrick at Dolwen, Abergele, in North Wales. His great-grandsire was the Cob, Eiddwen Flyer.

ON THE MOUNTAIN The Welsh Mountain Pony is a product of its early environment in terms of action, conformation, and constitutional hardiness. The wild terrain, the paucity of food, and harsh climatic conditions have also ensured a remarkably efficient nutrient conversion – the ponies are able to thrive on minimal rations.

Body *The body is notably compact with great depth through the girth, allowing ample room for powerful lungs and a heart that is large in relation to the pony's small stature. The short, powerful loin is a particular feature.*

Ears *Tiny, pointed ears, essential in the pony breeds, are a feature of the Welsh Mountain Pony.*

DYOLL STARLIGHT Dyoll Starlight marks the watershed between the old breed and the refined modern pony. The stud prefix Dyoll is the name of his breeder, Meuric Lloyd, spelled backward. Lady Wentworth, owner of the Crabbet Arab Stud, acquired Starlight, when Lloyd became terminally ill, on condition that the pony should not be sold. She broke the agreement by selling him to Spain in 1925. He died there in 1929.

ACTION The action of the Welsh Mountain Pony originates in the powerful hind leg, and exemplary hock joints engaged well beneath the body. The movement from the shoulder is remarkably free, but with the knee action necessary for the safe crossing of broken ground.

Feet *The feet, in common with those of most mountain breeds, are of dense, blue horn and are exceptionally hard.*

HEAD The head of the Welsh Mountain Pony is dominated by the large and luminous eyes, which are the glory of the Welsh breeds. The eyes and the wide, open nostrils, together with the dished face, reveal the strong influence of eastern blood in this kind but innately courageous and spirited pony, which is as beautiful as any in the world.

Welsh Pony

The Welsh Pony, Section B, is described in the stud book as a riding pony "with quality, riding action, adequate bone and substance, hardiness and constitution and pony character." Sometimes the modern pony may appear to be too close to the Thoroughbred-type riding pony (see pp.236–7), but there is no denying its commercial viability as a competition pony and a working hunter, as well as a show pony.

ORIGINS

The early ponies of the "old breed" were often the result of crosses between Welsh Mountain mares and small Welsh Cob stallions, upgraded by the use of Arabians and small Thoroughbreds. They lived on the mountain, and many carried men both shepherding and hunting. The modern ponies are much improved in quality, scope, and action. They are unequaled as riding ponies anywhere in the world, and most retain their original characteristic toughness and their typical pony qualities.

INFLUENCES

The "Abraham" of the Section B pony was Tan-y-Bwlch Berwyn, whose son Tan-y-Bwlch Berwynfa was the foundation of the famous Coed Coch Section B herd. Berwyn, and the Welsh Pony in general, relied on the eastern blood that complements the Welsh stock so well. Berwyn was foaled in 1924. He was by Sahara, a Barb (or more likely Arabian) stallion bought in Gibraltar in 1913, out of a dam who was the granddaughter of the Welsh Mountain Pony sire, Dyoll Starlight.

Criban Victor, a stallion almost as notable, arrived 20 years later. He, too, displayed the essential connections with the Mountain Pony. He was by Coed Coch Glyndwr's son, Criban Winston, although his dam was by the famous Welsh Cob stallion, Mathrafal Broadcast – a classic Welsh amalgam of the Sections comprising the stud book. Additional evidence of the strong and permeating eastern influence is provided by the lines that have derived from the world champion, Skowronek, and the illustrious Raseem.

Shoulders The Section B displays a greater length of rein than the Welsh Mountain Pony. The slope of the shoulder and the withers are more pronounced.

Ears Small, pointed pony ears.

HEAD The head of the Welsh Pony resembles in every respect that of the Welsh Mountain Pony, Section A. The small and pointed pony ears are of particular importance, and long horse-type ears are not tolerated. The whole head is clean-cut and there is no hint of coarseness.

Quarters Strength in the quarter, as well as the best of joints in the hind leg, are characteristic features of the Welsh breeds.

Color This pony is gray. All colors, except piebald and skewbald, are acceptable in the Section B Pony.

Tail The tail is set high and carried gaily.

AUSTRALIAN PONY The Australian Pony is related to Welsh Section A and B ponies (which were exported to Australia from at least the early nineteenth century). The first recorded pony import to Sydney, Australia, was made in 1803. By 1920 the Australian Pony had emerged as a definite and fixed type, and an Australian Pony Stud Book Society was formed in 1929. Its object was to produce a "home-grown" riding pony of high quality. There is no doubt that the Australian Pony fulfills that requirement. The ponies vary between 12 and 14hh.

CHARACTER Although the larger Welsh Pony may differ in proportions to the Welsh Mountain Pony, it retains the spirited pony character that typifies the Welsh breeds.

ACTION The action of the Welsh Pony, contributing to increased scope, is long and low in front with not much bend in the knees. Behind, the strong hocks provide powerful leverage. The action is notably straight.

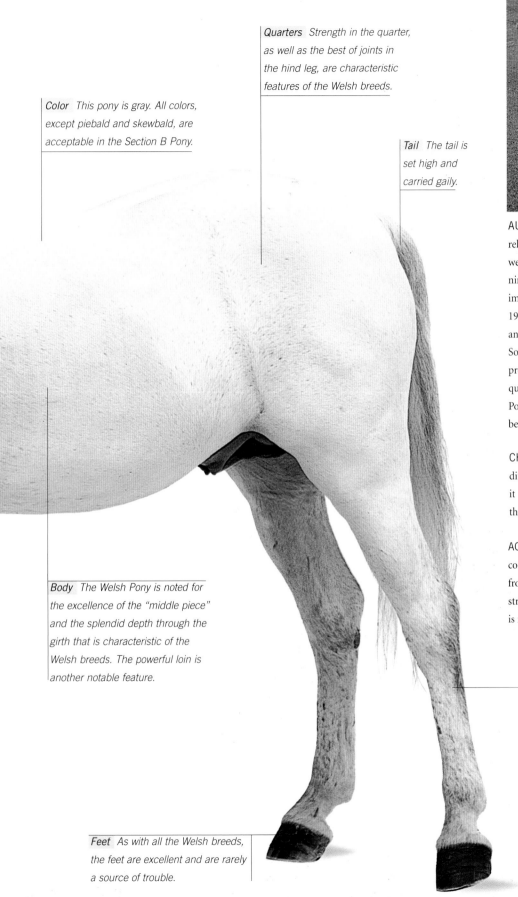

Body The Welsh Pony is noted for the excellence of the "middle piece" and the splendid depth through the girth that is characteristic of the Welsh breeds. The powerful loin is another notable feature.

Limbs While there is great length in the Section B proportions, the cannons are never long, and there is always a sufficiency of bone in the foreleg.

Feet As with all the Welsh breeds, the feet are excellent and are rarely a source of trouble.

Height does not exceed 13.2hh.

Mounted Games

Games on horseback have been a feature of horse cultures from the earliest time, and they are still traditional in many parts of Asia. Among regular mounted troops they were seen as useful training exercises, ideal for maintaining peak fitness, but increasingly in Western Europe mounted games are played almost exclusively by the young.

PONY CLUB GAMES

Mounted games, or *gymkhana*, (the word is of Indian origin), are almost central to the concept of the Pony Club, particularly in Australasia and in Britain (where the organization originated). In the UK, for instance, a Pony Club Mounted Games Championship was instigated in 1957 by HRH Prince Philip, Duke of Edinburgh, and is still called the "Prince Philip Games." The finals take place at London's Horse of the Year Show in October and are fiercely contested by enthusiastic teams from all over the country.

All kinds of games can be played from the back of a pony. The best known are probably the bending race, the sack race, and the various relay races, some reminiscent of military exercises. They are all fun events but they demand balance, agility, and highly developed riding skills, as well as quick, well-schooled ponies, temperamentally suited to the atmosphere of intense excitement.

TRADITIONAL CONTESTS

The games endemic to central Asia, Iran, and Afghanistan are more in the nature of brutal contest than fun, and call for exceptional riding skills as well as physical fitness of a high order.

The Afghan game of *buzkashi*, in which as many as 100 players do battle over a goat's carcass, is as ferocious a contest as any, but there are others that are less bloodthirsty.

Kyzkuu, played in various forms throughout Asia, is based on the bridal chase of the nomadic horse-peoples. Several men pursue the girl intent on claiming at least a kiss. She, however, may repel their advances with her heavy whip while riding for the finishing post – or, of course, she might decide to submit to a favored suitor. Wrestling on horseback, called *Oodarysh* or *Sais*, is popular in Kazakhstan and Kirghizia, while *Dzhigit*, acrobatic riding, is practiced all over central Asia.

TENT PEGGING

The spiritual home of the tent pegging sport is in India and Pakistan. It is practiced expertly by both civilians and the military, competing individually or as a team of four. The object is to strike a balsa peg set at the end of a prepared track (*pathi*) and, in order to gain full points, to carry it on the lance for a distance of 49ft (15m).

TENT PEGGING (Above) This contest was held at the Canberra Show, Australia, although the sport has its origins in Indian cavalry practice. Cavalry could cause chaos in an enemy camp by galloping through the tented lines and lifting the securing pegs, causing the tents to collapse on their occupants.

POLE BENDING (Above top) The bending race is popular with spectators wherever equestrian games are held. It is also an extremely good suppling and obedience exercise for the horse, as well as being a test of the rider's balance, control, and overall horsemanship.

PIGGYBACK (Left) This fast-moving game is a version of the "sharpshooter race," when two riders ride one pony, one of them leaping off to throw a ball at a target before remounting at speed to race to the finish line.

Welsh Cob

The Welsh Cob is a versatile family horse and, though spirited, is easily managed and economical to keep. The heartland of the Cob is Cardiganshire, where it is still integral to rural life.

ORIGINS

The Welsh Cob, Section D in the stud book, derived initially from the crossing of Welsh Mountain Ponies with Roman imports. Improvements were made in the eleventh and twelfth centuries using Spanish, Barb-type horses. These produced the Powys Cob – the remount of the English armies from the twelfth century onward – and the Welsh Cart Horse, a moderate-sized but powerful, now extinct, animal.

THE MODERN HORSE

The modern Welsh Cob came from a mix of the Powys stock with eighteenth and nineteenth century outcrosses to Norfolk Roadsters and Yorkshire Coach Horses. The four Cob lines stem from all those elements with an admixture of the ubiquitous Arabian blood. Yet the Welsh Cob remains, in perfection, a larger version of the base provided by the Welsh Mountain Pony.

In the past, the Welsh Cobs were in demand as heavy gun horses and for mounted infantry. There was also a large trade with the big city companies such as dairies and bakeries. The modern Welsh Cob is excellent in harness and makes a courageous, surefooted hunter.

Outline The outline of the Welsh Cob is identical to that of the Welsh Mountain Pony.

Technically, anything over 13.2hh. but usually between 14.2 and 15.2hh.

HEAD The arresting, quality head of the Welsh Cob reflects exactly the base stock represented by the Welsh Mountain Pony. Like that of the Mountain Pony (see pp.218–19), the face of the Welsh Cob is dished, the eyes are large, and the nostrils are wide and open.

Color *Welsh Cobs can be any color except piebald and skewbald. Blacks, bays, chestnuts, and palominos abound, and there are also creams and duns. This Welsh Cob is a dark liver-chestnut. Cymro Llwyd was dun or palomino and is largely responsible for those colors in the modern animal. Gray is rare in the Welsh Cob.*

FOUNDATION SIRES The foundation sires of Section D were: Trotting Comet (1840), with a background of Welsh Cart Horse and Norfolk Roadster blood; True Briton (1830), by a Yorkshire Coach Horse out of a reputed Arabian; Cymro Llwyd (1850), by the Crawshay Bailey Arabian out of a Welsh mare; and Alonzo the Brave (1866), a Norfolk Roadster.

WELSH PONY OF COB TYPE (Above) The small (13.2hh.) Welsh Pony of Cob Type, Section C in the stud book, is a splendid harness pony, ideal for trekking, and a wonderful riding pony and hunter for young people or small adults. It was the result of crossing Welsh Mountain mares with smaller trotting Cobs. Often called the "farm pony," it did every job on the hill farms and was used to cart slate from the mines of North Wales to the seaports. In 1949, when the type was in danger of disappearing, it was given a section in the stud book. Increasingly, Section C is bred to Section C, but the influence of the Welsh Mountain Pony is still strong.

THOROUGHBRED CROSS The Thoroughbred cross with the Welsh Cob, particularly the second cross, produces sound competition horses of the necessary size, scope, and speed.

ACTION Welsh Cob action is free and forceful. The whole foreleg is lifted from the shoulder and then fully extended before the foot touches down.

PERFORMANCE Before stallion licensing was introduced, breeding stock was often selected on the basis of performance over a given distance. A favorite route for the purpose was the 35-mile (56km) stretch uphill from Dowlais to Cardiff, which was completed in under three hours.

DRIVING Welsh Cobs, because of their activity, stamina, and courage, are ideal for competitive driving. A first cross to the Thoroughbred will increase the size and speed, but the Cob is the natural successor to the great trotting tradition of the Norfolk Roadster and remains a supreme harness horse in its own right.

Heels *A moderate amount of silky feather at the heel is permissible, but the hair must not be coarse and wiry.*

Dales

The Dales pony belongs to the Upper Dales of Tyne, Allen, Wear, and Tees in North Yorkshire. It is the larger, heavier-built neighbor of the Fell (see pp.228–9), with whom it shares common ancestors. Dales Ponies provided the power and sinews to operate the lead mines of Allendale and Alston Moor. They worked underground, once the horizontal levels were completed, and carried loads of lead ore to the Tyne seaports. They were also used in coal mines, as general farm animals, and in pack trains. They are capable of handling loads well out of proportion to their size; their packs weighed up to 224lb (100kg).

ORIGINS

The old-time Dales Pony was noted as a great trotter in harness or under saddle, and was well able to travel one mile (1.6km) in three minutes, carrying considerable weight. In order to improve on this ability, Welsh Cob blood was introduced in the nineteenth century, in particular that of the trotting stallion, Comet.

   Clydesdale outcrossing was practiced to the extent that in 1917 the Dales was regarded as being two-thirds Clydesdale. Nonetheless, it was also acknowledged as being, "for Army purposes, second to none in the country" because of the strength and quality of its feet, legs, and bone.

CHARACTERISTICS

The modern Dales Pony retains that wonderful bone and limb as well as its hard, blue feet. It is immensely strong and has a remarkable weight-carrying capacity, although its relationship with the Clydesdale is no longer apparent. A great and courageous performer in harness, it is also used increasingly as a riding pony. The Dales combines courage and stamina with a calm temperament. It is economical to keep, has a strong constitution, and is rarely sick. Because of these qualities, it is particularly useful as a trekking pony.

Color Alone among the British native breeds, the Dales' predominant coloring is black. Occasionally bays and browns, such as this dark brown, are found and, less usually, the odd gray pony – a possible legacy of the liaison with the Clydesdale.

Muzzle A muzzle of medium width without coarseness is desirable.

HEAD The head of the Dales owes nothing to the Clydesdale infusion of the past. There is width between the bright and docile eyes, and the small, pony ears are alert and mobile. The whole impression is one of intelligence.

Back The Dales pony has a particularly strong, short back and good conformation. This gives it a unique capacity for carrying weight, and contributes significantly to its true, powerful action, especially at the trot, a pace at which the breed excels.

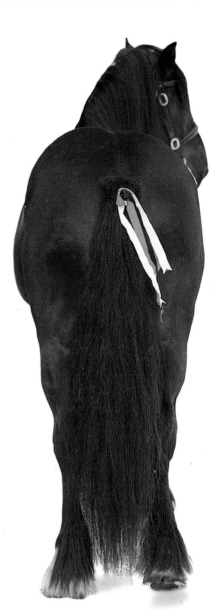

CARRYING BREAD TO LONDON This etching of packhorses carrying provisions to London in the 1840s may hardly represent the Dales accurately, but it does show the size of the load that a packpony was able to carry over the rough tracks of the day.

Girth An essential requirement for the breed is great depth of girth combined with well-sprung ribs.

REAR VIEW From the rear, the overall impression of the Dales pony is that of great strength concentrated within a compact form. It is enormously active in movement, going straight and true with much propulsive power from strong hocks and quarters.

Feet For centuries, Dales ponies have been famed for the excellence of their hard feet. A silky feather is carried on the heels.

Height does not exceed 14.2hh.

Fell

By tradition, the Fell is held to occupy the northern edges of the English Pennines and the wild moorlands of Westmorland and Cumberland, while the neighboring, and genetically related, Dales (see pp.226–7) belongs to the other side of the Pennines in North Yorkshire, Northumberland, and Durham. Both ponies are branches with the same root and have developed according to the uses that have been made of them.

ORIGINS

There is little doubt that the black, coldblooded Friesian (see pp.104–5), descendant of Europe's primitive Forest Horse, had an early influence on these northern breeds. The Frieslanders and their black horses were employed as auxiliary cavalry by the Roman legions stationed in northern Europe.

The greatest influence is that of the strong, swift Galloway, which remains particularly evident in the modern Fell pony. The Galloway was the mount of the border raiders and then of the Scottish drovers. It was bred between Nithsdale and the Mull of Galloway and, although it has been extinct since the nineteenth century, the qualities it bequeathed to British stock are still evident. The Galloway stood between 13 and 14hh. It was hardy, surefooted, possessed of great stamina, and very fast under saddle and in harness. It probably also formed part of the "running horse" stock that provided a base for the eastern sires of the seventeenth and eighteenth centuries and from which sprang the English Thoroughbred.

CHARACTERISTICS

In its time, the Fell was a pack pony, like its neighbor the Dales. Most probably, however, the Fell, which is lighter than the Dales and a tremendous trotter, was as much used under saddle as in harness on the rough fells. Today, it is sought after for both purposes and is, additionally, an excellent cross to produce horses of competition potential. Through the Wilson ponies, the Fell is at the base of the modern Hackney pony (see pp.98–9).

Shoulders An important point of conformation concerns the shoulder. In the Fell, it is well laid back and sloping, to give the riding action, but it is not too fine at the wither.

Ears The Fell has small, neat ears.

Jowls There is no coarseness around the jowls.

PROFILE The Fell is noted for its small, quality head – broad across the forehead and tapering down to the muzzle – and for its large, open nostrils. Its prominent, bright eye denotes intelligence and also reveals something of the equable temperament characteristic of the breed.

"AS HARD AS IRON" The breed standard states that "the Fell Pony should be constitutionally as hard as iron." In the eighteenth century, when Fells were used in pack trains, the average load was about 224lb (95kg) and the ponies covered some 240 miles (384km) a week.

LINGCROPPER The most famous of the early Fells was the eighteenth-century Lingcropper, who might have been a Galloway. He was found during the Jacobite uprisings "cropping the ling" at Stainmore, Westmorland, still carrying his saddle.

CARRIAGE DRIVING The swift, balanced trot of the Fell pony combined with its courage, endurance, and stamina make it an ideal driving pony. In past years, the Duke of Edinburgh drove a Fell team in competitive events.

PERSONALITY The overall impression of the Fell is that of enduring strength combined with quality and a general alertness of outlook.

ACTION The movement is described as "smart and true" with good knee and hock action, the pony going from the shoulder and strongly flexed hocks, and showing "great pace and endurance."

Color Fell colors are black, brown, as here, bay, and gray, without white markings, although a star is occasionally seen.

Tail The luxuriant mane and tail of the Fell pony are left to grow long.

Limbs A feature of the breed is the measurement of good flat bone below the knee. The official standard lays down a minimum of 8in (20cm).

Hocks The hocks of the Fell, because of their strength and ability to flex, contribute to the powerful drive of the hind leg.

Feet Feet are of the characteristic hard, blue horn, round, well formed, and capable of standing up to hard work over the high stony passes of the fells. Another characteristic is the generous growth of fine hair at the heels.

Height does not exceed 14hh.

Highland

The modern Highland pony has developed as a result of numerous outcrosses, though its origins are of great antiquity. There were ponies in northern Scotland and the Scottish islands after the Ice Age, and the pony bears a resemblance to the animals depicted 15–20,000 years ago in the caves at Lascaux in France.

Neck *The neck is strong, but never short, and the throat is clean.*

ORIGINS

Around 1535, Louis XII of France gave horses to James V of Scotland. These horses – a type of Percheron – were used to improve the native stock, as were Spanish Horses in the seventeenth and eighteenth centuries. The Dukes of Athol, foremost among the old Highland breeders, introduced oriental horses in the sixteenth century; and John Munro-Mackenzie used the Arabian Syrian in the late nineteenth century to establish the famous Calgary strain on the Island of Mull. Patriarch of the Highland breed was Herd Laddie by Highland Laddie, foaled in 1881 and bought by the Athol Stud in 1887.

AT WAR Highland ponies featured prominently in the Jacobite uprisings of the eighteenth century. In the Boer War in South Africa (1899–1902), both the Lovat Scouts and the Marquis of Tullibardine's Scottish Horse were mounted on Highland ponies.

CONFORMATION The compact conformation of the Highland, as well as its equable temperament, constitute an excellent base for crossing with the Thoroughbred. The first cross produces a sensible hunter, the second a potential competition horse.

CHARACTERISTICS

The Highland pony was Scotland's original all-purpose horse. Highlands are first-rate riding ponies, up-to-weight and surefooted. Hundreds are employed for trekking – a Scottish invention. They work in harness and forestry, carry game panniers, and are strong enough to carry deer carcasses weighing up to 252lb (126kg).

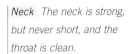

The Highland does not exceed 14.2hh.

IN THE HIGHLANDS Highland ponies are easily kept, thriving on rough pasture and needing little extra feeding. They have an ability to cross boggy land and are innately surefooted. Sound as a bell and free from hereditary disease, the Highland is a particularly long-lived breed. It is, moreover, docile and affectionate without being dull.

Color Few breeds have such a range of colors as the Highland. There are the duns in gray, as here, mouse, yellow, gold, cream, and fox. There are grays, browns, blacks, sometimes bays, and, occasionally, striking liver-chestnuts with silver manes and tails. Most have dorsal eel-stripes and some have zebra markings on the legs. Morelle, the first recorded sire at the Athol Stud in 1853, was a piebald – a color not now permitted.

Dorsal eel-stripe The dorsal eel-stripe is clearly visible on the back of this Highland pony.

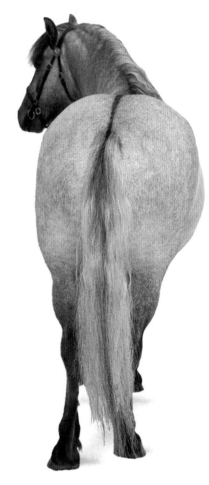

Nostrils The nostrils are good and wide.

HEAD A good Highland head shows nothing of an early Clydesdale influence. It is wide in the forehead, short between the eyes and muzzle, with good, wide nostrils and a kindly expression.

Limbs The Highland has short cannons with hard, flat bone and is very strong in the forearm. The knees are large and flat. The feather on the legs is soft and silky.

Feet Good feet reduce the incidence of foot disease to a minimum, as long as the ponies are not exposed to rich pasture and overfeeding.

REAR VIEW The thigh and second thigh are particularly well developed. The tail is usually set high and, like the mane and feather, is fine and silky, never coarse to the touch. The feather ends in a prominent tuft at the fetlock.

Connemara

The Connemara takes its name from the wild, empty part of Ireland to the west of Loughs Corrib and Mask. It is the sole "indigenous" equine of Ireland. A variety of breeds have been used to upgrade the Connemara pony to the point of excellence it has attained today.

ORIGINS

Crosses with Barbs and Spanish Horses resulted in the renowned Irish Hobby of the sixteenth and seventeenth centuries. The Hobby, forerunner of the Connemara, was a hardy, agile pony that, like the Galloway, played a part in the evolution of the Thoroughbred. Arabians were imported in the nineteenth century, and various government breeding programs brought in Welsh Cobs, Thoroughbreds, Roadsters, or Hackneys, and the less desirable Clydesdale cross in an attempt to check the degeneration of native stock. There were also Irish Draft sires and a line to the famous purebred Arabian, Naseel. The show jumper Dundrum was by the Thoroughbred stallion Little Heaven, and belonged to the Carna Dun line.

STUD BOOK

The Connemara Pony Breeders' Society was formed in 1923, and the English Connemara Society in 1947. The first stallion to be entered in the Connemara Stud Book was Cannon Ball, born in 1904. He won the Farmers' Race at Oughterard for sixteen years in succession. Rebel, born in 1922, and Golden Gleam, foaled a decade later, also had powerful influences on the breed development.

CHARACTERISTICS

The end product is probably the most outstanding performance pony available. The Connemara is fast, courageous, sensible, and a remarkable jumper. The natural environment of Connemara has given the pony hardiness, endurance, and its special character.

Neck The length of rein is exceptional in the Connemara.

Shoulders Good riding shoulders result in "a marked natural proclivity for jumping" – the hallmark of the modern pony.

Front Well-proportioned fronts are a feature of the Connemara.

Bone A bone measurement of between 7 and 8in (17 and 20cm) is not unusual.

HEAD The head of the Connemara is small and neat, revealing the influence of Oriental blood. Despite a background involving many breeds, the breeding pattern has produced, as was intended, a pony of fixed type. Furthermore, the versatile Connemara can be ridden by adults as well as children, which proves it to be a supremely tractable horse.

IDEAL COMPETITION MOUNT Connemara ponies have been exported extensively to Europe, where they are now bred in considerable numbers. They are regarded as the ideal competition mount for young people, and in Germany are subject to rigorous performance testing.

Color Coat colors are gray, as here, dun, black, bay, brown, and occasionally roan or chestnut. Piebalds and skewbalds are not accepted by the breed society.

FARM WORKER In remote Galway, the Connemara was used for every kind of farm task as well as being employed as a pack animal to carry seaweed, potatoes, peat, and corn. Of the old dun-type Connemara, Professor Cossor Ewart wrote, "they are capable of living where all but wild ponies would starve…strong and hardy as mules, fertile and free from hereditary disease, their extinction would be a national loss." (Royal Commission report, Congested Districts Board, 1897.)

TOP-CLASS HORSES The Connemara is a natural cross with a Thoroughbred to produce a top-class competition horse.

TYPE "… an extremely hard, wiry type of pony showing a great deal of Barb and/or Arab blood." (Evidence of Mr. Ussher C.B. to 1897 Royal Commission.)

CONFORMATION Elegance combined with substance, good proportions throughout, and true riding action summarize the qualities of this excellent performance pony. The compact body is notable for its depth.

Feet As with all the native breeds, the feet are excellent and the Connemara is surefooted to a degree.

The Connemara can stand between 13 and 14.2hh.

New Forest Pony

New Forest Ponies have been subject to outside influences for centuries because of the position of the forest in southwest Hampshire, England, an area crossed by routes to the west of the country.

THOROUGHBRED (Left)
The sire of Eclipse, probably the greatest racehorse of all time, was Marske, who was used on Forest mares for a short time from 1765. Once Eclipse's reputation was established, Marske was returned to stud in Yorkshire.

ORIGINS

There have been continual efforts to improve the Forest stock ever since the proclamation of Canute's Forest Law in 1016. As early as 1208, Welsh mares were put into the Forest; in the eighteenth century the Thoroughbred stallion, Marske, served Forest mares for a short time; and in the nineteenth century Queen Victoria loaned Arabian and Barb stallions. However, the principal development was due to Lord Cecil and Lord Lucas, both great, if rather innovative, "improvers." Between them, they introduced Highlands, Fells, Dales, Dartmoors, Exmoors, and Welsh Ponies. Lord Lucas even brought back a Basuto pony when he fought in the Boer War. Surprisingly, a distinctive type emerged from this potpourri of breeds.

CHARACTERISTICS

The modern, commercially viable New Forest Pony is, for the most part, stud-bred but still retains the character and movement inherited from its natural environment. The ponies have real riding shoulders and a typically long, low action made very evident at the canter, the "Forester's" best pace. Very used to human contact, the ponies are easily handled and are less sharp, or cunning, than some native breeds. They are excellent performers and are very strong; the larger ones can easily carry adults.

The upper height limit is 14.2hh. Forest-bred stock may be smaller.

FOUNDATION STALLIONS
Foundation stallions are Denny Danny, with a line to the Welsh Pony, Dyoll Starlight; Goodenough and Brookside David, both connected to Field Marshall; Brooming Slipon, and Knightwood Spitfire, grandson of the Highland, Clansman.

POLO PONY BLOOD
A major influence in the evolution of the Forester was the polo pony stallion, Field Marshall, out of a Welsh mare. He stood in the forest in 1918–19.

DIET Forest-bred ponies live on the moor grasses around the numerous bogs and are particularly fond of gorse tips.

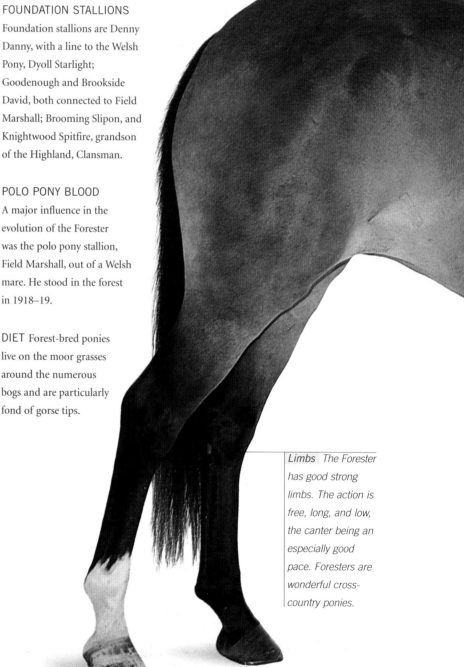

Limbs The Forester has good strong limbs. The action is free, long, and low, the canter being an especially good pace. Foresters are wonderful cross-country ponies.

Shoulders The shoulders, which are long and sloping, are real riding shoulders.

BREED SOCIETY The breed society is the New Forest Pony Breeding and Cattle Society, formed after the amalgamation of earlier societies in 1938. It produced its own stud book in 1960.

Head The New Forest Pony varies in type and is occasionally somewhat "horsy" about the head. The overall impression is of intelligence, and the ponies are easily trained. The modern Forester, because of its scope and ability, is in great demand throughout Europe.

Color New Forest Ponies are any color except piebald, skewbald, or blue-eyed cream. Bays, as here, and browns predominate.

Body The Forester is an all-around riding pony and has plenty of depth through the girth.

ENVIRONMENTAL INFLUENCES The New Forest, providing sufficient if not abundant food, has influenced the essential character and the distinctive movement of the versatile and surefooted New Forest Pony. Despite the presence of so many contributing breeds, it is the New Forest that provides what Lord Cecil observed as "the mysterious power of nature to grind down and assimilate all these types to the one most suited to the land."

Feet As with most ponies, this one is very surefooted.

Riding Pony

The Riding Pony was developed for the show ring. It is the juvenile rider's equivalent of the Thoroughbred show hack. It is probably the most perfectly proportioned equine in the world, particularly in the middle height limit from 12.2 to 13.2hh.

ORIGINS

The evolution of the Riding Pony over a period of no more than a half century is an object lesson in the judicious melding of selected bloods to produce an end product suited to the purpose required. The Riding Pony is based on a mix of native British blood (Welsh, and to a lesser degree Dartmoor), Arabian, and Thoroughbred. The establishment of so unique a pony may not be classed as an achievement in quite the same category as that of the "invention" of the English Thoroughbred, but it remains a remarkable and largely unparalleled accomplishment in the history of horse breeding.

CHARACTERISTICS

The Riding Pony moves gracefully and in perfect balance from the shoulder with the free, long, low action of the English Thoroughbred. It has inherited all the presence of its hotblood ancestors, but it has to be perfectly mannered and retain the bone, substance, and good sense of its native forebears.

Average height is 13.2hh. Show classes have three height divisions: up to 12.2hh., 12.2–13.2hh., and 13.2–14.2hh.

Neck *The neck is long, the graceful curve joining into the body at withers and shoulder.*

PROFILE The outline of the Riding Pony is that of the perfectly proportioned Thoroughbred in miniature. However, it is not a horse, and there is no loss of the essential pony look.

Mane and jowl *The mane is soft and silky. There is no thickness through the jowl to prevent poll flexion.*

Ears and eyes *The ears are small and mobile, and the eyes large and well spaced.*

Shoulders *The shoulder exemplifies that of the supreme riding animal. The shoulder blade is long and well sloped, and the humerus is short.*

Muzzle *The muzzle is small with large nostrils capable of great dilation to assist air intake.*

Knees *Above the knee, the muscles are big and long; below it the cannons are short. The knee itself is flat and large to allow for the passage of the tendons.*

HEAD The skin covering the head is thin, the veins easily seen. The impression is of great refinement and intelligence, but the essential pony character is retained. A horse head on a Riding Pony should never be seen.

PRESENCE Presence is an essential attribute of the Riding Pony. It is the personality and the star quality that demands attention and says uncompromisingly, "Look at me."

Quarters Quarters are well muscled but not heavy or excessively rounded. They run into similarly muscled gaskins.

Tail The tail is well set, high on the quarter. A low-set tail denotes a conformational defect.

COLOR The pony in this illustration is palomino. Riding ponies can be any color: black, brown, bay (as main picture), gray, palomino, and even shades of roan. White markings are permissible but skewbalds and piebalds are not.

Body The withers in the Riding Pony are clearly defined, the back of medium length, the trunk well ribbed, and the girth deep. In a good example, the body is as near to perfection as can be imagined.

Hock The hock is big, free from any lumpiness, and not puffy. It is low to the ground, the point in line with the chestnut on the inside of the foreleg.

Hind leg The hind leg is inclined to speed. That is, there is length from hip to the point of the hock for maximum propulsion.

Feet Riding pony feet are of the best. They are equal in size, open, well formed, and hard. There is no feather at the heel.

REAR VIEW The view from behind presents a picture of symmetry. The action is straight and true, with the hind feet following exactly in the track made by the fore shoes.

Eriskay

The ponies of Scotland's Western Isles are of ancient origin and formed the basis for the bigger and better-known Highland pony (see pp.230–1). Crossbreeding caused a reduction in their number until eventually only a handful of the old purebred ponies were left on the tiny island of Eriskay.

CROFTERS' PONY

These ponies were called Eriskay when enthusiasts sought to reestablish the breed in 1968. There is now an active Eriskay Pony Society and the number of ponies has risen to over 300, although it is still classified as a threatened rare breed.

In the nineteenth century, Western Isles ponies were used for work on the croft (tenant farm). But a call for larger, stronger ponies encouraged crossbreeding of native stock with Clydesdales, Fjords, and some Arabians. Eriskay, however, was too remote to be affected and there was no introduction of outside blood. By the 1970s, the herd on Eriskay was reduced to around 20 ponies. The present position of the Eriskay establishes it as the original survivor of the Western Isles breed, a distinct, primitive pony. It is still listed as "critical" by the Rare Breeds Survival Trust but with more foals born each year its future seems assured.

Forehand The neck, giving a good length of rein, is set high on a sloping shoulder, the chest is not too wide, and the head is in proportion.

The Eriskay stands between 12 and 13.2hh.

TEMPERAMENT Since the men of Eriskay earned their living from the sea, the work in the fields was left to the women, children, and the ponies. As a consequence, the ponies, living in close proximity with their handlers, had to be of good and friendly temperament. With no room for sentiment in this harsh environment, ponies unsuitable in this regard were swiftly culled.

Back The back is a good feature of the breed, for the structure, with its powerful short loin, is very strong. It is of moderate length and not overly broad.

Quarters The croup slopes gently to the tail and to strong, active quarters. The hips are wide enough and enhance the four-square impression. The balance of proportions in the quarters is good.

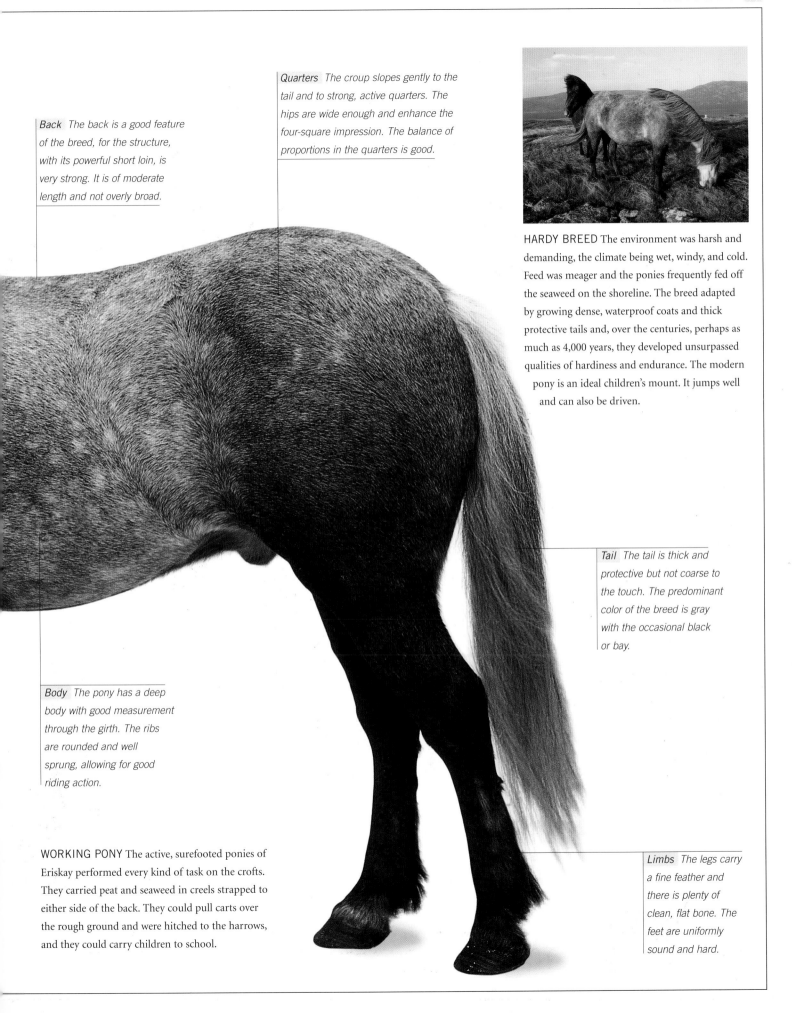

HARDY BREED The environment was harsh and demanding, the climate being wet, windy, and cold. Feed was meager and the ponies frequently fed off the seaweed on the shoreline. The breed adapted by growing dense, waterproof coats and thick protective tails and, over the centuries, perhaps as much as 4,000 years, they developed unsurpassed qualities of hardiness and endurance. The modern pony is an ideal children's mount. It jumps well and can also be driven.

Tail The tail is thick and protective but not coarse to the touch. The predominant color of the breed is gray with the occasional black or bay.

Body The pony has a deep body with good measurement through the girth. The ribs are rounded and well sprung, allowing for good riding action.

WORKING PONY The active, surefooted ponies of Eriskay performed every kind of task on the crofts. They carried peat and seaweed in creels strapped to either side of the back. They could pull carts over the rough ground and were hitched to the harrows, and they could carry children to school.

Limbs The legs carry a fine feather and there is plenty of clean, flat bone. The feet are uniformly sound and hard.

Lundy Pony

Lundy Island, is described as a lump of granite 3½ miles (5.6km) long by ½ mile (0.8km) wide, rising out of the sea where the Bristol Channel meets the Atlantic. Situated due north to south it is open to the ferocity of the southwesterly gales on the west side but is more sheltered on the east. It is rich in flora and fauna, and since 1928 it has supported a pony herd.

THE LUNDY HERDS

In 1928 the island's owner, Martin Coles Harman, bought New Forest stock to put on Lundy. After an eventful sea trip the ponies swam from boat to shore. One of the two stallions used in the experiment was a Thoroughbred and, not surprisingly, he and his stock did not thrive in the hard winter conditions. Welsh and Connemara stallions taken there later were far more successful, and it is the Connemara cross that is responsible for the distinctive Lundy Pony type, largely through the influence of the stallion Rosenharley Peadar, although New Forest stallions were used in the 1970s.

There have always been "experiments" to improve the native stock and the New Forest, in its native habitat, has been subjected to more than most (see New Forest, pp.234–5), but there is no doubt that the Lundy initiative, and the introduction of the Connemara, has produced a valuable and distinctive product that has quality and is tough and hardy.

The Lundy Pony Preservation Society is responsible for the herd and also for the Lundy herd bred on the mainland. The latter has used only Connemara stallions.

The Lundy Pony stands at 13.2hh. average.

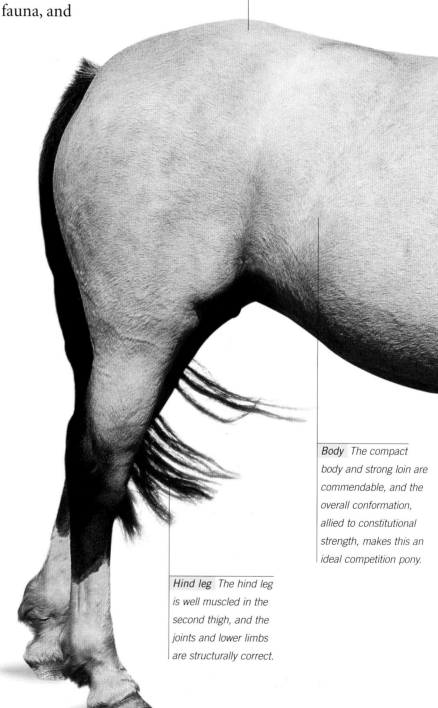

Quarters The quarters and the pleasing, symmetrical outline are reflective of the powerful Connemara influence on the New Forest base. Here, the quarters are well made and make for show-jumping potential.

Body The compact body and strong loin are commendable, and the overall conformation, allied to constitutional strength, makes this an ideal competition pony.

Hind leg The hind leg is well muscled in the second thigh, and the joints and lower limbs are structurally correct.

Neck The neck is a particularly good feature. It is of adequate length, muscled, and elegant and gives a useful length of rein from wither to poll.

Head A real knowing pony head. It is neat and gives a wonderfully alert expression.

Shoulder The strong, sloping shoulder is a characteristic of the Connemara and this one is especially well formed. The depth of girth is more than sufficient.

DISTINCTIVE While the Lundy ponies are distinctive, the mainland ponies, improved by the Connemara cross, are different in type and appearance from the island herd, now numbering about 20 animals. The present Lundy stallion is a grandson of Rosenharley Peadar.

Forelegs An excellent pair of forelegs. The forearm is muscled, and the chest is open and not too broad. Feet, joints, and bone are all of high conformational standard.

COLOR The Lundy Preservation Society runs a thriving sponsorship program, and the ponies are ideal, good-tempered, all-around mounts for children. The predominant colors of the island herd are cream and golden dun, bright and dark bay; when New Forest stallions were used the principal colors were dark dun and bay. The mainland herd retains the dark dun color as well as bright bay and some black.

Shetland

The Shetland Isles, the original habitat of the smallest of the British pony breeds, and about 100 nautical miles (185km) north-east of Scotland, is bleak and gale-swept. The land has no trees; it abounds with rocky outcrops and much of the soil is thin and acid, supporting little more than rough grasses and heather. So heather, grasses, and mineral-rich seaweed formed the diet of the original Shetland and this, with the inhospitable environment, has governed its character.

ORIGINS

Shetlands probably came to the Shetland Islands from Scandinavia perhaps as much as 10,000 years ago, before the ice fields had receded. These first ponies would have been of pronounced Tundra-type (see Origins, pp.10–11). The Shetland still retains the extra large nasal cavities, which allow the air to warm before entering the lungs, that are common to equines of the northern latitudes.

CHARACTERISTICS

Shetland Ponies are naturally hardy and constitutionally strong. They move with a quick, knee-lifting action that is free and straight fore-and-aft.

The Shetland is traditionally measured in inches. The average height is 40in (101cm), but the best in terms of conformation are usually 1–2in (2–5cm) smaller.

Head The head is well shaped and sensible; the ears are small and neat, and the forehead is broad, denoting intelligence.

Shoulders Shoulders are strong, well laid, and oblique, not upright or loaded. There is great depth through the girth.

Neck The neck is crested, particularly in stallions. It is also strong, muscular, and in proportion to the pony's size.

Chest The Shetland is broad between the forelegs – never narrow.

PEAT FETCHING On the Shetland Isles, Shetland ponies did every kind of work, including carrying seaweed and fetching peat for fires. For their diminutive size they are one of the most powerful equines, capable of carrying a man over rough country and able to work under heavy panniers.

Color Shetlands come in a variety of colors. Black, as here, is the foundation color, but brown, chestnut, and gray can be found as well as skewbald and piebald.

Body A short back with exceptionally muscular loins is characteristic of the Shetland. It has a thick-set, deep-ribbed body that gives an impression of strength.

Quarters The tail is well set on the broad quarters, which run into well-developed gaskins.

MINIATURE SHETLANDS (Above) In recent years, there has been a movement toward the breeding of "miniature" Shetlands, which are even smaller than the general breed standard. These animals have an obvious curiosity value, but there is a danger of their losing type.

Tail The tail and mane are especially full and profuse for protection against the weather.

Coat The coat changes according to the season. It is smooth in summer, but a thick, wiry, double coat is grown in winter.

Limbs The limbs are short and set at each corner. They have large, sharply defined joints and strong, flat bone.

PONY OF THE AMERICAS The first Pony of the Americas was foaled in 1954 and was the result of a cross between a Shetland stallion and an Appaloosa mare. There are now stringent standards calling for a miniature horse, with Appaloosa coloring and characteristics, whose conformation is between that of a Quarter Horse and an Arabian. The height is set at between 11.2 and 13.2hh.

Feet The Shetland has round, tough feet of hard, blue horn with pasterns that are normally sloped, not upright.

American Shetland

By far the most popular pony in the US is the Shetland (see pp.242–3), which originated in the Shetland Isles of Scotland. The first import of Shetlands to North America was made in 1885. The American Shetland Pony Club was formed three years later, and today there are well in excess of 50,000 Shetlands in the US. Shetlands are also very numerous in Europe, most particularly in the Netherlands. However, no attempt has been made to cross the breed except in the US.

MORE LIKE A HACKNEY In essence, the American Shetland is not much more than an American variation on the Hackney pony. It is said, however, to be intelligent, spirited, adaptable, and very good natured. The action, in harness, is high, extravagant, and flashy.

ORIGINS

Few of the Shetlands in the US today bear much resemblance to the tough Shetland Isles pony whose character was formed by its harsh environment where the winter weather is severe and sustaining feed is minimal. Indeed, the American Shetland is a purely artificial, man-made product, and while it is claimed that it retains the native hardiness and constitution of the pure Shetland, that is arguable and most unlikely. The breed was created by first selecting the finer types of Island Shetland and then crossing them with Hackney ponies, and adding a dash of Arabian and small Thoroughbred blood to the mixture.

The "new-look" American Shetland is primarily a harness pony of pronounced Hackney character and with much the same brilliance of action. However, it is also raced in harness and shown under saddle.

FEET The feet are grown artificially long, and heavy shoes are used to accentuate the trotting action of the American Shetland.

Hind leg Greater length has been introduced in the hind leg by the use of Hackney ponies, Arabians, and small Thoroughbreds.

Frame The overall frame of the American Shetland is narrower and longer than that of the broad-beamed, short-legged Island Shetland and there is obviously a greater refinement and structural delicacy.

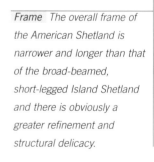

Tail The luxurious growth of mane and tail are reminders of the true-bred Shetland of the Islands. The harness ponies are shown with artificially set tails.

HACKNEY PONY The breed was created in the nineteenth century as the pony counterpart of the renowned and brilliant Hackney (see pp.98–9), and used to breed the American Shetland.

Neck The neck is long and graceful, blending well into the shoulder and with the head well set on.

Withers The withers are unusually pronounced for a pony. They run into a short, well-made back with good loins and contribute to the slope of the shoulder.

Head The head is relatively long and the profile is straight or slightly dished. There is some loss of pony character.

Forehand The chest is broad and the conformation of the forehand, though not of Shetland character, is correct and pleasing.

Body The girth is adequate in depth and the limbs are long and slender. The joints, however, do not approach those of the Island Shetland in size or strength. The artificially stretched stance shown here is typical of the harness pony.

Colors All kinds of colors occur in the American Shetland: brown, as here, black, bay, chestnut, roan, cream, dun, and gray are all found.

FLASHY ACTION American Shetlands are shown in harness-pony classes in which much emphasis is placed on style and flashy action – they can also be shown in pony-roadster classes in which a less exaggerated gait is allowed. The action is encouraged by artificial "aids" in the shoeing.

The average height is around 42in (103cm) at the wither but smaller specimens can be found.

Falabella

Miniature horses have been bred as pets and for their curiosity value at various periods of equine history, but the best known is the Falabella. Despite its size, the Falabella is not a pony but a miniature horse, having the horse's characteristics and proportions. The "breed" is named after the Falabella family, who developed the little animals on its Recreo de Roca Ranch, outside Buenos Aires in Argentina.

JULIO CESAR FALABELLA Julio Cesar Falabella is a member of the family that first developed the miniature "breed." He is pictured here with a mare and foal that still bear some resemblance to the original Shetland foundation.

ORIGINS

The basis of the Falabella was the Shetland Pony and possibly, at one time, a very small, freak Thoroughbred. The Falabella came about through deliberate down-breeding with crosses of the smallest animals and thereafter through close inbreeding. In the process, strength and vigor have been lost, and the animals have lost any of the Shetland's hereditary toughness.

Falabellas are popular in the United States and are bred in England, as well as being exported elsewhere. It is said that they can be used in harness, but they are unsuitable for riding.

Quarters Here is a good example of a miniature horse although it lacks correctness and some strength in the quarters and hind limbs. The aim of the breeders is to produce a near-perfect specimen in miniature.

Color Most colors occur including bay, black, brown, gray, and part-colors, but the spotted Appaloosa-type coat pattern, as here, is increasingly sought after.

Hocks The hocks tend to be weak and held close together, that is, cow-hocked.

Tail Luxurious growth of the mane and tail is usual on the Falabella.

FALABELLA FOALS These Falabella foals are appealing, but the practice of down-breeding and inbreeding has resulted in conformational weaknesses even in these carefully reared animals. Breeders have also to consider the effects on the constitution and guard against inherited loss of vigor.

SUGAR-DUMPLING A noted breeder of midget horses was Smith McCoy of Roderfield, West Virginia. His smallest horse was a mare called Sugar-Dumpling. She weighed a mere 30lb (13.5kg) and stood only 20in (51cm) high.

PET Although the Falabella has no practical use, it can be an attractive and engaging pet, and it is reputed to be a most friendly and intelligent little creature. The head and general expression are particularly pleasing.

Coat Falabella coats are often long and silky, but they do not have the Shetland's thick, warm undercoat and they do not approach that breed in terms of hardiness or strength of constitution.

HEAD This Falabella head is not unlike that of the Shetland, from which the breed was derived. In the best Falabella specimens, the head is in proportion to the small body; in the poorer ones, it is large in comparison.

Limbs The limbs are not always the best, a common failing being the tendency toward lack of bone, and bowlegs in front – deficiencies that breeders are trying to eliminate.

Feet The feet may be acceptable in terms of size and shape, but are occasionally inclined to be boxy.

The height of the Falabella does not exceed 30in (76cm).

Landais

The Landais was originally a semiwild pony that lived in the heavily wooded Landes region in France, south of Bordeaux and running down the Cote D'Argent to Biarritz and the barrier of the Pyrénées. It may have descended from the Tarpan and possibly the same is true of the bigger Landais, often called Barthais, which used to be found on the better grazing of the Chalosse plain.

INFLUENCES

In the nineteenth century, Arabian blood was introduced and repeated in 1913, when there were some 2,000 ponies in the area. After World War II, the Landais came near to extinction; at one time there were no more than 150 ponies. To avoid the dangers of inbreeding, the breed enthusiasts outcrossed to Welsh Section B stallions, strongly supported by the Arabian.

The formation of French pony clubs in the early 1970s encouraged the breeding of the Landais for use by children. The breed represents a significant base stock in the French Riding Pony (Poney Français de Selle), which, it is hoped, will one day rival its British counterpart.

The present-day Landais is a pony of improved quality, showing Arabian character and retaining the neat, pointed ears of the Welsh breeds. It remains a hardy breed and adapts easily to varying temperatures. Economical to keep, the Landais is, it is claimed, both docile and intelligent.

Topline The topline of the pony is acceptable in terms of the length of rein – from the withers over the neck to the poll. This counteracts, to a degree, the failings in the shoulders.

Neck The neck is relatively long and thickens significantly at its base to join a somewhat loaded shoulder.

HEAD The Landais head is small, neat, and finely chiseled, showing the strong Arabian influence. The short, pointed ears are entirely Welsh in character, and the eyes are widely spaced. The profile is straight but the overall appearance is not unattractive. Generally, the head joins smoothly to the neck without there being fleshiness through the jowl.

The height of the Landais is 11.3–13.1hh.

Back There is usually a straightness of the back, which, combined with the flat withers, poses a problem with regard to the fitting of the saddle. In general, the conformation tends to place the pony on its forehand.

Color Predominant colors are dark bay, brown, black, and chestnut. This pony is liver-chestnut.

Quarters The quarters slope downward from the croup and have insufficient length, a matter now being corrected by outcrosses of better quality. The tail is held high in movement.

POTTOCK (Above) The semiwild Pottock belongs to the mountainous, Basque region. It is one of the few remaining, indigenous ponies of France. It has been improved by crosses to Welsh Section B stallions and Arabians. There are three types: the Standard and the Piebald, which are between 11.1 and 13hh., and the Double, a bigger pony of 12.2–14.2hh. The Pottock is less refined than the Landais, but very tough.

Limbs The pony appears to be very light of limb, although the breed standard stipulates 6 ½ – 7in (16.5–18cm) of bone on the forelimbs as being desirable. There is a tendency for the elbow to be "tied-in," restricting the freedom of movement.

Feet On the whole, the feet remain indicative of the Landais' primitive ancestry, being hard and well shaped.

REAR VIEW A thick mane and tail and a silky coat are a feature of the Landais; the tail is often grown very long. Generally, the quarters are inclined to be weak, the hind leg often inheriting this worst characteristic of the Arabian.

Ariègeois

The Ariègeois, sometimes called cheval de Mérens, has its home on the eastern edge of the Pyrenean chain that divides France from Spain. It takes its name from the Ariège river. The old-type of Ariègeois, so accurately described in Caesar's *Commentarii* *(Commentaries: notes on the Gallic and Cini Wars)*, is found only in the high valleys of the Spanish border toward Andorra.

HISTORY

Carvings and wall pictures at Niaux in the Ariège, made about 30,000 years ago, show the black, mountain pony in winter order, characteristic "beard" and all. Its substance was probably achieved by crossings with the Romans' heavy pack mares, and Oriental blood was added to the pony at various times. The Ariègeois' home is not unlike the high fells of Cumbria in northern England. Indeed, the black Ariègeois is very similar to the British Fell (see pp.228–9) and almost an exact replica of the Dales (see pp.226–7).

Primarily a pack pony, the Ariègeois is employed on upland farms for cultivating steep slopes, where tractors are impractical. When smuggling was an accepted occupation along the Spanish border, the movement of contraband depended on the surefooted Ariègeois – and it may still be so.

Outline The outline is similar to that of the British Dales pony. As befits an animal used for pack transportation, the back is long but strong. Usually, the croup is sloped and the tail set somewhat low in consequence.

Tail Like most inhabitants of the high mountains, the Ariègeois grows a thick, harsh mane and tail as protection against the cold winter weather.

Limbs The limbs are less massive than might be expected, and there is a tendency to cow-hocks – so often a characteristic of the mountain-bred pony.

Feet The breed is exceptionally surefooted and traverses the steep and icy mountain paths without difficulty. The density of the horn is exceptional and makes shoeing unnecessary.

IMPERVIOUS TO THE COLD The Ariègeois is impervious to the severe winters and is quite at home in its steep mountain home. However, it is not resistant to heat and needs shelter from the summer sun.

Neck *The neck is fairly short and straight, and lacks any elegance.*

Mane *The mane is exceptionally heavy and adds to the impression of coarseness about the head.*

Body *Despite the broad chest, straight and upright shoulders, and flat withers that have considerable width between the shoulder blades, the girth of the Ariègeois is fairly deep.*

Color *The coat is solid black with reddish highlights in winter. White markings are exceptional. The flanks, however, may be lightly flecked with white.*

HEAD The head can be coarse but it is light-boned and expressive. The forehead is flat, the ears fairly short and very hairy, and the profile straight. The eyes are bright and alert with a gentle expression. In winter, a hairy "beard" growth covers the jawbones.

The height of the Ariègeois is 13.1–14.3hh.

HARDY BREED The breed is versatile, easily managed, and constitutionally hardy. It can work on minimum rations of relatively poor quality.

Haflinger

The Haflinger has its homeland in the southern Austrian Tyrol, around the village of Hafling in the Etschlander Mountains. The principal Haflinger stud farm is at Jenesien. The pony has an innate ability to work on the steep mountain slopes, and it is used for riding and driving.

ORIGINS

The modern Haflinger, although a coldblood, has an eastern foundation through the Arabian stallion El Bedavi XXII, to whom all purebred Haflingers can be traced back. Otherwise the base stock originates in the indigenous, but now extinct, Alpine Heavy Horse and a related pony breed. There are later infusions of smaller Norik horses and Hucul, Bosnian, and Konic ponies, which may be regarded as being of a similar genetic background.

CHARACTER

The close-knit character of the Haflinger family and the mountain environment ensures a fixed type of unmistakable appearance. The breed is enormously sound and hardy, the youngstock being raised on the Alpine pastures (a practice known as *alpung*) where the thin air develops their hearts and lungs.

Head The large eyes, big, open nostrils, and small ears give the Haflinger a lively, intelligent appearance and reflect its kindly temperament.

Color The color is always chestnut or palomino with a characteristic flaxen mane and tail. This makes the Haflinger one of the world's most attractive ponies.

AVELIGNESE (Left) The Avelignese is the Italian version of the Haflinger and is often bigger than its cousin from over the mountain (up to 14.3hh.). They share a common ancestor in El Bedavi XXII, and have much the same background and an almost identical appearance. A mountain horse used in draft and under pack, the Avelignese is bred in mountainous areas of northern, central, and southern Italy.

EDELWEISS BRAND (Right) The Haflinger is sometimes called the Edelweiss Pony. All Hafling-bred ponies bear a brand mark featuring Austria's native flower with a letter H at its center.

Back The Haflinger is strong and notably muscular. The back is inclined to be long as befits a pony that is often used for pack purposes.

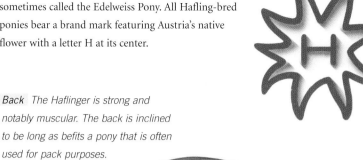

WILLING WORKER The Haflinger is a versatile and willing worker. It will draw a sleigh, pull wheeled vehicles, or work in forestry or on the farm. In Austria, ponies are not worked until they are four years old, but it is not unknown for them to be healthy and active at 40 years of age.

Body The Haflinger is powerfully built, being especially strong and muscular in the loins and with well-formed quarters. There is good depth through the girth.

Feet The limbs of this very sound pony are well made, and the feet are excellent. Bred and reared on mountain slopes, it is naturally surefooted.

REAR VIEW A full and flowing, flaxen tail that is well set into strong quarters is a feature of Austria's hardworking Haflinger pony.

ACTION The action of the pony is exceptionally free, and it maintains its long-striding walk even when working on rough and steep mountain slopes.

The height of the Haflinger pony is up to 13.3hh.

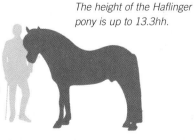

Fjord

Of the modern horses, none bears so striking a resemblance to the Asiatic Wild Horse as the Norwegian Fjord pony, which may also have a connection with the Tarpan, as it retains both their coat color and much of their primitive vigor. The Fjord was the Vikings' horse and is recognizable in runestone carvings in Norway, many of which depict fights between stallions. The Fjord went with the warriors in their longboats when they raided Scotland's Western Isles. Its influence remains in Scotland's Highland pony and in the ancient Icelandic Horse.

Color The Fjord color is dun, in all its shades, accompanied by a dorsal eel-stripe running from the forelock to the tip of the tail. There are often zebra bars on the legs, as here.

CHARACTERISTICS

In its native land, the powerful Fjord carries out every kind of work, taking the place of the tractor on mountain farms. It will draw a plow and carry a pack load though rivers and along precipitous, mountain tracks. It is also used under saddle and excels in long-distance events, which suit its courage and stamina. It is an excellent performer in harness and can hold its own in competitive events.

The Fjord is found in variant types throughout Scandinavia but is bred principally in Norway. A great number are exported to Germany, Denmark, and central European countries, where their qualities have made them popular.

GOTLAND PONY On the Swedish island of Gotland in the Baltic Sea, the Gotland Pony has existed since the Stone Age and is probably Scandinavia's oldest breed. At one time it ran wild, and there is still a wild herd in the Lojsta Forest. Like the Fjord, it is possibly a descendant of the Tarpan. It walks and trots well but is no galloper.

REAR VIEW The tail is often silver and is thick and full but is occasionally low set. The dorsal eel-stripe is typical of the breed and revealing of the Fjord pony's primitive ancestry. The quarters reflect the short, compact conformation and the overall strength of build. Light feather occurs on the heels.

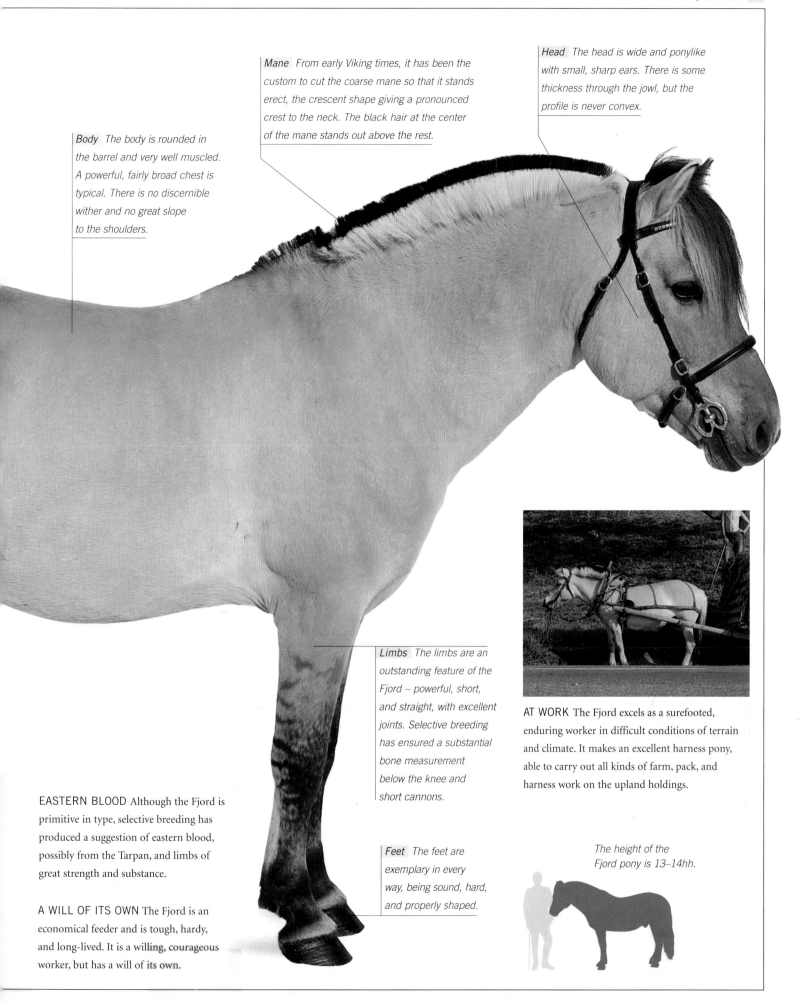

Mane From early Viking times, it has been the custom to cut the coarse mane so that it stands erect, the crescent shape giving a pronounced crest to the neck. The black hair at the center of the mane stands out above the rest.

Head The head is wide and ponylike with small, sharp ears. There is some thickness through the jowl, but the profile is never convex.

Body The body is rounded in the barrel and very well muscled. A powerful, fairly broad chest is typical. There is no discernible wither and no great slope to the shoulders.

Limbs The limbs are an outstanding feature of the Fjord – powerful, short, and straight, with excellent joints. Selective breeding has ensured a substantial bone measurement below the knee and short cannons.

AT WORK The Fjord excels as a surefooted, enduring worker in difficult conditions of terrain and climate. It makes an excellent harness pony, able to carry out all kinds of farm, pack, and harness work on the upland holdings.

EASTERN BLOOD Although the Fjord is primitive in type, selective breeding has produced a suggestion of eastern blood, possibly from the Tarpan, and limbs of great strength and substance.

A WILL OF ITS OWN The Fjord is an economical feeder and is tough, hardy, and long-lived. It is a willing, courageous worker, but has a will of its own.

Feet The feet are exemplary in every way, being sound, hard, and properly shaped.

The height of the Fjord pony is 13–14hh.

Icelandic Horse

Although the Icelandic Horse stands no more than 13.2hh., it is never referred to as a pony by the Icelanders. The horses came to this volcanic island in the longboats of the Norsemen, who settled there between AD860 and 935. It has occupied a central place in the lives of the Icelanders for over 1,000 years.

HISTORY

The strong, Icelandic horse culture has an extreme purity of stock as it received no outside blood for over 800 years. There was an attempt to add eastern blood but it proved so disastrous that the *Althing*, the world's oldest parliament, prohibited the import of horses in AD930.

From an early date, selective breeding seems to have been practiced, using fights between stallions as a basis for selection. Selective breeding on a practical scale began in 1879 in the most famous breeding area, Skagafjördur, in northern Iceland. The programs were largely based on the quality of the five gaits peculiar to the Icelandic Horse. Many studs breed strictly to a specific color, of which there are 15 basic types and combinations.

The Icelandic Horse, often kept in semiwild conditions, is used for every kind of work. Sport is equally important. Competitive events are held frequently and include racing, cross-country, and even dressage competitions. As cattle cannot be wintered out in Iceland, and the Icelandic Horses can, horse herds are also kept for meat; horse flesh has always been a staple of the Icelandic diet.

Mane Both mane and tail are full and abundant.

Head The head is distinctive but plain and heavy in proportion to the short, stocky body.

Forehand The shoulders appear to be relatively straight rather than otherwise. The neck is short and carried well but is usually thick through the jowl.

The height of the Icelandic Horse is 12.3–13.2hh.

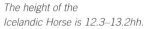

SEMIWILD HORSES About half of Iceland's horses live out all year in a semiwild state, without receiving any conventional supplementary feed to sustain them through the harsh winters. Occasionally, however, they are given the highly nutritious herring, with which the Icelandic seas abound.

Color Color is a feature of the Icelandic breed and there are 15 recognized combinations. Chestnut accompanied by a flaxen mane and tail, as here, is popular. There are also duns, bays, grays, and blacks. Sometimes palomino and albino are found as well as piebald and skewbald.

Body The girth is always deep and the back is short.

Quarters The quarters of the Icelandic Horse are peculiarly wedge-shaped and sloping but are, nonetheless, very strong and muscular. The animal has a notable ability to engage the hind legs well under the body.

TOLT The *tolt*, pictured here, is the specialized four-beat running walk used by the Icelandic Horse to cross broken ground swiftly. It is a "gait which with unaltered footfall can escalate its swiftness from a mere stop to great speed." (Icelandic Pony Society breed standard.)

Limbs Although small, the Icelandic Horse is able to carry full-grown men at speed over long distances and difficult terrain. Its compact body is carried on strong limbs, notable for their short cannons and strong hocks.

Feet The feet are exemplary and the breed is noted for its agility and surefootedness over rough country.

FIVE-GAITED HORSE The five Icelandic gaits are: *fetgangur* (walk) used under pack; *brokk* (trot) for crossing rough country; *stökk* (gallop); and the two gaits of antiquity, the *skeid* (pace), which covers short distances at speed, and the *tolt*, the famous running walk.

RACING THE ICELANDIC HORSE
The first modern race-meeting of Icelandic Horses was held at Akureyri in 1874. Racing takes place at different venues between April and June, the biggest being in Reykjavik on the Monday after Pentacost.

Caspian

It was a matter of enormous scientific and historical importance when the Caspian Miniature Horse, now termed a "pony" on account of its size, was discovered by Mrs. Louise L. Firouz at Amol on the Caspian littoral in 1965. The Caspian is certainly the most ancient breed in existence.

HISTORY

It is generally accepted that just prior to the domestication of the horse, four subspecies were in existence (see Origins, pp.10–11). There were two pony types and two horse types. The last of these, Horse Type 4, was the smallest of all, standing no more than perhaps 9hh., but it was a horse with respect to its proportions. It was the most refined of the four, had a high-set tail, and a distinctly concave profile. Its habitat was in western Asia, and it is suggested that this was the Arabian prototype. The trilingual seal of Darius the Great (c.500BC) shows very small horses pulling the royal chariot; and Egyptian artefacts, dated 1,000 years before Darius, depict similar horses of small stature but full of quality.

Research seems to point to the Caspian as being the far-off ancestor, far off by some 3,000 years possibly, of the Arabian horse. It has physical characteristics different to other equines. There is an extra molar in the upper jaw, a pronounced difference in the shape of the scapula, and a different formation of parietal bones of the head.

There are thriving Caspian societies in Britain, Australia, New Zealand, and the US. Stud farms exist in Iran.

The height of the Caspian is 10–12hh.

Neck The neck is usually arched and graceful, flowing into the fairly sharp wither formation.

Shoulders The Caspian has very good, sloping shoulders with well-formed withers. The shape of the scapula is more like that of a horse than a pony. This produces a longer stride, resulting in relatively great speed for its size.

Ears The breed standard calls for very short ears.

Limbs The Caspian has slim, lithe legs that look almost fragile but are, nonetheless, inherently sound and strong.

Bone The bone below the knee is dense and strong, and there is little or no feathering at the fetlock.

HEAD The Caspian head is very distinctive. It is short and covered with fine, thin skin. The forehead is peculiarly vaulted and the eyes are large and gazellelike, while the muzzle is small and tapered with the large nostrils set low. The breed standard calls for very short ears, actually stipulating that they should not be more than 4½in (11.4cm) long.

TEMPERAMENT The Caspian is a kind, highly intelligent and willing animal. It is spirited but never unruly, and the stallions can be both handled and ridden by small children.

Color Principal colors are bay, as here, gray, and chestnut, with occasional blacks and creams. White markings can occur on head and legs.

Back The back is straight and the tail is usually carried high, like that of the Arabian.

ARABIAN PROTOTYPE (Above) The well-proportioned Arabian may have originated with the Caspian and it has many of the latter's characteristics. The Caspian has a similar symmetry and is more a miniature horse in its proportions than a pony. Although the Arabian is an ancient breed, it has been claimed that it could have been preceded by the Caspian.

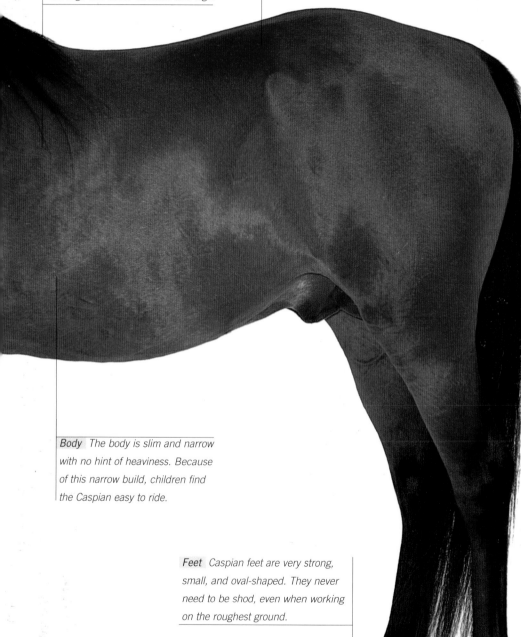

Body The body is slim and narrow with no hint of heaviness. Because of this narrow build, children find the Caspian easy to ride.

Feet Caspian feet are very strong, small, and oval-shaped. They never need to be shod, even when working on the roughest ground.

ACTION The action is natural and floating. The walk and trot are long-striding, the canter is smooth, and the gallop very rapid. Despite its size, the Caspian can keep up with an average horse at all gaits other than the full gallop. It is a natural jumper of exceptional and extraordinary ability.

REAR VIEW Narrow and light, the quick-moving Caspian is built for speed, although it is also a very capable performer in harness. The breed has a full and flowing mane and tail, the latter being carried high.

Batak

The entire existence of the Batak pony of central Sumatra is intricately involved with the life of the Batak people. The ponies are raced, they are appreciated as "the most exquisite meat," and they also serve as the central sacrifice to the trinity of Toba gods, for which purpose each Batak clan keeps three sacred horses.

THE SACRIFICIAL PONY

While the Batak people are known to eat, deify, and sacrifice their horses, they also ride them, being particularly fond of racing and gambling.

Horses, most probably of Mongolian extraction, were introduced to Southeast Asia from India during the first three centuries of the Christian era. Arab traders came later to Indonesia, bringing horses with them and encouraging their use in the islands.

ARABIAN INFLUENCE

The early Dutch colonists imported Cape Arabians, and Arabian stallions were stood at the stud farm established in Minankabu, Sumatra. Not surprisingly, the Arabian influence is very evident in the spirited and agile Batak stock, which has the reputation of being docile and good natured. Like all the Indonesian ponies the Batak is both economical to feed and easily managed.

At one time there was a heavier strain of Batak, less Arabian in character, to be found in the north of the island. This was the Gayoe, but it is now doubtful if this strain exists in its original form.

The Batak stands at about 13hh.

Neck The mane hair is fine but the neck is weak when compared to the heavy head.

Head Although the head is large, the Arabian influence and character is very evident in the profile, muzzle and eyes.

Shoulder The shoulder tends to straightness, but the chest is broad enough and the forelegs are clean with acceptable joints. The conformation is not exemplary but the pony has a certain refinement.

RACING STOCK The Sandalwood ponies, pictured above being ridden by children, were similarly improved by the introduction of Arabian blood. The breed is raced extensively in Indonesia over distances of 2½–3 miles (4–5km) and are usually ridden bareback (as seen with the second pony) in the traditional bitless bridle.

Back *The back is long, straight, and lacking in muscular development, and, although the overall impression is still one of some refinement, there is evidence of degeneration as a result of climate, soil, and general environment.*

Quarters *The quarters give an immediate impression of weakness. They are meagerly built and slope away to a low-set tail. Although no one color predominates, the fine, silky coat of the Arabian remains evident.*

WORKING PONY As well as being ridden, the Batak pony can be driven in harness or act as a pack pony. While stock degenerates in the local environment without regular infusions of outside blood, the ponies remain tough, durable, and constitutionally sound.

Body *The body is tubelike, the ribs not well sprung, and there is insufficient depth through the girth. Despite these conformational failings the Batak ponies remain hardy, enduring, and full of spirit.*

Hind leg *The hind leg used to be the worst feature of the Cape Arabian, and this is reflected here in the pronounced lack of muscular development.*

Lower limb *The lower limb is correspondingly poor, the shank is overlong, and the very moderate hocks are carried high off the ground.*

GAMBLING The Batak people are obsessive gamblers, but there was once a salutary penalty to be paid by anyone unable to pay his debts. He could be sold into slavery unless the creditor allowed him to repay the debt by providing a horse for the purpose of a public feast.

Feet *The feet are as good a feature of the pony as any, being of hard, durable horn.*

Timor

The Timor pony belongs to the Indonesian island of that name. Even today, it is an important element in the island's economy, and the number per head of population remains high. At one time the ratio was estimated as being one horse to every six people. Although the savannahs provide good grazing, the Timor pony is small and does not exceed 12hh.

INDONESIA'S DWARF PONY

In the sixteenth and seventeenth centuries Timor came under the influence first of Portuguese and then of Dutch colonists. Both introduced Arabian blood to the Indonesian islands to upgrade the existing stock, which had a background of the Mongolian and Indian ponies derived from an admixture of the primitive Asiatic Wild Horse and Tarpan.

Despite the existence of extensive savannah providing wiry but nutritious feed, the Timor is the smallest of the Indonesian ponies, just as the anoa, an inhabitant of the Celebes mountains, is the world's smallest buffalo. It is the buffalo, and the "cowboys" involved in their husbandry, that provide much of the employment for the almost dwarf-sized ponies. They are used for working cattle and, as in the American West, the Timor cowboy employs a rope lasso as the main tool of his trade.

UP TO WEIGHT

Despite a diminutive size, the ponies are tough and agile, and they routinely carry full-grown men. They are usually ridden in the bitless bridles, which are traditional to the islands and reminiscent of those used in central Asia 4,000 years ago. Recognizable saddles are not much seen, and the riders' feet often touch the ground. Timors are exported to Australia and are said to make good children's ponies.

Neck The neck is short, corresponding with the undistinguished shoulder. The mane is full and the coat fine.

Head The head is heavy and out of proportion to the frame but in itself it is not an unattractive feature.

Shoulder The shoulders are upright despite a reasonably prominent wither. The limbs are not exemplary but they are tough and clean.

HANDSOME IS… There is some evidence of the Arabian influence in the Timor, but, despite its acknowledged qualities of endurance, agility, and strength, the Timor remains an unprepossessing specimen exhibiting what might be considered degenerative characteristics. It is, nonetheless, a remarkable equine.

Back The back is straight with a distinctively level croup, but the loin is nonetheless remarkably strong and is possibly the saving grace of the structure.

Quarter The tail, so as to conform with the level croup, is placed well up the quarter and in movement is carried high. The top of the quarter and thigh carry muscle.

PONY OF THE ISLANDS There is a large pony population throughout Indonesia. This pony is from Java, the home of a race of strongly built ponies, where saddles are more evident than elsewhere. Like all the Indonesian ponies, the Java is a strong, willing worker – hardy, sound, enduring, and very cooperative.

Thigh The second thigh is light and not very well shaped but it is long and muscled. The tail is full and carried well from the high croup placement. The quarter is not perfect, but is far from being inferior.

Body There is not much depth through the girth but, despite the length, the body is well enough formed and the ribs reasonably sprung.

Joints The hock could be larger but it is not incorrectly formed and it is undeniably serviceable, while the fetlocks are acceptable enough.

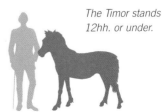

The Timor stands 12hh. or under.

Sumba

The Sumba and Sumbawa ponies of Indonesia inhabit adjacent islands and are widespread throughout the archipelago, being particularly numerous in Sumatra. Of all the Indonesian ponies these reveal more clearly than any other their primitive ancestry, most being pronouncedly Mongolian in appearance and having the characteristic dun coat color. They are not dissimilar to the Chinese pony but are better made and more agile.

THE GAME'S THE THING

The ponies are small, carrying large Mongolian-type heads that are often convex in profile, but they are strong out of all proportion to their size and easily able to carry grown men as well as heavy pack loads.

They are ridden without saddles, being controlled by the traditional braided leather bridle acting on the nose, and similar to nosepieces employed as far away as California, Mexico, and South America. Their speed and agility make them suitable for the popular local sport of lance throwing, which is played on Sumba. Two sides, armed with blunted lances, ride against each other. The game is over when all the members of one side have been struck by their opponents' lances.

THE DANCING STARS

Carefully selected Sumba ponies are trained to perform traditional dances. The ponies are chosen for their elegance and lightness of foot and are highly prized. They dance to the beat of the drums with tinkling bells attached to the lower limbs. The owner conducts the dance holding the pony on a loose long rein, while a small boy rides it with great suppleness and balance. The tradition is an old one found in many central Asian horse cultures.

Head The head is usually coarse and convex in profile, and bigger than in this example with a definite thickening through the jowl. Here, the ears are pricked and alert, and the large eyes are not set too far to the side of the head. The neck, though short, is necessarily muscular to support the weight of the head.

Limbs The limbs, characteristically black in color or even zebra-striped, are serviceable, but not exemplary. The feet and joints are hard and rarely subject to lameness.

COLOR The coat color is predominantly dun, usually accompanied by a strong dorsal stripe, dark mane and tail, and either black or zebra-striped lower limbs. Grazing is of poor quality, hence the small stature, but the ponies are exceptionally hardy and enduring.

Croup Here the croup is short and runs down to a poorly carried, low-set tail, a failing that may be corrected by the introduction of Arabian blood, for instance.

Back The back is straight but muscled on either side of the spine and of considerable strength. The pony is easily able to carry heavy weights and to do so at speed.

RIDING PONIES Despite poor feed, which might be expected to result in stunted growth and conformational deficiencies, the ponies have great freedom and elasticity of movement. They make good riding ponies that can be handled easily by children. In temperament, they are pleasantly docile and cooperative, in contrast to what might be expected from their primitive ancestry. The Asian Wild Horse, for example, is aggressive and retains those characteristics even in captivity.

Hind leg Although it is not the best of hind legs, it does have its compensations in a pair of clean hock joints, hard lower limbs, and flat fetlocks that are in no way disposed to being lymphatic.

Body The body is surprisingly compact, and though the slope of the shoulder leaves something to be desired, the action is not unduly inhibited.

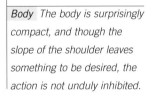

The Sumba stands at about 12.2hh.

Hokkaido

The first horses to arrive in Japan came in the third century AD with a Korean people from central Asia. Their burial mounds, after the fashion of the steppes, contain *haniwa*, terra-cotta figures of both humans and horses. In the thirteenth century Mongolian ponies brought with Kublai Khan's attempted invasions of the country, may have supplemented the local stock. The Hokkaido is probably the best of the Japanese breeds, (the others are Kiso and Kagoshima) but none is of particular distinction.

The open ground of Hokkaido in the north of Japan, unlike the mountainous central area of Kiso-Sanmya and the impoverished area of Kyushu in the south, is the area best suited to animal raising. It provides sufficient nutritious grazing for the ponies, which are still used on the small farms, for haulage, and for pack work. They are used in sleds and also, until recently, were employed in the small coal mines of the area.

At one time, Japanese cavalry were mounted on crosses, or second crosses, with the better quality Hokkaido, and there is evidence of an Arabian outcross in the appearance of the best Hokkaido ponies. In themselves, however, they are rarely suitable for comfortable riding.

The early Japanese practiced horse sacrifice in order to propitiate the gods. "Within living memory, the country custom was observed of hanging the heads of horses at the entrances of farmhouses. The horse possessed the qualities of an agricultural god, and his head acted as a charm." (Kendrick, 1964).

The Hokkaido stands at around 13hh.

Quarters and limbs This is the best type of "improved" Hokkaido. It has a good, well-made quarter, with the tail well set, and acceptable, muscled hind legs and joints.

Body A compact, well-ribbed-up body is an attractive feature of this pony, but it lacks depth through the girth and the wither is ill-defined.

Feet Japanese ponies always have good feet. They are hard, of bluish horn, nicely rounded, and with a very correct angle of slope.

Head *The head, in this instance, does not betray primitive ancestry but is instead the result of outside crosses.*

Muzzle *The muzzle is neat and tapered, and the profile more Arabian than Mongolian!*

Shoulder *The shoulder is not notably sloped and the legs are light and perhaps too slender with a tendency to roundness at the knee joints.*

JAPANESE TRADITION The Japanese were never noted horse people, although today all kinds of riding, as well as racing, is popular in Japan and is of a high standard. The Samurai tradition included "skill in horsemanship" as well as the other military arts, the *bujutsu*.

Knees *These knees are rounded rather than flat and not sufficiently prominent. The bone is adequate in size, and the pasterns are correctly sloped.*

CIVILIAN RIDING Traveling civilian dignitaries rode sitting on top of wide, wooden, pack-type saddles, precarious arrangements covered with cloths, bedding, and anything else that had to be transported with them. They sat cross-legged or, as here, with their legs held on either side of the horse's neck. Only fighting men held the reins; otherwise the horse and its "rider" were led to their destination by a footman.

Index

Acknowledgments

Dorling Kindersley would like to thank Janos Marffy, Sandra Pond, Will Giles, Richard Tibbits and David Ashby for illustrations; Dr James Bee of the Royal Veterinary College, London, UK for his advice on the foal development sequence; Robert Oliver for the use of his stable yard; Giles Hine for help with the horses; Graham Young the blacksmith; Monsieur Mauget in France; Gaetano Manti in Italy; Pat Renwick and the Shetland pageant; The Kentucky Horse Park, Lexington; Steven Cluett, Tracey Hambleton, Gill Sherman, Diana Weeks and Kevin Williams for additional design assistance; Paul Dewhurst for shadow artwork; Sharon Lunn for silhouette diagrams; Irene Lyford for the index; Emma Matthews for keying-in and Jenny Speller for picture research.
Studio Cactus would like to thank Kate Grant and Chris Stafford for help with the American photography. Thanks also to Mic Cady, Kate Hayward, Jane Baldock, and Laura Seber.
And, of course, thanks to all the horses and ponies we photographed and their owners who were so patient (these are all acknowledged in the picture credits below). Thanks also to those we were, unfortunately, unable to include in this book.
Bob Langrish would like to thank Sally Waters, Janet Lorch, Dr Mikhail Alexeev, Colin Wares, Dinny Lund, Evegeny Lepetukhin. Thanks to Jo Walton and Louise Thomas for additional picture research and to Hilary Bird for revising the index.

Picture Credits
Animal Photography includes photographs by Sally Anne Thompson.

b bottom, *c* center, *l* left, *r* right, *t* top

Agence France Presse: 43tr; **American Museum of Natural History**: 10b, 10tc; **Ardea**: 11br; **Jenny Barnes**: 66/67, 196tl, 222/223; **Bewick Woodcuts**: 99tr, 268, 271; **Bob Langrish**: 17br, 22cra, 22bl, 22br, 42/43, 71tr, 96/97, 180/181, 196cl, 223cr, 261tr, 265tr; **Clix**: Shawn Hamilton 70/71, 80/81; **CM Dixon**: 8/9; **Corbis**: Tony Arruza 55cr; Felice Beato / Hulton Deutsch Collection 267br; Ric Ergenbright 55tr; Jack Fields 89tl; Kevin Fleming 159tl; Owen Franken 263tr; Kit Houghton 54/55, 71cr, 146/147, 152bc; David Katzenstein 147cr; Michael St Maur Shiel 81tl; Johnathan Smith / Cordaiy Photo Library Ltd 81cr; Ted Spiegel 88/89; Brian A Vikander 147tr; **Dale Durfy**: 141tr, 142bc, 143tr; **Empics**: 49tr, 49cr; **Mary Evans Picture Library**: 11bl; **Elwyn Hartley Edwards**: 16b; **Kit Houghton**: 2/3, 17tr, 17bl, 17bc, 57tr, 63tr, 64bc, 89cr, 97tr, 97cr, 100/101, 101tr, 101cr, 153tr, 162/163, 181tr, 213br; **Frank Lane Picture Agency**: J McDonald / Sunset 4/5; Peter Newark's Historical Pictures: 43cr, 173br, 183bl;

pp.16 Standardbred (Trotter) – *Raffaello Ambrosio*
Ambrosio Racing Stables, Peninsula Farm, Lexington, Kentucky

pp.26–7 Tennessee Walking Horse – *Dot Com*
Nicole Carswell, 7th Heaven Farm, Morehead, Kentucky;
Saddlebred – *Yorktown Tempest*
Marylee Wilkinson, Rancho Del Rio, Oconomowoc, Wisconsin
Quarterhorse – *Smart Lil Macolena*
Ben Bowman, Bowman & Sons Training, Bloomington, Indiana

pp.40–1 Arab – *Persimmon*
Pat and Joanna Maxwell, Lodge Farm Arabian Stud, Oxon, UK; *tr* Mary Evans

pp.44–5 Barb – *Taw's Little Buck*
Kentucky Horse Park;
tl Peter Newark; *bl* Bruce Coleman; *cr* Ardea

pp.46–7 Thoroughbred – *Lyphento*
Conkwell Grange Stud, Avon, UK;
tr, br Peter Newark

pp.50–1 Andalucian – *Campanero XXIV*
Nigel Oliver, Singleborough Stud, Bucks, UK; *bl* Andalucian – *Adonis-Rex*
Welshpool Andalucian Stud, Powys, UK
tr Kit Houghton

pp. 52–53 Lusitano – *Montemere-O-Thurman*
Turnville Valley Stud, Oxon, UK;
br **Hispano-Arab** – *Ultima*
Mr & Mrs Davies

pp. 56–57 Alter Real – *Casto*
Portuguese National Stud, Portugal

pp.60–1 Shagya Arab – *Artaxerxes*
Jeanette Bauch & Jens Brinksten, Denmark; *br* Only Horses

pp. 62–63 Belgian Warmblood – *Trudo Darco*
Paesen Martinus, Peer, Belgium

pp. 64–65 Welsh Part-Bred – *Taurus*
Sian Thomas BHSI, Snowdonia Riding Stables, Waunfawr, Gwynedd, UK

pp.68–9 Dutch Warmblood – *Edison*
Mrs Dejonge; *tl* Mary Evans

pp.72–3 Selle Français – *Prince D'elle*
Haras National De Saint Lô, France

pp.74–5 Danish Warmblood – *Rambo*
Jorgen Olsen, Denmark; *bl* Einer Anderssons Pressbild

pp.76–7 Trakehner – *Muschamp Mauersee*
Janet Lorch, Muschamp Stud, Bucks, UK; *br* Animal Photography

pp.78–9 Hanoverian – *Défilante*
Barry Mawdsley, European Horse Enterprises, Berks, UK

pp.82–3 Holstein – *Lenard*
Sue Watson, Trenawin Stud, Cornwall, UK; *tr* Mary Evans

pp.84–5 Oldenburg – *Renoir (Modekönig)*
Louise Tomkins; *tr* Animal Photography

pp.86–7 Hunter – *Hobo*
Robert Oliver; *bl, tc* Mary Evans

pp.90–1 Hack – *Rye Tangle*
Robert Oliver

pp.92–3 Cob – *Silvester and r Hunter Ovation*
both owned by Robert Oliver

pp.94–5 Lipizzaner – *Siglavy Szella*
John Goddard Fenwick & Lyn Moran, Ausdan Stud, Dyfed, UK;
bl Animal Photography;
br Only Horses

pp. 98–99 Hackney – *Hurstwood Consort*
Mr & Mrs Hayden, Hurstwood Stud, UK

pp.102–3 French Trotter – *Pur Historien*
Haras National De Compiègne, France;
tr Peter Newark; *bc* Woodcut

pp.104–5 Friesian – *Sjouke*
Sonia Gray, Tattondale Carriages, Cheshire; *trl* Mary Evans; *trr* Animal Photography

pp.106–7 Irish Draught – *Miss Mill*,
bl (foal) – Gort Mill Mr R J Lampard

pp.108–9 Norman Cob – *Ibis*
Haras National de Saint Lô, France;
bl Mary Evans; *tr* Mary Evans/Bruce Castle Museum

pp.110–11 Cleveland Bay – *Oaten Mainbrace*
Mr and Mrs Dimmock

pp112–13 Gelderlander – *Spooks*
Peter Munt, Ascot Driving Stables, Berks, UK; *trr* Mary Evans

pp.114–15 Frederiksborg – *Zarif Langløkkegard*
Harry Nielsen, Denmark;
bl Mary Evans; *tr* Animal Photography

pp.116–17 Maremanna – *Barone*
Mr Attilio Tavazzani, Centro Ippico Di Castelverde, Italy; *br* Kit Houghton

pp.118–19 Murgese – *Obscuro*
Istituto Incremento Ippico di Crema, Italy; *tr* Istituto Geografico de Agostini

pp.120–21 Camargue – *Redounet*
Mr Contreras, Les Saintes Maries de la Mer, France

pp.122–23 Furioso – *Furioso IV*
A G Kishumseigi, Hungary;
tl Mary Evans

pp.124–25 Nonius – *Pampas*
bl foal both owned by A G Kishumseigi, Hungary

pp.126–27 Knabstrup – *Føniks*
Poul Elmerkjær, Denmark;
br Animal Photography

pp.128–29 Akhal-Teke – *Fakir-Bola*
Moscow Hippodrome;
bl Animal Photography; *t* Peter Newark

pp.130-31 Budenny – *Barin*; *bl* Tersk
both at Moscow Hippodrome;
tr Animal Photography

pp.132–33 **Kabardin**
Moscow Hippodrome;
tl Mary Evans

pp.134–35 **Don** – *Baret*;
bl Karabakh
both at Moscow Hippodrome;
tr, bc Mary Evans

pp.136–37 **Orlov Trotter**
Moscow Hippodrome;
tl Mary Evans; *bl* Animal Photography

pp.138–9 **Bashkir** – *Mel's Lucky Boy*
Dan Stewart Family, Kentucky Horse
Park

pp. 140–41 **Kathiawari** – Mounted
Branch, New Delhi Police, India

pp. 142–43 **Marwari**
Capt. Sandeep Dewan, 61st Cavalry,
Ahmednagar, India

pp.144–45 **Australian Stock Horse**
(photographed by Hawkesbury
Photographics) – *Scrumlo Victory*
Mrs R Waller, Ophir Stud, Australia;
bl, tc Mary Evans; *tr* Auscape

pp.148–49 **Morgan** – *Fox Creek's
Dynasty*
Darwin Olsen, Kentucky Horse Park; *tl*
Bewick Woodcuts

pp. 150–51 **Galiceno** – *Java Gold*
Billy Jack Giles, Godley, Texas

pp.152–53 **Criollo** – *Azuleca*
Claire Tomlinson, Westonbirt, Glos, UK

pp.154–55 **American Crème** –
Sheridan's Valor
Tracey L. Burchell, Blue Moon Farm,
Nicholasville, Kentucky

pp.156–57 **Quarter Horse** – *Eye Dun
Time*
Dorothy & Ronald Wilcheck,
Whitesville, Kentucky;
bl – *Hez Totally Supreme*
Burgess Blanton, Houser Halter Horses,
Ohio; *br* – *Ticket Chex*
Betty Miller, Stamping Ground,
Kentucky

pp.158–59 **Quarter Horse** sliding stop
sequence – *Smart Lil Macolena*
Ben Bowman, Bowman & Sons
Training, Bloomington, Indiana

pp.160–61 **Standardbred** – *Rambling
Willie*
Farrington Stables and the Estate of
Paul Siebert, Kentucky Horse Park; *tl*
Bewick Woodcuts

pp.164–65 **Saddlebred** – *Kinda Kostly*
Kentucky Horse Park

pp.166–67 **Missouri Fox Trotter** – *Cast
Iron Camelot H*
Bobby & Brenda Copple,
Dawsons Springs, Kentucky;
br – *Easy Street*
Ruth Massey, Kentucky Horse Park

pp.168–69 **Tennessee Walker** –
Delight's Moondust
Andrew & Jane Shaw, Kentucky Horse
Park; *bl* Animal Photography

pp.170–171 **Peruvian Paso** – *Gavulan
de Campanero*
Snr. Juan E. Villanueva,
Association of Horses and Paso Finos,
Puerto Rico

pp.172–73 **Mustang** – *Mestava*
Rowland H. Cheney, Stockton,
California

pp.174–75 **Morab** – *Moss Casidy Rose*
Lisa A. Kuduk, White O' Mornin Farm,
Winchester, Kentucky

pp.176–77 **Rocky Mountain Pony** –
Mocha Monday
Rea Swan, Hope Springs Farm,
Kentucky Horse Park

pp.182–83 **Pinto** – *Hit Man*
Boyd Cantrell, Kentucky Horse Park;
tr Tobiano – *MTP Late for a date*
Caryn Vecchio, Caraway Farm, Paris,
Kentucky

pp.185–85 **Palomino** – *Wychwood
Dynascha*
Mrs G Harwood, Wychwood Stud, Glos,
UK;
tr Ardea

pp.186–187 **Appaloosa**
(photographed by Stephen Oliver) –
Golden Nugget
Sally Chaplin;
tr Bewick Woodcuts

pp.188–89 **Shire** – *Duke*
Jim Lockwood, Courage Shire Horse
Centre, Berks, UK;
bc Mary Evans

pp.190–91 **Suffolk Punch** –
Laurel Keepsake II
P Adams and Sons;
tl Bewick Woodcuts

pp.192–93 **Clydesdale** – *Blue Print*
Mervyn and Pauline Ramage, Mount
Farm Clydesdale Horses,
Tyne and Wear, UK

pp.194–95 **Percheron** – *Tango*
Haras National de Saint Lô, France;
tl Mary Evans; *br* Kit Houghton

pp.198–99 **Ardennais** – *Ramses du
Vallon*
Haras National de Pau, France;
bl Kit Houghton

pp.200–1 **Breton** – *Ulysses*
Haras National de Tarbes, France;
bl Kit Houghton

pp.202–3 **Boulonnais** – *Urus*
Haras National de Compiègne,
France; *tr* Einar Anderssons Pressbild

pp.204–5 **Poitevin** – *Vitrisse*
Haras National de la Roche sur Yon,
France

pp.206–7 **Jutland** – *Tempo*
Jørgen Neilsen, Denmark;
tr Animal Photography

pp.208–9 **Belgian Draught** – *Roy*
Kentucky Horse Park;
bl Animal Photography

pp.210–11 **Italian Heavy Draught** –
Nobile
bl **Bardigiano** – *Pippo*
both at Istituto Incremento Ippico di
Crema, Italy

pp.212–13 **Noriker** – *Dinolino*
Josef Waldherr, Wackersberg, Germany

pp.214–15 **Exmoor** – *Murrayton
Delphinus*
June Freeman, Murrayton Stud, Herts.,
UK

pp.216–217 **Dartmoor** – *Allendale
Vampire*
Miss M Houlden, Haven Stud,
Hereford, UK

pp.218–9 **Welsh Mountain Pony** –
Bengad Dark Mullein
Mrs C Bowyer, Symondsbury Stud,
Sussex, UK;
bl, tr Animal Photography

pp.220-21 **Welsh Pony** – *Twyford Signal*
Mr and Mrs L E Bigley, Llanarth Stud,
Hereford, UK;
tr Bruce Coleman

pp.222–23 **Quarter Pony** – *tr Do A
Little Dance*
Katie Wilhelm, Plain City, Ohio

pp.224–25 **Welsh Cob** – *Treflys Jacko*
Mr and Mrs L E Bigley (see pp.146–7);
tr **Welsh Pony of Cob Type** – *Llygedyn
Solo* Kitty Williams, Glebedale Stud,
Gwent, UK

pp.226–27 **Dales** – *Warrenlane Duke*
Mr Dickson, Millbeck Pony Stud,
Yorks, UK; *tr* Mary Evans

pp.228–29 **Fell** – *Waverhead William*
Mr and Mrs S Errington

pp.230–31 **Highland** – *Fruich of Dykes*
Countess of Swinton;
bl Animal Photography

pp.232–33 **Connemara** – *Spinway
Bright Morning*
Miss S Hodgkins, Spinway Stud,
Oxon, UK;
tr Kit Houghton

pp.234–35 **New Forest Pony** –
Bowerwood Aquila
Mrs Rae Turner, Bowerwood Stud,
Hants, UK; *tl* Bewick Woodcuts; *br*
Animal Photography

pp.236–37 **Riding Pony** – *Brutt*
Robert Oliver; *tr* Animal Photography

pp.238–39 **Eriskay** – Kirsty and
Donald John Rodgers, Isle of Eriskay,
Western Isles, UK

pp.240–41 **Lundy** – c/o The Warden,
Lundy Island (administered and
maintained by The Landmark Trust,
Maidenhead, Berks, UK.)

pp.246–47 **Falabella** – *Pegasus of
Kilverstone*; *bl* foals – *l Cleopatra of
Kilverstone*; *r Bernardo of Kilverstone* all
owned by Lady Fisher, Kilverstone
Wildlife Park, Norfolk; *trl* Ardea

pp.248–49 **Landais** – *Hippolyte*
tr **Pottock** – *Thouarec III*
both at Haras National de Pau, France

pp.250–51 **Ariègeois** – *Radium*
Haras National de Tarbes, France;
bl Only Horses

pp.252–53 **Haflinger** – *Nomad*
Miss Helen Blair, Silvretta Haflinger
Stud, W Midlands, UK;
bl **Avelignese** – *Noaner*, Istituto
Incremento Ippico di Crema, Italy;
tr Animal Photography

pp.254–55 **Fjord** – *Ausdan Svejk*
John Goddard Fenwick and Lyn Moran,
Ausdan Stud, Dyfed, UK;
bl Einar Anderssons Pressbild; *br* Animal
Photography

pp.256–57 **Icelandic Horse** – *Leiknir*
Kentucky Horse Park, USA;
bl, tr Animal Photography

pp.258–59 **Caspian** – *Hopstone Shabdiz*
Mrs Scott, Henden Caspian Stud, Wilts,
UK; *tr* Woodcuts

pp.260-261 **Batak** – *Dora*
Tung Kurniawan, Sumatra, Indonesia;

pp.262–63 **Timor** –
Meriam Bellina, Pelita Jaya Stable,
Jakarta, Indonesia

pp.264–65 **Sumba** – *Mitzi*
Tung Kurniawan, Sumatra, Indonesia

pp.266–67 **Hokkaido** – *Ayme*
Japanese Racing Association,
Tokyo, Japan